362.5

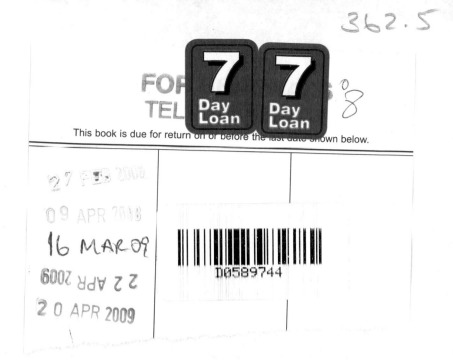

LONGMAN SOCIAL POLICY IN BRITAIN SERIES

Series Editor:
Jo Campling

Published Titles:
The Personal Social Services
Robert Adams

Health Policy and the NHS
Judith Allsop

Housing Problems and Policies
Brian Lund

Crime and Criminal Justice Policy
Tim Newburn

Foundations of the Welfare State
Pat Thane

Older People in Modern Society
Anthea Tinker

Forthcoming Titles:
Equal Opportunities and Social Policy
Barbara Bagilhole

New Directions in Educational Policy
Paul Lodge

Lone Mothers
Jane Millar

LONGMAN SOCIAL POLICY IN BRITAIN SERIES

Responding to Poverty
The Politics of Cash and Care

Saul Becker

London and New York

Addison Wesley Longman Limited,
Edinburgh Gate, Harlow,
Essex CM20 2JE, England
and Associated Companies throughout the world.

Published in the United States of America
by Addison Wesley Longman Inc., New York

First published 1997

ISBN 0 582 24322X PPR

British Library Cataloguing-in-Publication Data
A catalogue record for this book is
available from the British Library

Library of Congress Cataloging-in-Publication Data
Becker, Saul.
    Responding to poverty: the politics of cash and care/Saul
Becker.
        p.   cm. — (Longman social policy in Britain)
    Includes bibliographical references and index.
    ISBN 0–582–24322–X
    1. Poverty—Great Britain.   2. Poor—Services for—Great Britain.
3. Public welfare—Great Britain.   4. Great Britain—Social
policy—1979–   I. Title.   II. Series: Longman social policy in
Britain series.
HV4085.A5B43   1997
362.5'8'0941—dc21   96–50040
                                                          CIP

Set by 8 in 10/11pt Times
Produced through Longman Malaysia, PP

To the memory of my grandparents, Julia and Solomon Wrobel, and for my mother, Annette.

CONTENTS

Acknowledgements   ix
Introduction   xi

1   The construction of 'poverty' and the 'poor': politics,
    ideology and social attitudes   1

2   The politics of poverty: definitions, measures and effects   21

3   Cash, care and welfare: continuity and change in
    historical perspective   38

4   Regulating the poor: the politics of social security   57

5   Managing the poor: social services and social work with
    poor families and children   88

6   Excluding the poor: social services and community care   121

7   Towards a social reaction model of poverty and exclusion   157

Documents   **167**
List of Documents, 1–13   167

Bibliography   189
Index   215

ACKNOWLEDGEMENTS

I am grateful to many people for helping me with this book. In particular I want to record my gratitude to Ruth Lister for all her comments and suggestions, and for her ongoing support and encouragement. Bill Silburn and Arthur Gould also commented on a draft of some early chapters, and David Trenery made invaluable comments on the community care chapter. Thanks also to Jo Campling for encouraging me to write the book in the first place.

Many others sent me material or indulged my requests for further information, including Pete Alcock, Sue Balloch, Jean Carabine, Gary Craig, Geoff Fimister, Isobel Freeman, Peter Golding, Adrian Harvey, Chris Hollins, Bob Holman, Brian Jones, Stephen McKay, Keith Moore, Carol Walker and Jane Tunstall.

I am grateful to the employees of the Department of Social Security who attended my study groups on 'cash and care', held at the 1995 and 1996 DSS Summer Schools at King's College Cambridge, and who shared their ideas with me: Gill Brown, Michele Davies, Clare Devlin, Doug Ellis, Rachel Frost, Colin Herring, Dave Higlett, Joe Johnson, Jackie Kenny, Elaine Lawson, Alison Lomax, Dawn McDonnell, David McNab, Jayne Morrisey, Judith Perry, Clare Pyrah, Patricia Scarrow and Linda Turner.

I owe a particular, and long-standing debt to Hilary Waring and Liz Pritchett of Nottinghamshire County Council's Local Government Library. For many years Hilary and Liz have helped me keep up to date (insofar as is possible) with the publications relating to social services and social care.

I must apologise to, and thank, Jo Aldridge, Chris Dearden and Betty Newton, my colleagues in the Young Carers Research Group at Loughborough University. For some time they have had to carry a disproportionate load of our research commitments while I got on with the book. Thanks also to Betty for all her help with the bibliography and to Chris for all her proofreading. I must also acknowledge my employer, Loughborough University, which gave me a period of three months study leave in 1995 to start work on the book.

Others have helped me to survive the experience of writing this book, including Jon North – who has taught me a great deal about the voluntary sector – and Arthur Gould, who has taught me a great deal about some very strange things indeed! For two years my family have looked forward to the day when the writing would all be over. Thanks to Fiona for her patience, and apologies to Jessica, Sophie and Zachary for my impatience during the last two years.

INTRODUCTION

For the last 14 years, two thousand people per day have joined the ranks of Britain's poor. One in four of the population – over 14 million people – now live in poverty.[1] Every day, one in three children is born into a poor family. This book is about poverty and the poor in Britain. It is about what poor people can expect to receive from the state in terms of 'cash' and 'care', and what they must give in return.

The primary focus is on policy formulation, implementation and change during the 1980s and 1990s in three key areas of British social policy: social security, personal social services (including social work), and community care. These three areas are of strategic importance in promoting the well-being and welfare of citizens, particularly the poorest. It is poor people who make heaviest use of state provision in 'cash' and 'care'.

The intention is to provide new insights into the social and political processes that maintain poverty and exclusion for millions of people; the impact of policy, organisation and change on the poor; and the achievements and limits of social policy. Chapter 1 examines the social construction of 'poverty' and the 'poor' in the 1980s and 1990s. It is concerned with how the terms have been framed and used in political and policy debates, and how their meaning and use reflects wider social attitudes and welfare ideologies. It explores the views on poverty and the poor held by those on the political right and left, and examines how these views are being translated into particular responses and political approaches to welfare reform. The exploration of the politics of poverty is continued in the second chapter, where the long-standing debates and disagreements over definitions, measures and effects of poverty are reviewed. In particular the contention that 'there is no such thing as real poverty in Britain today' is examined. The contribution and role of academics studying poverty, and how they and their work have been drawn into the political arena, is also considered.

Chapter 3 provides a historical context to the subsequent three chapters. It examines the importance to poor people of the state's social security system and personal social services in meeting needs and promoting welfare. By providing a historical overview of some of the main concerns and policy developments in cash and care, it shows how the relationship between state, independent and informal provision has changed over time, and the consequences of these changes for poor people.

Chapters 4, 5 and 6 focus respectively on the politics and policies of social security, personal social services and community care during the 1980s and 1990s. Throughout these chapters the key political and professional concerns, ideas and debates which have helped to shape policy formulation, implementation and change during these decades are examined in detail, and the impact on the poor is assessed.

The final chapter presents a new model that is intended to help us better understand the relationships between cash, care and poverty. Poverty and exclusion need to be understood as the consequences of social reactions, social and individual attitudes, policies, practices and structures, which act as barriers to independence and security for millions of citizens on low income. Policy, organisation and change within cash and care have become part of the problem, rather than the solution, of poverty and social exclusion.

1 When measured as those living below half of average income after housing costs.

CHAPTER 1

The construction of 'poverty' and the 'poor': politics, ideology and social attitudes

Introduction

'Poverty' is a political issue. Poverty, and the fear of poverty, could largely be abolished in British society if there were a political commitment to the task. For centuries, poverty and the poor have been taken for granted by politicians, policy makers and the public more generally. The existence of poverty is widely believed to be an inevitable aspect of British society, associated with the notion that 'the poor are always with us'. Since the late 1970s the 'social' problem of poverty has been depoliticised in the United Kingdom. Given that poverty was only 'rediscovered' as a social issue in the mid-1960s, its prominence as a social problem, demanding political attention, was relatively short-lived. Today, the consideration of poverty has been recast in technical language and debates concerned with definitions and measurement, in the images and symbols of individual failure and culpability, and in a concern for the reform of welfare, particularly 'cash' and 'care' for poorer people.

For centuries the poor, in the United Kingdom and elsewhere, have been defined as lazy, criminal and responsible for their circumstances. More recently, governments and opposition parties have drawn upon these images to divert attention away from the process of social policy formulation and implementation, and the social issue of poverty, to focus instead on the 'subjects' of the policy process, namely people on low incomes and the poor. Academic concerns – in particular with the lifestyles, living standards and consumption of the poor – have unwittingly aided the 'individualisation' of poverty, have helped to fuel a political rhetoric which constructs the poor as 'different' and defines poverty in personal, rather than social terms. Some academics have attempted to reframe the discussion of poverty in terms of social exclusion and social polarisation, to help rescue the poverty debate from 'the intellectual and political ghetto of its own and others' making' (Williams and Pillinger 1996: 1).

This chapter examines the social construction of 'poverty' and the 'poor' in the 1980s and 1990s, and explores how the terms have been framed and used in political and policy debates. I argue that the prevention or eradication of poverty poses a number of interrelated challenges, on the political, moral, practical and personal levels, but that first and foremost preventing or eradicating poverty is a political matter, and then an issue for social policy. Unless governments are willing to act politically, then poverty will continue as a condition of partial citizenship and exclusion for millions of fellow citizens (Golding 1986). The failure of successive Conservative administrations since the end of the 1970s to combat poverty is not just a matter of policy inertia or lack of political will. It also reflects the deep-rooted and politically charged disagreements surrounding the very concept itself, how poverty is defined and measured, its causes and effects, and most importantly, what should be done about it. It is necessary to first understand the social construction of poverty and the poor if we are later to explain the state's *responses* to poverty, particularly in the fields of social security and personal social services. We also need to understand the construction of poverty, and responses, as a reflection of wider social attitudes and reactions, political and welfare ideologies, which define the poor as responsible for their poverty, and view many as 'undeserving'.

The challenges of poverty

Much social policy in Britain, and elsewhere, 'flows' from the problems associated with poverty (Alcock 1993: 5). But poverty *per se* is not inevitable, nor is it an intractable problem for social policy. Nor is poverty just a problem about how individuals, families and communities manage their financial and other resources. The UN Economic and Social Council has recognised that: 'The eradication of poverty is a crucial and attainable goal of the international community ... The struggle against poverty is a struggle for peace and sustainable development ... All governments, public and private institutions and members of civil society ought to be involved' (International Year for the Eradication of Poverty UK Coalition 1996). The eradication of poverty is first and foremost a political and ideological challenge, requiring political, central and local government commitment, and coordinated responses. It is also a moral challenge, concerned with the extent to which, as individuals and as a society as a whole, we are willing to tolerate the existence and experience of poverty for millions of fellow citizens. Poverty is furthermore a practical challenge, concerned with devising and implementing policies which will either prevent poverty, relieve it, or reduce it, rather than making it worse. Finally, poverty is a personal challenge, concerned with the degree to which all of us, as citizens, are enabled to maximise our own agency, abilities and aspirations, to make best use of the available opportunities, for the benefit of our families, ourselves and each other. During the 1980s and 1990s much of the focus has been on practical issues, particularly the types of policies that can be used to relieve, and sometimes to prevent, poverty. This has been dominated by the ideas and proposals of 'experts' – academics, researchers, policy think-tanks and others. Far less attention has been given to the political and moral dimensions, and the need to empower all citizens, including the poor, to have a stake, and play a part in, the discussions about poverty and the future of welfare.

The post-war Beveridge settlement was one attempt to grapple with the problem of poverty and the other 'giant evils', including ignorance, idleness, squalor and disease (Timmins 1995). It combined a political and moral commitment with practical policies designed to prevent want and the fear of want. Since then, however, there has been little political consensus about the means and ends for abolishing or preventing poverty. The post-war sense of optimism, that 'things could only get better' (Stevenson 1995: 2) has turned to confusion and uncertainty as the Beveridge ideal has increasingly been shown to fail society as a whole, and to fail the poor in particular. Deakin suggests that, notwithstanding post-war welfare collectivism, 'however you mark the card, the giants have it by a clear margin' (1993: 21). Despite the claims by modern would-be reformers, including Norman Fowler in the 1980s and Peter Lilley in the 1990s, there has, as yet, been no New Beveridge, no new political, ideological, moral or social consensus on which to build a popular and politically acceptable programme to abolish poverty and the fear of poverty.

This is not to say that there are no *ideas*. Indeed, there has been no shortage of suggestions and recommendations designed to make Britain a 'better place' or a more 'just society' for all citizens, including the poor and the poorest. Some of these reports, from think tanks, social policy academics, researchers, pressure groups, politicians and others, now reveal considerable overlap in their prescriptions for reform and change. There is an increasing emphasis on 'routes out of poverty' through the labour market and paid employment in particular; the need for adequate and affordable child care; the need to move people off social security benefits and into paid employment wherever possible; and the need for better training and preparation for work and for home (Commission on Social Justice 1994, Barclay 1995, Labour Party 1996). Groups such as the Child Poverty Action Group, Low Pay Unit, Disability Alliance, Citizens Income Trust, Institute for Public Policy Research, Institute of Economic Affairs, Adam Smith Institute and Social Market Foundation have all promoted particular policies and approaches for some years (see, for example, Parker 1989, Hadjipateras and Witcher 1991, Becker and Bennett 1991, Green 1993).

Others across the political spectrum have suggested different approaches to social and economic restructuring. On the left, Labour's Social Justice Commission has argued for an 'Investors' Britain' with a greater need for training and getting people back into the labour market (Commission on Social Justice 1994). The Liberal Democrat-inspired Dahrendorf Commission urged fundamental changes to investment policy, pensions provision, reform of the City and lifelong access to learning (Dahrendorf 1995). Commission member Will Hutton also outlined his own agenda for the restructuring of city institutions and for a 'stakeholders' society' in a separate book, which went on to become a best seller and the basis for a television series (Hutton 1995). Another Dahrendorf Commission member, Labour MP and chair of the House of Commons Social Security Committee, Frank Field, outlined his proposals in a separate book where he argued for a radical restructuring of the national insurance system. Field believes that the main cause of the 'crisis' in welfare is the perverse incentives created by means-tested benefits, incentives for people not to work, train or save (Field 1995). He suggests that if welfare reform programmes are to be successful then they must be seen as relevant to the majority of society, not just the poor: 'changes for the poor will only come about if the self-interest of the majority is mobilised in a way which also promotes the common good' (p. 2). Consequently, 'Welfare has to cease specialising in poverty alleviation and become more generally concerned with underpinning living standards ... Moving away from an exclusive debate about poverty is therefore a first priority' (Field 1995: 22/76) [Document 1]. Some of Field's views and proposals have found favour with the 'New' Labour Party (Labour Party 1996) [Document 2], as will be seen later in this chapter.

On the right, while there are no Commissions, there is nonetheless a welfare debate. In the 1990s, Peter Lilley, as Secretary of State for Social Security, has argued for greater selectivity and targeting of benefits – not through greater use of the means-test – but based rather on excluding certain types of need by redefining conditions of entitlement:

The government does not agree that means-tested benefits are destructive. These, as with all statutory benefits, have disincentive effects. That is why the government's reforms have focused, not on extending means-testing, but on changing the conditions of entitlement to benefit. The real issue to be addressed is not means-testing versus contributory benefits, rather the issue is how to reduce dependency on state benefits.

(DSS press release 1995d)

There has been no shortage of practical ideas and policy prescriptions. Many proposals for reform, from think-tanks and others, are concerned with complex technical considerations about the relationships between tax and benefits, between benefits and work incentives, between different types of benefits, in cash and in kind. Other proposals, more notably from politicians, are concerned with the battle for ideas, to establish the 'moral high ground', the framework and boundaries for the proper relationship between the individual and the state, and between the state and the markets. Despite calls for welfare reform from across the political spectrum and elsewhere, there is, however, a lack of political will among those in government, and opposition, to come to terms, and grapple with, *poverty* as a social problem. There is little sense of urgency that something must be done about poverty in the United Kingdom, and that something must be done soon. The major concern that has dominated policy discussions of the 1980s and 1990s is that the poor are becoming a group dependent increasingly on welfare

– a group apart – and one which the nation can no longer afford, nor should wish, to maintain. Policy responses, and the debate about welfare reform, have focused increasingly on technical and discretionary arrangements for restricting access by certain social groups; for excluding certain kinds of need from both the cash and care systems of the British welfare state; for getting people off welfare and into work; and for tackling fraud and abuse. The emphasis is on exclusion rather than inclusion (Lister 1990).

Genuine movement for the benefit of poor people will only be possible when there is the political, moral and personal commitment to act. This may require a 'great reforming government' (Field 1995: 20), one with a clear framework of values and a mandate and strategy for change. But it will also require a broader social consensus that action on poverty is necessary, and that the poor are worth the investment. Poor people, as with all citizens, need to be included in this process. They need to be empowered to take greater control over their circumstances and environments, not just on the basis of self-interest, but for the collective good. This will require a fundamental shift in the way the poor are perceived, from passive 'victims' or active 'villains', to people with agency and potential, a 'resource' rather than a 'cost'. In the past poor people have most often been excluded from such discussions, their voices seldom heard in the policy and political debates. The 1995 Rowntree Inquiry into Income and Wealth, and Labour's Social Justice Commission, for example, both failed to include poorer people in their teams; they embodied the 'top-down' response to the challenges of poverty (Beresford and Green 1996).

Politics and politicians: the political construction of poverty

To what extent have politics and politicians fuelled the growth of poverty during the 1980s and 1990s? This is not the same as to ask 'what are the causes of poverty?'. To understand the *causes* of poverty we need to examine such issues as labour market restructuring, the growth of flexible employment, low pay, the extra costs associated with bringing up children or living with sickness, disability or old age, unemployment, and so on (Oppenheim and Harker 1996). Increasingly, we also need to consider the wider socio-economic, cross-national and global institutions that govern the relationships and exchange between individuals, states and international markets, as these too play a critical role in causing and maintaining poverty for millions of people in the UK and abroad. Policies to remedy poverty may need to be collaborative and multi-national, rather than emphatically home-based (Townsend 1993a, 1993b, Townsend and Donkor 1996). Our concern here is not with causes of poverty *per se*, but is about the *political* construction of poverty. At one level this is about the politics and policies that governments pursue, or don't pursue, and the effects that these have on the poor. At another level it is about how governments, politicians and others in the policy process construct poverty through their discourse and rhetoric, through ideas, themes, images and symbols. I shall take these in turn.

As I have already indicated, there has been little, if any, political and moral commitment by governments to combat poverty as a social problem during the 1980s and 1990s. Those in government, and the agencies and agents that support policy formulation and implementation, have considerable power and influence to prevent, relieve or eradicate poverty, and to determine the types of services, in cash or kind, that are provided, or denied, to poor people. There is considerable evidence to suggest that, rather than preventing or reducing poverty, government actions, policies and inaction have made matters worse for many poor people since the end of the 1970s. The Child Poverty Action Group has, for three decades, highlighted systematically the effects that government policies, particularly social security changes, have had on the lives of the poor (Bull and Wilding 1983, Walker and Walker 1987, Becker 1991, Oppenheim and Harker 1996). Others have shown how government policies in taxation, child support and other policy fields impact separately and collectively, and very often negatively, on poor people (Barclay 1995, Kempson 1996).

Successive Conservative governments since the end of the 1970s cannot avoid collective responsibility for the growth in poverty and the 'privatisation of human misery' (Craig 1995). Indeed, it is these governments that have consistently blocked any real progress on combating poverty. In 1995, for example, the Prime Minister refused to attend the United Nations Summit on Social Development in Copenhagen, which was working to combat poverty at the international level. While Britain signed the joint declaration committing itself 'to enact national plans for the substantial reduction of overall poverty and the eradication of absolute poverty', the government did nothing to introduce measures designed to honour this agreement during 1996, the International Year of Poverty Eradication. When confronted by an anti-poverty coalition as to its inaction, the government replied that it saw any anti-poverty drive as a matter for Third World countries, not the UK: 'The UK [already has] the infrastructure and social protection systems to prevent poverty and maintain living standards', commented Peter Lilley, Secretary of State for Social Security (*Guardian* 1996a: 7/16). Indeed, the government attempted to block measures to combat poverty. It took legal action against the European Commission (EC) on a number of occasions in 1996, because the EC had attempted to commit expenditure to a further (fourth) programme to combat social exclusion in member states, without the necessary consent of national governments in the Council of Ministers. Lilley observed: 'The challenge is not aimed at stopping sensibly planned funding in support of disadvantaged people. The government is already funding many projects to combat social exclusion in the UK through inner city challenge, adult training, health care, housing and literacy programmes' (quoted in DSS press release 1996g).

Government politics, policies, actions and inaction do not operate in a vacuum. Social attitudes towards poverty 'sets the limits within which legitimate politics can act' (Golding 1995: 212). Politicians and governments are voted in by citizens, and the Conservative Party has won three consecutive elections since 1979. At the same time as wanting more action to prevent poverty and provide better welfare services for all, the electorate has persistently voted for a party committed to cutting back public expenditure, particularly on state welfare programmes. Social attitudes towards poverty and the poor are critical in understanding the social construction of poverty, and in particular the responses of politicians, policy makers and those who implement social policy.

Social attitudes and welfare ideologies

Golding asserts: 'Poverty is itself experienced as a reflection of attitudes and beliefs held both by those enduring deprivation and by those in the wider society' (Golding 1995: 213). The dominant images of the poor are informed by historical and economic processes, as well as social, material and cultural traditions. Studies of social attitudes in Britain and abroad show the existence, and persistence, of a 'core' of beliefs about poverty and the poor which construct poverty as a personal problem, and define the poor as responsible for their situation. This has been characterised as 'blaming the victim' or an individualised, medical-pathology model of poverty. This pattern of beliefs has existed for as long as researchers have studied attitudes towards poverty, and is a cross-national phenomenon (see, for example, Lauer 1971, Alston and Dean 1972, Feagin 1972a, 1972b, Goodwin 1972, Miller 1978, Feather 1974, Sinha, Jain and Pandey 1980). The poor have been perceived as lazy, lacking drive and ambition; lacking morals, thrift and the skills of good financial management; and lacking in integrity and honesty.

Studies in Britain have, for many years, also confirmed this pattern of beliefs. In 1971, for example, a Gallup poll found that a third of all respondents thought poverty was due to lack of effort (Gallup 1976: 1456), while a survey of perceptions of poverty in Europe found that there was far greater hostility to the poor in the UK than any of its European neighbours, indeed 49 per cent of UK respondents believed that poverty did not exist at all (EEC 1977). Where poverty is acknowledged, the explanations for its existence and persistence are most often phrased in moralistic terms; subjective factors and beliefs, including prejudice, overrule any objective evidence (EEC 1977: 19, Golding 1991: 39). Golding and Middleton (1982) found that the most common explanations for poverty made reference to the financial ineptitude of the poor and their failure to control money going out of the home, rather than society's failure to get a decent income into it

(p. 195). Indeed, a significant number believed that the poor 'have only themselves to blame so there's no reason why society should support them' (p. 167).

There is evidence to suggest that, by the mid-1980s, there was some shift in social attitudes, with greater sympathy for the poor, and the public being more inclined to view poverty in social terms (Mack and Lansley 1985, Lipsey 1986). In 1986, for example, 55 per cent of the public agreed that there was 'such a thing as real poverty in Britain today'. By 1989, 63 per cent agreed that 'there is quite a lot of real poverty in Britain today' (Jowell *et al.* 1990: 7). Jowell and colleagues suggest that: 'It is, perhaps, the growth in large cities of beggars and of homeless people, (particularly 16–18 year olds, most of whom since 1988 no longer get Income Support) that has helped to increase public awareness of poverty' (Jowell *et al.* 1990: 7). There is evidence that the shift towards greater sympathy for the poor, no matter how precarious, continued into the 1990s (Golding 1994). A number of surveys show that the British public are now more likely than in the 1980s to view poverty in structural terms, although a significant proportion – one in five – still define poverty in terms of laziness and lack of willpower (Golding 1994, 1995). Moreover, there is still a large proportion of the British public who do not believe that there is such a thing as 'real' poverty in Britain. One third of UK respondents in the 1993 Eurobarometer survey, for example, thought that nobody in the UK lived in poverty (Golding 1995).

The 'deserving' and 'undeserving' poor

While social attitudes towards the poor as a whole may be shifting, slowly and precariously, towards more sympathy, there is still considerable hostility towards some *groups* of the poor, particularly those seen as 'undeserving'. The distinction between the 'deserving' and 'undeserving' poor has been characterised as a demarcation between those who are seen as 'copping out' or 'chipping into' society. Those who appear to be trying are held in far greater esteem than those who fail to make a contribution (Tropman 1977, 1981). It is the need for reciprocity which lies at the heart of the distinction between the 'deserving' and 'undeserving' poor. The deserving are those who 'by virtue of helplessness, are exempted from the requirements of reciprocation inspired by the market ethic' (Redpath 1979: 48). Only the deserving poor are exempted from the need to participate and chip in. The general 'culture of contempt' (Golding and Middleton 1982) towards many claimants maintains these distinctions; generally older and sick people are seen as the most deserving, while the non-disabled ('able bodied') and unemployed ('jobseekers') are seen as the least deserving (Schlackman Research Organisation 1978, Golding and Middleton 1982).

In the 1970s and early 1980s many of the so-called 'undeserving' poor were labelled as 'scroungers' and inspired a moral panic. These claimants, viewed as people who were 'out to get everything they could' from the welfare state while giving little or nothing in return, were seen as requiring regulation and control, to prevent a widescale crisis in the welfare state (Deacon 1978, Golding and Middleton 1982). Social security was enlisted as one weapon in the battle against 'scroungers', and this itself helped fuel images of the 'undeserving' poor: 'The notion of social security as a policing mechanism creates the complementary image of the claimant as criminal, to be policed, checked, investigated, suspected and controlled' (Golding and Middleton 1982: 97). This image has affected some of the poor themselves. Many claimants experience feelings of stigma when claiming; while 85 per cent of supplementary benefit claimants in Mack and Lansley's (1985) study saw receiving benefit as their right, 40 per cent were nonetheless embarrassed to claim. In the 1990s the panic over 'scroungers' has been substituted by panics over the 'underclass' and the 'dependent poor', groups of poor people, including lone parents, whose so-called 'deplorable' behaviour, fecklessness or 'benefits dependency' has put them outside the accepted, and acceptable, norms and conventions of society. Some of these images will be examined later in the chapter.

Attitudes to welfare

The study of social attitudes suggest the coexistence of both sympathetic and hostile views towards the poor – the notion of the poor being victims *and* villains – although the balance between these two positions may change at any time depending on the prevailing political, economic, social and moral climate, and whether the group in question is considered as deserving or not. Attitudes towards the systems of welfare that support the poor are also fluid and contradictory. There is differing support for the various sectors and services of the British welfare state. Golding observes that 'Consistently through the 1980s, only about one in seven people gave social security as a first or second priority. Health, education and housing all significantly preceded social security in their rankings. In other words, general public services appear more popular than selective or income maintenance provision' (1991: 44). In the field of social security, benefits perceived to be targeted at the 'deserving' attract the most support; retirement pensions and benefits for disabled people generally arouse stronger public support than unemployment benefit or child benefit (Piachaud 1974, Cooke 1979, Jowell and Airey 1984, Golding 1991). When asked to give the three worst and best things about social security, the respondents questioned as part of the 1980s Fowler review of social security expressed the most concern at help going to people 'who didn't need it'. One in ten thought that the system encouraged scroungers (DHSS 1985b: 84). Golding and

Middleton also found that people generally felt that benefits were too high and too easy to get; nearly half of their respondents thought too much was spent on welfare and social security, over twice the proportion who felt too little was being spent. There was particular resentment of Black people or immigrants receiving benefits (Golding and Middleton 1982: 164, 171). Taylor-Gooby (1985a, 1985b) confirms that there is low enthusiasm for meeting minority needs (not just ethnic minority needs). Where people are seen as different, with special needs, there is some ambivalence in meeting these needs; two-thirds of the Fowler review respondents preferred a general benefits system which made no provision for special or unique needs. They also had mixed views about child benefit; support varied according to who was being asked, with strongest support, not surprisingly, from families with children, and least support from elderly people (Taylor-Gooby 1985a: 33, DHSS 1985b, see also Golding 1991: 45).

Attitudes to welfare in general and to benefits in particular, as with attitudes towards poverty, are complex, contradictory and fluid. The public support both collective and private provision of welfare – a mixed economy – but their support is tinged with a moralistic concern for excluding the 'undeserving'. Moreover, there is concern that welfare itself may encourage dependency and 'remove the incentive for people to help themselves' (Mack and Lansley 1985: 217). The proportion of people believing this declined only slightly from 52 per cent in 1983 to 46 per cent in 1994 (Taylor-Gooby 1995: 9).

Attitudes towards welfare, and extra spending on welfare, are tinged, therefore, with a concern to ensure that social programmes benefit the 'deserving', exclude the 'undeserving' and offer taxpayers some personal return on their investment. Antipathy towards welfare is greatest among those who felt they 'had more to lose as the payers than to gain as beneficiaries' (Golding and Middleton 1982: 165). On the one hand people want more spending on welfare services, but on the other hand they do not want to pay *too* much more to secure services or benefits, particularly where the costs to them as taxpayers outweigh the potential benefits, in the short or long term. The public support the welfare state not because of altruism but because of enlightened self-interest (Lipsey 1994, Taylor-Gooby 1995). So, for example, over one in five of those in households in the lower half of the income distribution put benefits as their first or second priority for extra spending, compared with only five per cent of those in the top half of the income scale (Taylor-Gooby 1995: 5). Indeed, it seems that social attitudes endorse a welfare state that aims to meet widespread need, rather than one which just focuses on the needs of poor or disadvantaged groups, and that provision should be expanded, even if it means paying more in taxes: 'If public opinion has its way, then both rich and poor alike would prefer the structure of the welfare state to remain largely as it is, with the bulk of its resources devoted to mass services from which all can benefit ... Popular support for 'old welfare' has proved to be robust because it is rooted in the self-interest of Britain's contented majority' (Taylor-Gooby 1995: 16–17). Consequently, Frank Field's (1995) proposals that any reform of welfare must be directed at benefiting the majority of society, not just the poor, is likely to find widespread and popular support.

Political ideologies and attitudes to poverty

Academics and researchers have attempted to understand and explain these beliefs about poverty, the poor, the 'undeserving' and support for welfare programmes by making reference to the influence on attitudes of a range of socio-economic characteristics of the survey respondents. So, for example, age, gender, income, occupation, educational level and other factors have all been associated with a particular attitude. More sophisticated analyses have explored the interaction of many of these variables, including race, class, area of residence, general ideology, political attitudes, beliefs in the work ethic, beliefs in a 'just world', partisanship, among others. So, for example, there is evidence to suggest that those who are strongly committed to the work ethic tend to believe that the poor are low in their motivation toward work; those with left of centre political views are more likely to view poverty in structural terms; those with right of centre political views are more likely to view poverty in individualistic terms, and are less likely to believe that 'real' poverty exists at all (Williamson 1974, Whiteley 1981, Furnham 1982, Wagstaff 1983, Golding 1991). In 1986, for example, 59 per cent of Conservative voters thought that there was 'very little poverty in Britain today', compared with 27 per cent of Labour voters (Jowell, Witherspoon and Brook 1987: 9), while by 1994, 54 per cent of Conservative identifiers believed that 'there is quite a lot of real poverty in Britain today' compared with 79 per cent of Labour identifiers (Taylor-Gooby 1995: 8). The authors of the 1990/91 British Social Attitudes Survey comment that party political divisions in attitudes to poverty are still surprisingly large: 'Almost four times as many Labour as Conservative identifiers attribute poverty to injustice in society, and three times as many Conservative as Labour supporters attribute poverty to laziness' (Jowell, Witherspoon and Brook 1990: 8). So, in 1989 for example, 30 per cent of Conservative identifiers saw poverty in terms of laziness, compared with only 9 per cent of Labour identifiers: 'These ideological divisions are all the more interesting when we see that attitudes vary little according to income level. In other words, working-class Conservatives are similar to middle-class Conservatives in their view of the extent of poverty in Britain and its causes' (Jowell *et al.* 1990: 8). By 1994, the proportion of Conservative identifiers defining poverty in laziness terms had dropped to 18 per cent, but was still larger than the 12 per cent of Labour identifiers with the same view (Taylor-Gooby 1995: 8).

Conservative voters also have stronger beliefs that the world is a 'just place', and that 'outcomes' in life, and death, are directly related to behaviour. These 'just world beliefs' are themselves strongly associated with more negative attitudes towards the poor (Furnham and Gunter 1984, Harding, Phillips and Fogarty 1986). Political ideologies exert a strong influence on welfare ideologies (and vice versa), and these are strongly associated with attitudes towards poverty and the poor. Conservative identifiers are traditionally more likely to view poverty in individual terms and to promote a 'residual' state welfare system (George and Wilding 1994), although the ideological differences between right and left are becoming more blurred as all political parties have moved to embrace the ideology of a mixed economy of welfare.

Left and right on welfare, poverty and the 'undeserving' poor

Dominant social attitudes towards poverty, and political ideologies, help to shape the construction of, and responses to, poverty and the poor. As will emerge later in this book, they also shape the interventions by welfare professionals in cash and care. If poverty is constructed as a private, individual problem (in terms of its cause or effect), then what politicians, policy makers and professionals do about it, if anything, will be quite different to what actions would be taken if it were defined in social, structural terms.

If we trace the patterns of political rhetoric in Britain during the 1980s and 1990s we can identify a number of themes around poverty and the poor, and around welfare reform, which have dominated concerns across the political spectrum. As we have already seen, there is a contradiction in social attitudes which simultaneously construct the poor as victims and villains. Despite some movement towards greater sympathy with the poor as a whole, there is still a profound reluctance on the part of many citizens, particularly those with Conservative political views and the associated anti-collectivist welfare ideology, to regard poverty in anything more than 'absolute' terms (see chapter 2). Moreover, the *cause* of poverty is still very often viewed as the consequence of individual behaviour or culpability. The result of this individualised focus is to relegate in importance the structural and socio-economic characteristics of poverty, and devalue the shared collective experience of exclusion among the poor. Moreover, it leads to the separation and categorisation of the poor into sub-groups, divided along the lines of 'deserving' and 'undeserving'.

The view from the right

Increasingly, the Thatcher and Major governments of the 1980s and 1990s, supported and encouraged by New Right thinkers from the United States and Britain, have questioned whether the welfare state is sustainable on economic and moral grounds. Glazer, for example, has argued that: 'A greater degree of voluntarism and of self-help and expansion of the non-statutory sector can do a great deal to provide for needs and services ... We should think of ways to meet needs with a lesser degree of dependence on public action' (1988: 139). This analysis, and that adopted by the Conservatives, derives from a deep concern with the consequences of state-provided welfare and social policy; the apparent capacity of welfare to increase 'dependency'; its ability to weaken established valued institutions and the threat this poses to the social, economic and moral order. According to Glazer even people with disabilities are guilty of 'dependency' and welfare manipulation. Many, he argues, have taken advantage of the US system to receive assistance: ' ... in the 1970s surprising increases in the numbers who get social security payments on the basis of disability suggested that not all disability is beyond control of the disabled, or incapable of being affected by incentives and disincentives' (Glazer 1988: 102). At the heart of this critique and concern with the destructive potential of social policy and welfare provision is a philosophical liberalism which seeks to limit the role of the state to sustaining the conditions required to protect individual freedoms. Central to this is the belief that individuals make decisions and operate within a context of self-interest. If, through a free market, they are allowed and enabled to pursue self-interest within the confines of the law, their individual efforts will benefit society as a whole (Green 1993). The role of the state is therefore a limited one, to protect the freedoms of the individual from interference by others [Document 4]. The duty to help any so-called 'victims' of this process rests predominantly with families, the 'active citizen' and charities, rather than with the state.

This critique is reflected in the rhetoric, politics and policies pursued by successive Conservative governments in the 1980s and 1990s. An early indication of the Conservative's approach was contained in their strategy for social security reform during the 1980s. The government argued that: 'In building for the future we should follow the basic principle that social security is not a function of the state alone. It is a partnership between the individual and the state – a system built on twin pillars ... it should not discourage self-reliance or stand in the way of individual provision and responsibility' (DHSS 1985c: paras. 1.5/1.7). This strategy, of promoting pluralism and partnership between the state, the citizen, the markets and other welfare providers (family, the private, voluntary and charitable sectors) is at the heart of Conservative social policy with regards to cash and care. Individuals have been encouraged to take responsibility for their own welfare, and for the welfare of their families, through combinations of informal arrangements of kith and kin, private insurance, or purchases through the quasi markets in health and social care (Johnson 1990, Deacon 1991, Deakin 1993, Le Grand and Bartlett 1993).

In a further review of social security policy initiated in 1993, the Prime Minister, John Major, spoke about the need for a greater role for the market in welfare provision and for a further review of public expenditure: 'We utterly reject the idea that the State can manage economic and personal relations between people better than businesses or families'. He also referred to the need to explore workfare-type schemes: 'I increasingly wonder whether paying unemployment benefit, without offering or requiring any activity in return, serves unemployed people or society well' (Major, quoted in *Daily Telegraph* 1993). Just days later, the then Chief Secretary to the Treasury, Michael Portillo, announced to the House of Commons a 'sweeping' public spending review. The purpose of the review was to: 'Distinguish between the essential costs of high priority spending, which we will continue to fund, and avoidable spending which we cannot afford ... We will be seeking to identify areas where better targeting can be achieved or from which the public sector can withdraw altogether' (Portillo, quoted in *Guardian* 1993a) [see also Document 4]. In a later speech Portillo suggested that:

The trend of legislation over 30 years has been to put more responsibility on Government. The scope of Government has vastly increased. The safety net has become thicker, higher and wider. Help from Government has become widely available with scant regard to whether the recipients have behaved reasonably, or unreasonably, responsibly or irresponsibly. As a result, the penalties for fecklessness have been diminished and the rewards for personal responsibility devalued.

(quoted in *Guardian* 1994c)

Referring to Portillo's comments, the Director of the Child Poverty Action Group (CPAG) suggested that Portillo was using the 'deserving' versus 'undeserving' debate to 'divide and rule in order to justify cuts in benefits' (*Guardian* 1994c). However, Portillo's views hold widespread currency among other Conservative ministers and outside. The then Chief Secretary to the Treasury, Jonathan Aitken, confirming CPAG's fears, stressed that there would need to be substantial expenditure cuts in the social security budget and warned against the creation of 'in effect a benefit dependence culture and society' where people become 'too comfortable with benefits' (*Guardian* 1994f).

The view that the poor have become 'too comfortable with benefits'; and the associated images of a 'dependency culture', reinforce the view that the poor are different and subordinate, and that 'their' poverty is an individual problem of laziness, fecklessness, lack of effort, and even dishonesty. One particularly powerful image, drawing on many if not all of these concerns, is that of the 'underclass'. Perhaps the most vociferous proponent of the 'underclass' thesis is the American political scientist Charles Murray. His first essay relating to Britain was published in the *Sunday Times*, and given further weight through an influential pamphlet published by the right-wing Institute of Economic Affairs (Murray 1990). This pointed to the dangers of an American-style 'underclass' developing in Britain. Murray's argument is that the 'underclass' does not refer to a degree of poverty, but to a *type* of poverty. He defined the characteristics of the 'underclass' in terms of high rates of illegitimacy, of crime, and dropping out from the labour market. Murray argues that poverty is a consequence of the behaviour of individuals: 'When I use the term "underclass" I am indeed focusing on a certain type of poor person defined not by his condition, e.g. long-term unemployed, but by his deplorable behaviour in response to that condition, e.g. unwilling to take the jobs that are available to him' (Murray 1990: 68). Murray argues that there is an increasing number of people in Britain who are becoming detached from the values of work, decency and community, and form an 'underclass' where crime and illegitimacy is rife. In a second essay published in 1994, he updated his thesis and concluded that the picture had deteriorated significantly since his first study. Again, he argued that illegitimacy was the key measure of the 'underclass' and that 'the civilising process that begins in infancy and is completed by marriage ... cannot occur in societies where the two-parent family is not the norm' (Murray 1994: 26). Those communities in which 'the family has effectively collapsed' (p. 11), Murray believes, would become increasingly chaotic and violent, degenerating into what he termed the 'New Rabble'.

Many of these images of the 'underclass', of 'benefits dependency' and of family and social disintegration, have been associated particularly with lone parent families. There are about one and a half million lone parent families in the UK, and most – 90 per cent – are headed by women. Nearly three-quarters of these families are in receipt of income support, while another quarter of a million are receiving family credit because of low wages. Most lone parents and their children could be considered to be living in poverty (Bradshaw and Millar 1991, Oppenheim 1993a).

Charles Murray has been especially concerned with the dangers posed by lone-parent families: 'long-term welfare dependency is a fact, not a myth, among young women who have children without husbands ... a series of changes in the benefit rates and collateral housing benefits lifted a large proportion of low-income young women above the threshold where having and keeping a baby became economically feasible' (Murray 1990: 8/30). For Murray, governments and social policy have encouraged more women to *choose* lone parenthood as a way of life; benefits have then maintained them in a 'dependency culture'. Murray's analysis is shared by Glazer and others who also argue that such developments are profoundly damaging to children, the family and society more generally: 'There is sufficient evidence that the welfare culture itself ... the experience of living in poor female-headed families dependent on income transfers and living in concentrations of such people, serves independently to damage the children in these settings' (Glazer 1988: 85). Dennis and Erdos (1992), in an Institute of Economic Affairs publication, have also argued that the growth of lone parenthood is undesirable and dangerous: the presence of the natural father is critical for the child's development. According to Dennis and Erdos, academics and 'conformist intellectuals', by accepting lone parenthood as a legitimate family formation, have helped to undermine the family, social stability and common sense, and have encouraged irresponsibility and selfishness (Dennis and Erdos 1992, Dennis 1993).

Many social policy academics and others have challenged the very concept and meaning of an 'underclass'. Frank Field (1989) has viewed the 'underclass' as a structural phenomenon, resulting from social and economic restructuring. Those most likely to comprise the 'underclass' include long-term unemployed people, lone parents and elderly people dependent on social security benefits. Others have argued that there is no evidence to support the view that claimants and other welfare users have a different behavioural and moral code to the rest of society. Indeed, the evidence seems to show quite the opposite, that people on low incomes aspire to a job, a decent home and an adequate income, as do the 'non-poor' (Dean and Taylor-Gooby 1992, Kempson 1996). Moreover, the diverse ways in which the concept has been used, by those on the left and right, leads to confusion and uncertainty about what the term actually means and how it should be applied (Oppenheim and Harker 1996: 17–18, Lister 1996a). The concept of an 'underclass' is as yet unproved, and perhaps unhelpful: 'It may provide a convenient focus for public expressions of anxiety about the alleged culture of dependency, but it conveys a powerful and apocalyptic image of social breakdown and decay that has been more useful to leader-writers than to policy makers' (Silburn 1992: 138).

Proven or not, the image of the 'underclass' and benefits dependency has had a strong influence on the political rhetoric relating to poor lone parents. The Conservative Party Conference has often been a centrepiece for the attack on lone parenthood and poor lone mothers in particular. In October 1993, for example, ministers deplored lone parents 'married to the state'. Michael Howard, as Home Secretary, linked lone parenthood – and illegitimacy in particular – with rising crime and the decline in morality, despite no rigorous evidence to support either. At the same conference the Housing Minister, Sir George Young, announced plans to review the housing priority of lone mothers: 'How do we explain to the young couples who wait for a home before they start a family that they cannot be rehoused ahead of the unmarried teenager expecting her first, probably unplanned child?', he asked (quoted in the *Guardian* 1993d). By 1995 it became clear that lone parents were to be targeted for further cuts in benefits, despite the publication of research showing that lone parent families face substantially higher child costs in relative terms than two parent families, and that the single parent premium and one parent benefit were critical for maintaining the living standards in lone parent households (Dickens, Fry and Pashardes 1995).

Perhaps one of the most radical ways of dealing with the 'problem' of lone parents and their 'benefit dependency' was a suggestion put forward by the Institute of Economic Affairs, and already widely advocated in mainstream US politics, that lone mothers give up their children for adoption, to help provide children with two parents and a stable, permanent home – the 'ultimate privatisation' (*Independent on Sunday* 1995b, see also Morgan 1995). Peter Lilley, as Secretary of State for Social Security in John Major's government, has echoed Murray's analysis of the dangers of lone parenthood when he observed that more young women were having children outside wedlock because many young men were not worth marrying (because of their low earning capacity), and that many unskilled young women could receive as much on benefits as in paid employment (Lilley 1995a: 26). John Redwood MP, the failed challenger to John Major in the 1995 Conservative leadership competition, fully endorsed suggestions that lone mothers should consider giving up their children for adoption. Within days, a Conservative member of the House of Commons Social Security Committee was calling for lone parents to receive a lower level of benefit if they refused to place their children for adoption (*The Independent* 1995d). The next year, just after the 1996 Adoption Bill was published, junior health minister John Bowis fuelled the debate by suggesting that single mothers-to-be might consider giving up their 'unwanted' babies for adoption rather than bringing them up alone (*Community Care* 1996a).

There is a strong belief, especially among those on the right, that lone parents have only themselves to blame for their situation, and that their feckless and irresponsible behaviour damages not only themselves and their children, but, like the 'underclass', is a danger to the values and security of the wider society. Their actions, activities and choices need to be regulated and controlled, particularly through welfare reforms designed to deprive them of any 'preferential' status within the social security system, and get them back into work.

The view from the left

While Labour would not endorse a philosophical liberalism, there is evidence that there has been some convergence between Conservatives and New Labour in the 1990s concerning the need for, and strategies towards, welfare reform [Documents 2 and 7]. When Labour's Social Justice Commission published its final report in 1994 it was described by the Chairman, Sir Gordon Borrie, as a plan for the 'biggest shake up of welfare for 50 years'. The report was concerned to combine 'the ethics of community with the dynamics of a market economy'. It viewed social justice not just as being about how much society spends on other people, but about 'how much we invest in ourselves'. The report's proposals, firmly embedded in a 'mixed economy of welfare', included: the taxation of child benefit for those in the higher rate tax bracket, a national minimum wage and a minimum pension guarantee, among others (Commission on Social Justice 1994). Similarly, when the Rowntree Foundation published its report some months later, there appeared to be an emerging consensus on the need to redesign social security to promote work, enterprise and personal responsibility (see also McCormick and Oppenheim 1996, Beresford and Green 1996). Responding to the Borrie report, Tony Blair, Labour's new leader, welcomed this 'truly remarkable piece of work':

> Second generation welfare is about giving people a hand up and not just a handout ... It means services and not just cash – child care as well as child benefit, training as well as unemployment benefit, care in old age as well as a pension. Welfare should be a springboard to success and not a safety net to cushion failure. It should provide the stability within which families and communities can cope with a world of change.

> (quoted in the *Daily Telegraph* 1994b).

A radical restructuring of the welfare state was now firmly on the agenda of all the main political parties. Blair confirmed 'New Labour to modernise welfare, not a debate about paying more benefits, but giving each and every able-bodied person the chance to work and to do without benefits' (Blair 1995). He also pledged a 'wholesale review' of the welfare state if Labour were elected to power: 'If the benefit system means that people are better off on benefits than they are in work, then it is failing' (*Financial Times* 1995a). Blair's review of the welfare state would be based on six principles: promoting personal responsibility and deterring fraud; enhancing the role of the family and protecting children; greater use of the private sector to provide services or benefits; rewarding moves from benefits to work; better services, including child care for working mothers and long-term care of vulnerable groups; greater flexibility to tackle emerging problems such as the increasing use of life savings to pay for nursing care for the elderly. Labour's reluctance to commit itself to a more generous benefit system was especially clear in the Party's reaction to the publication of the 1995 Rowntree Inquiry Report. Labour called for people on benefits not to be excluded from increases in national wealth, but would not promise to uprate payments to promote participation and citizenship if it gained power (*Daily Telegraph* 1995a). Shadow Chancellor Gordon Brown argued that what was needed was a 'new war on poverty', based on a string of measures to get people off benefits and back to work, in the interests of social justice and economic efficiency (*The Independent* 1995a).

By the end of 1995 Blair had ordered a radical rethink of Labour's policy on welfare in general and social security in particular. He told Chris Smith, shadow social security secretary, to 'think the unthinkable' and produce a comprehensive blueprint within six months. Many of the ideas to be examined, including those of Frank Field, were a far cry from the suggestions of Labour's Social Justice Commission, whose findings already seemed relegated to a distant memory. Indeed, in Chris Smith's letter to constituency Labour parties and affiliated organisations, he reminded them that 'the Commission's Report does not represent Party policy'. The Terms of Reference for the new review contained 10 principles that would govern Labour's approach to social security, including: a recognition of the fundamental Beveridge insurance principle; a benefits-to-work strategy; the long-term sustainability and affordability of provision that is made; the genuine security provided by the system, particularly in terms of planning for old age; the promotion of personal responsibility; and a real assault on fraud and error (Smith 1995). In the area of personal pensions Labour appeared to be moving closer to supporting Frank Field's (1995) proposals for compulsory contributions to private pensions. Field had also proposed compulsory insurance for unemployment and long-term care in old age, suggestions endorsed by the Dahrendorf Inquiry and appearing quickly to become the new orthodoxy among the government and opposition parties.

When Chris Smith announced the principles governing Labour's proposed overhaul of the social security system, on the same day as the government announced its proposals for private insurance and pensions to pay for care in old age, some commentators judged this to be 'the end of the welfare state' (*Guardian* 1996b). Both parties had moved some way from the comprehensive, state-run social insurance model that had informed policy since the 1940s. Both now placed greater emphasis on the use of private insurance as a means to secure stability and independence throughout the life cycle. Smith commented: 'Surely it is time to get away from the sterile battle lines of public and private and, instead, to look at how the two can best work together in the interests of the citizen – and in the interests of all citizens at that' (*Guardian* 1996b). One month later Labour published its proposals for encouraging claimants to move from welfare to work (Labour Party 1996) [Document 2]. The package included measures to merge benefit and employment advice offices in one stop shops and introduce a single claim for all main benefits; encourage jobless people to study and do voluntary work, removing existing penalties which limit both; make it easier for people to return to income support if temporary or uncertain employment did not work out; and provide 'flexible benefits' whereby unemployed people would be able to make flexible local use of benefit and training money. This last measure would allow local decision makers ('case managers') to use local resources for benefits, training and special employment measures, to tailor a package for individual claimants, thus introducing local variation into the social security system, an idea also popular with Peter Lilley (see chapter 4). An earlier commitment to abolish the government's controversial jobseekers allowance had been dropped.

Both the rhetoric of the government and New Labour supported a mixed economy of welfare and a greater role for the private sector, particularly private insurance, in the provision of cash and care. Labour's social security agenda mirrored increasingly that of the Conservatives. Frank Field's ideas, particularly those concerned with fraud and abuse of the welfare state, had strong overtones of the speeches of Social Security Secretary, Peter Lilley (see for example the debate on benefit fraud, *Commons Hansard* 18 June 1996: cols 688–741). Indeed, at times both Field and Lilley seemed to be engaged in their own exclusive debate about the future of welfare, with a series of articles in the press and cross-referencing to each other's stance, and with Field writing an introduction to Lilley's own 1995 collection of essays on the future of welfare (Lilley 1995a).

Labour's social security agenda mirrored that of the Conservatives, or was it – as Blair suggested – the other way round, with the Conservatives sounding more like Labour? Blair argued that Labour needed to reclaim 'language and attitudes that used to be ours but in the 70s and 80s became associated with the Tories' (*Financial Times* 1995a). Rather than New Labour stealing the clothes of the Conservatives, Blair was suggesting that the Conservatives had stolen Labour's clothes. However, Peter Lilley counter-argued that it was New Labour which was the real thief: 'Mr Blair's other device is to sing Tory tunes using Tory rhetoric about the need for "wholesale reform of the welfare state". But why should the electorate prefer karaoke Conservatism to the real thing?' (*The Times* 1995b). While there was evidence of some convergence in welfare thinking, particularly on the need for welfare-to-work strategies and a growing role for private insurance, the Conservatives appeared to go further than Labour in their proposals for structural reform. In 1996 they initiated action to privatise the administration and delivery of social security benefits and to introduce a purchaser–provider split in the field of social security, similar to their approach in the fields of health and community care (see chapters 4 and 6, and Documents 6 and 7). In terms of poverty, the view from the right and left was one of encouraging citizens, including the poorest, to take responsibility for themselves, to leave welfare and get back to work. The political and moral commitment to abolish poverty as a social problem, and the challenge of including the views of poor people themselves, was not on the political agenda of either party. Both seemed oblivious to the implications and consequences of their proposals for poor people. Indeed, there were some, particularly those on the right, who argued that there was no such thing as 'real' poverty in Britain anymore. This is the subject of the next chapter.

CHAPTER 2

The politics of poverty: definitions, measures and effects

Introduction

An apparently simple set of questions concern us here: what is 'poverty' and does it exist in Britain today, how can it be measured, and what are some of its effects? Answering these questions is, however, fraught with difficulties, not least because the very terms 'poverty' and 'the poor' are social constructs, dominated by ideological and political disagreements.

In this chapter we examine the 'politics of poverty' as it relates to the debates and confusion over definitions, measures and the effects of poverty. We see how concepts and terms have been used, and misused, by politicians and others to promote the view that 'real' poverty no longer exists in late twentieth century Britain, and that 'relative' poverty is not really 'poverty' at all. We also consider the role of academics studying poverty and the poor, the evidence they have gathered on the extent, nature and effects of poverty, and the way in which they, and their work, have been drawn into the politics of poverty.

Defining poverty

Our starting point is concerned with definitions. Alcock has suggested that: 'Arguably it is the issue of definition which lies at the heart of the task of understanding poverty. We must first know what poverty is before we can identify where and when it is occurring or attempt to measure it; and before we can begin to do anything to alleviate it' (1993: 57). Defining poverty – and whether or not it exists at all – has been fraught with difficulty and controversy. The answer to the question 'does poverty exist in Britain today?' depends on how poverty is defined and by whom; and how it is defined depends, partly, on the political values, welfare ideology and beliefs of the person making the definition (see chapter 1).

There are some who argue that poverty, as a concept and condition, is only meaningful in an 'absolute' sense. This view is based on the belief that 'real' poverty is linked with 'subsistence'; poverty occurs only when and where people have insufficient resources to provide the minimum necessary to sustain life. This conceptualisation draws heavily on the late nineteenth and early twentieth century work of Booth and Rowntree. People were said to be in poverty if they had insufficient resources to meet basic physical requirements. In 1901, for example, Rowntree proposed that a family would be considered to be living in poverty if its total earnings were insufficient to obtain the minimum necessary for the maintenance of merely physical efficiency (Rowntree 1901).

In the late twentieth century, 'absolute' poverty, equated with extreme need – starvation, hunger and destitution – is still widespread in many countries, particularly 'Third World' and some former Soviet bloc countries. People are considered to be 'poor' if they do not have sufficient resources to be able to provide food and water, shelter, clothing, warmth or other 'necessities' to sustain life for themselves or for their family. Comparisons with the very public squalor and suffering of the poor in these countries, and indeed in Britain during the 1930s, reinforces the view that, in Britain today, 'Absolute poverty ... has been virtually eliminated by the welfare state' (Prescott 1994: 26). Any 'absolute' poverty that does exist is viewed as a residual problem affecting just a small group of people (for example homeless and destitute people, and some elderly people). Media images of elderly people who die in the winter because they cannot afford to heat their home, and homeless people sleeping in boxes under bridges or in the doorway of shops, support the view that while these may be considered as examples of 'real' poverty, they are relatively small-scale or isolated. Moreover, the concern in many of these cases is not so much one of 'poverty', but rather of the poor themselves, and particularly about their lifestyles – how they 'choose' to live their lives.

The 'absolute' concept of poverty has, in the 1980s and 1990s, been hijacked by some on the right to support their view that there is no such thing as 'real' poverty in Britain. The argument goes that, because absolute poverty has been virtually eliminated, there is no 'real' problem of poverty in late twentieth century Britain. For most of the 1980s the word 'poverty' was rarely used by Conservative politicians or in official reports; rather the talk was of 'low income families', quite a different notion to 'the poor', as we shall see later. The argument that real poverty has been eradicated in modern Britain also informed the British Government's response to calls for it to implement anti-poverty policies during 1996, the International Year of Poverty Eradication. As we saw in chapter 1, the government declined to take any new action, arguing that this was an issue for Third World countries, not for Britain. Similarly, when the Rowntree Foundation published its influential 1995 report on income and wealth the findings prompted some in government and elsewhere to label the inquiry as a 'fatally flawed' exercise – one which had fundamentally misunderstood the true nature of poverty:

... the Rowntree report falls at the same fences – relative poverty, average incomes, absolute poverty – that brought down its predecessors in their attempts to prove that the lives of poor people are getting worse, and that the government is to blame ... *And real poverty is, surely, absolute poverty – not a relative decline, nor statistical gymnastics performed with rising average incomes or poverty lines, but actual drops in living standards* ... In short, the report has failed to make any significant discovery about poverty in Britain; and its findings themselves are based on dubious foundations.

(*Sunday Telegraph*, 1995, my emphasis)

In the late 1980s the then Social Services Secretary, John Moore, also argued that 'real' poverty had been eradicated in Britain by Western material capitalism. He suggested that language had been shaped and facts manipulated deliberately by academics and others, in order to present as poverty what was in reality simply inequality: 'I suggest that what happened was that by the 1960s the gulf in living standards between countries under socialist governments and those with capitalist systems had become glaringly apparent ... At this point of crisis for socialism, academics came to the rescue. Realising that poverty was on the wane, academics helpfully discovered a new kind of poverty' (Moore 1989). This 'new kind of poverty', Moore believed, was little more than inequality. In fact, he misunderstood, or chose to misrepresent, the nature of 'relative' poverty being put forward by a number of academics, particularly by Peter Townsend. 'Relative' poverty, as we shall see, is quite different to inequality.

Relative poverty

Those academics and others who conceptualise poverty in relative terms argue that poverty, in Britain and elsewhere, cannot simply be equated with starvation and destitution. The argument goes that there is 'real' poverty in Britain today, and that this is best understood as a condition of exclusion from social participation, or partial citizenship (Townsend 1979, Golding 1986, Lister 1990, Oppenheim and Harker 1996). In a reconceptualising of Rowntree's work (Veit-Wilson 1986, Spicker 1993, Stitt and Grant 1993) it has been identified that Rowntree himself observed that there was a difference between subsistence and 'living': 'My primary poverty line represented the minimum sum on which physical efficiency could be maintained. It was a bare standard of subsistence rather than living ... such a minimum does not by any means constitute a reasonable living wage' (Rowntree, quoted in Oppenheim 1993a: 7). Rowntree saw that his primary poverty line did not allow for anything 'extra'; in his own admission it did not allow for a 'reasonable' living wage.

Academics developed the relative approach in more depth from the 1960s, but their purpose was not, as Moore had suggested, to 'helpfully' discredit capitalism, but was rather one stage in an academic process of understanding, and coming to terms with, the continued existence of poverty amidst affluence. Interest in poverty was also part of the development of social policy and administration as an academic field of study (Bulmer, Lewis and Piachaud 1989, Brown and Payne 1990).

Peter Townsend and others were developing an alternative conceptualisation of poverty which challenged the dominant absolute-subsistence
paradigm (Abel-Smith and Townsend 1965, Coates and Silburn 1970,
Townsend 1979). This critique argued that the absolute approach could
not be sustained in theory or in practice; the very process of quantifying
and calculating an individual's need for food or other necessities
involved judgements (usually by experts) based upon changing dietary
requirements, and assumptions of a *socially* determined kind about
eating habits and styles. In other words, people's needs for 'necessities'
were conditioned by the society in which they lived and to which they
belonged; both 'needs' and 'necessities', like 'poverty', are social
constructs (Doyal and Gough 1991). It is not possible to divorce the
determination of even basic physical or biological needs – of necessities
– from the conventions of society in which those needs are defined and
in which they have to be met. Over time, even absolute conceptualisations of poverty change as living standards improve (Fiegehen, Lansley
and Smith 1977, Veit-Wilson 1986). Nor is it possible to make absolute
pronouncements (indeed, who should be allowed to make them?) on
what is a 'subsistence lifestyle', what minimum level of income ensures
subsistence (and nothing better or worse) for *all* citizens?

The deeper the analysis of 'absolute' poverty, the more the concept
becomes fragile and unsustainable. Its usefulness to guide policy formulation and implementation is especially problematic when specific
policy options are considered. Consequently, poverty has to be understood as a dynamic concept, and measured in relation to the living
standards which are generally accepted in the society, and at the time, in
question. Townsend has suggested that:

> Individuals, families and groups in the population can be said to be in poverty
> when they lack the resources to obtain the kinds of diet, participate in the activi-
> ties and have the living conditions and amenities which are customary, or are at
> least widely encouraged and approved, in the societies to which they belong ...
> Their resources are so seriously below those commanded by the average indi-
> vidual or family that they are, in effect, excluded from ordinary living patterns,
> customs and activities.

(Townsend 1979: 31)

Townsend's relative definition of poverty is based upon what he calls a
'deprivation standard' (Townsend 1979, 1993a). He argues that as
people descend the income scale, more families reduce disproportionately their participation in the community's styles of living – in effect
they are forced to drop out of participation or are excluded. He argues
that there is a threshold at which non-participation – or relative deprivation – increases sharply. That level of income can be said to constitute
poverty. It is this level, this threshold, and the *effects* on people of
having to live on incomes at or below this threshold, which distinguish
relative poverty from inequality: 'is there a threshold of income which
really does have an effect in terms of mortality, of the isolation of
people, their withdrawal from citizenship roles, family roles and so

on? ... This to my mind is the essence of any rational investigation of poverty – which distinguishes it from an investigation of inequality' (Townsend 1993b: 49–50). Poverty is a prescriptive concept, carrying with it a moral imperative that something needs to be done about it. Inequality is a descriptive concept – a state of affairs – and whether it is acceptable or not is a matter of opinion, and some debate (Alcock 1993: 6). The Thatcher administrations of the 1980s believed that inequalities were necessary to encourage a dynamic enterprise economy, where income would trickle down from the better off to the poorest (Johnson 1990, Deacon 1991, Lilley 1996). Following many years of a narrowing in inequalities, the gap widened from the late 1970s to 1992, to the extent that inequality was at its widest since the Second World War (Millar 1991, Barclay 1995). It was only after the publication of the 1995 Rowntree report into income and wealth that Prime Minister John Major accepted publicly for the first time that too much inequality is also a cause for concern, and that it is a responsibility of government to reduce inequality (Oppenheim and Harker 1996: 166, Beresford and Green 1996).

Today, the concept of poverty, in its relative sense, centres on the notion of exclusion from social participation. The European Commission definition of poverty confirms that: 'The poor shall be taken to mean persons, families and groups of persons whose resources (material, cultural and social) are so limited as to exclude them from the minimum acceptable way of life in the member states in which they live' (Golding 1995: 213). Academics, pressure groups and others have published numerous reports in the 1980s and 1990s which analyse how poor people are excluded from full participation in the life of the community (some of their evidence is outlined in more depth later in the chapter). Moreover, this exclusion has to be seen in the context of power and powerlessness, not just financial resources: 'Poverty is not only about shortage of money. It is about rights and relationships; about how people are treated, and how they regard themselves; about powerlessness, exclusion and loss of dignity' (Church House 1985: para. 9.4). While the concept of 'powerlessness' is widely accepted as an important factor in the contemporary discussion of poverty, there have been those who have argued that there is a danger in going too far down this path. So, for example, a number of authors have begun to emphasise the strengths and 'agency' of poor people themselves, the need for them to have a say in how services are constructed, run and managed, and in the definition of poverty itself (Lister and Beresford 1991, Beresford and Croft 1986, 1995). Lister suggests that: 'The question is how we can combine a structural analysis with recognition that poor people do have agency and in many cases are using it' (Lister, quoted in Friedrich Ebert Foundation 1993: 51). At one level, while poor people may be 'victims' of structural forces or oppression, they are also actors in their own right (Jordan 1990, Lister 1994, Williams and Pillinger 1996). Consequently: '... the achievement of lasting solutions may rest not in what can be done *for* the poor but what is done *by* the poor' (Deakin 1993: 28, my emphasis). This movement, to include poor people, has parallels in other spheres of social policy, for example the emphasis on including social services' users and family carers in decision making and service arrangements for community care (see chapter 6).

Towards a synthesis of absolute and relative conceptualisations

Absolute conceptualisations of poverty necessarily involve relative judgements to apply them to any particular society and 'relative definitions require some absolute core in order to distinguish them from broader inequalities' (Alcock 1993: 62, see also Sen 1983). In their 1980s study of 'Breadline Britain', Mack and Lansley attempted to bridge the conceptual gap between absolute and relative poverty. They tried to define poverty by reference to what the general public, rather than so-called 'experts', saw as necessities and a minimum standard of living. The authors found general agreement about what constituted this minimum. At least two out of three people surveyed thought the following were necessities: self-contained damp-free accommodation with an indoor toilet and bath; weekly roast joint for the family and three daily meals for each child; two pairs of all-weather shoes and a warm, waterproof coat; sufficient money for public transport; adequate bedrooms and beds; heating and carpeting; a fridge and washing machine; enough money for special occasions (e.g. Christmas); and toys for the children (Mack and Lansley 1985). Mack and Lansley went on to define poverty as a situation in which people were forced to live without the items/ services which *society as a whole* regarded as necessities. In 1983, they found that 7.5 million people – one in seven of the population – lacked three or more of these necessities. By 1990, the number of people lacking three or more of these necessities had increased to 11 million – one in five of the population (Mack and Lansley 1985, Millar 1991, Golding 1991). Despite being consensually defined necessities, these judgements involve relative, cultural and time-specific considerations by the public at large. There has been controversy surrounding the inclusion of certain items as necessities, not least a 'Sunday joint' or a washing machine. The 'consensus' on what is a necessity not only changes over time but varies between different groups and cultures (Walker 1987).

A further attempt to synthesise the absolute and relative approaches can be found in contemporary use of the 'budget standard'. The budget standard approach is based on a specified basket of goods and services which, when priced, can represent a standard of living (Piachaud 1979, Bradshaw 1993, Oldfield and Yu 1993, Middleton, Ashworth and Walker 1994). Judgements about the goods and services to be included are made by a panel of experts, supplemented by behavioural measures of the goods and services which people actually buy. The approach, attempting to synthesise notions of necessities with items and services commonly consumed, is a reformulation of the approach adopted by Rowntree almost a century ago. Where it differs is in its deliberate attempt to take full account of evidence about people's *actual* spending behaviour – including spending on non-essentials. Different types of budget can be determined, for example a low cost budget or a modest but adequate budget. The approach can also be used to evaluate the adequacy or otherwise of social security benefit levels. So, for example, Middleton and her colleagues have drawn up a budget standard of essential items agreed upon by mothers ('real' experts rather than 'professional' experts). Compared to income support rates the resulting budget produces an average shortfall for children under 11 of £7.92 per week and as much as £11.57 for a boy aged two to five. Mothers from all social backgrounds agreed that there was no way they could reduce their minimum budget any further (Middleton, Ashworth and Walker 1994). The levels of benefit provided by the state were far too low to enable mothers to buy the items that they had defined as essential.

The budget standard approach offers a way to bring together the relative and absolute notions of poverty and link these with wider issues concerned with the adequacy of benefits. Veit-Wilson (1994) has suggested a reformulation of the budget standard approach, with an emphasis on minimum income standards – the lowest income level required for people to take part in ordinary social life and thus be kept out of poverty (see also chapter 7). He argues that social assistance in Britain was never intended to provide for day-to-day needs. In the absence of an 'official' minimum income standard it is difficult to make definitive pronouncements about the adequacy of income support because we cannot be certain about what needs income support is intended to cover. However, the findings of academics, budget standard researchers and others do indicate strongly that social assistance is too low to provide for a minimally adequate level of living in Britain today. To avoid poverty, citizens on social assistance would need higher levels of benefit; for families with young children they would need incomes about a third higher than their income support levels.

Not surprisingly, these findings and conclusions are viewed with suspicion by some, particularly those in government. Controversy has been generated by the methodology, results and policy implications of both Mack and Lansley's work and the budget standard approach. What should be included in the list of necessities, or in the budget, and who should decide? There is 'plenty of scope for argument and disagreement' (Silburn 1993: 16). Moreover, as more people, including the poorest, have been able to purchase 'consumer durables', this has been used, particularly by those on the right, to challenge whether people on the lowest income are, in fact, poor at all. In 1996, Peter Lilley, Secretary of State for Social Security, in a speech highly reminiscent of John Moore's earlier lecture, commented:

I have always avoided sterile debates about how best to define poverty ... Over the same period [1979–92/3] the proportion of people in the bottom tenth of income who own consumer durables has risen enormously. For example fewer than a third had a fridge-freezer in 1979. Now the overwhelming majority (84 per cent) do. Almost no low income household in 1979 had a video. Now nearly three quarters have one. Some 40 per cent had a car in 1979. Now 57 per cent have one. To most people the idea that well over half the group alleged to demonstrate ever-deepening poverty nonetheless have a car – at least gives pause for thought!

(Lilley 1996: 2, 3) [Document 3]

The resource and policy implications for a government attack on poverty as 'social exclusion' would be immense. Consequently, the political manipulation of the debate over definitions, and whether or not poverty exists in Britain today, may be a deliberate attempt to define 'poverty' out of existence. Lilley, like John Moore before him, has linked the relative approach with the 'politics of envy', a matter of inequality, not real poverty (Lilley 1996: 1, 6). This is in sharp contrast to those proposing the relative conceptualisation of poverty as 'real' poverty. They view poverty – as exclusion from social participation – as having profound consequences for the lifestyles, opportunities and well-being of the poor, particularly children, as they experience multiple deprivations, including ill health, and other negative and destructive effects.

Measuring poverty

Even though there is no universally agreed or politically neutral definition of poverty, or an official poverty line in the UK, there are measures which are used to indicate the existence and extent of poverty. These are derived largely from official and other sources of statistics. One measure, the 'Low Income Families' statistics, is derived from official data (the Family Expenditure Survey), and shows the number of people living on, below or just above social assistance (supplementary benefit/income support) levels. From 1972 to 1988 these figures were produced by the Department of Health and Social Security. They are now regularly produced by the Institute for Fiscal Studies for the House of Commons Social Security Committee. A second 'proxy' poverty line is the 'Households Below Average Income' statistics (HBAI). Under this measure people could be considered to be living in poverty if they are living below half average income after meeting housing costs. Since 1988, the Households below Average Income statistics have been published by the Department of Social Security. Using these two approaches it is possible to derive two cash-based proxy poverty lines for all family types, for any year.

Low Income Families

According to the Low Income Families/income support poverty line, a couple could be considered to be living in poverty if they had an income after housing costs of £66.60 per week or less in 1992–3; £69 per week or less in 1993–4; or £73 per week or less in 1995–6 (Oppenheim 1993a, Oppenheim and Harker 1996: 27). The corresponding figures for a lone parent with one young child aged under 11 are £71.05 in 1992–3, £73.60 in 1993–4 and £77.90 in 1995–6 (Oppenheim and Harker 1996: 27). It is possible to derive figures for any type of household using this approach. Under this measure 13.7 million people – almost a quarter of the UK population in 1992–3 – were poor (measured as living on or below income support levels) (Social Security Committee 1995). Nearly 3.7 million children (29 per cent of all children) lived in families on or below income support levels. The figures also show that 4.74 million people (8.3 per cent of the population), including more than 800,000 children, lived on income *below* the 'safety net' of income support. One main reason for this is the low take-up of some means-tested benefits. According to government estimates as many as one in four people eligible for income support do not claim it. The average number of people not claiming income support though entitled was between 770,000 and 1.57 million in 1993–4; the total amount of unclaimed income support was between £740 million and £1,660 million (DSS 1995a).

The findings of academics and others involved in budget standard work and poverty research confirm the proposition that those living on, and especially below, income support levels, can be considered to be living in poverty. One study after another has shown that those living on or below income support levels will be unable to afford a modest but adequate standard of living – in other words a standard which keeps them out of poverty. Where children are present the low level of income support can have particularly damaging consequences on health and lifestyles (Graham 1996). Budget standards research suggests that 2.7 million children living in families on income support are receiving some 25 per cent less than is required for a basic level of subsistence (Oldfield and Yu 1993). On a 'low cost' weekly expenditure, a couple with two children would require an extra £34 per week in 1993 over the income support level in order to afford the budget. A lone parent would require an extra £23. This 'low cost' budget does not allow extravagance. It provides for the minimum basics of housing, food, fuel and clothing, very few toys, no outings, one return bus fare a week and a day trip to the seaside as the annual holiday. If a slightly higher budget was taken – one which allows for a few more clothes and educational visits a year – then the cost of a child under 11 would be £56 per week in 1993. Consequently, the shortfall in actual income support levels would be even greater (see also Bradshaw 1990, 1993, Kumar 1993). Those with the lowest incomes – those living below social assistance levels – will, according to Townsend's deprivation threshold, be those who are most likely to experience deprivation, exclusion from social participation and the damaging consequences of poverty.

This pattern has been confirmed by numerous research studies and through the voices and testaments of poor people themselves. However, the seriousness of the situation has been ignored, indeed disbelieved, by governments throughout the 1980s and 1990s. For example, when Malcolm Wicks MP, Labour spokesperson on child support, presented figures in the House of Commons on the number of children living on income support, he also asked: 'Would the Minister care to bring up a child on income support levels? Why have the government deliberately created mass child poverty?'. The reply from the government front bench was scornful and dismissive: 'The Hon. Gentleman puts his argument at the most exaggerated level possible, but that is typical of the Labour Party' (*Hansard* oral answers, 23 April 1996: col. 182).

Households Below Average Income (HBAI)

The HBAI figures show the living standards of people in the lower half of the income distribution. Data are available on the number of individuals in various income bands, such as those living in the bottom 10 per cent, 20 per cent and so on, up to 50 per cent of the income distribution. Many poverty commentators have chosen 50 per cent of average income as a proxy poverty line. So, for example, under this measure a single person could be considered to be poor if their income in 1992–3, after paying for housing costs, was £61 per week or less (£65 at 1995 prices). A couple with three young children aged 11 or under could be considered to be in poverty if their income after housing costs was £183 or less in 1992–3 (£196 at 1995 prices) (Oppenheim and Harker 1996: 33).

According to the HBAI measure, in 1979, 5 million people (9 per cent of the population) were living in households with below half average income. By 1992–3, the figure had risen to 14.1 million people, 25 per cent of the population (DSS 1995e). Those most vulnerable to poverty on this measure include unemployed people, those in part-time work, lone parent families and single pensioners. Many of these groups are dominated by women (Glendinning and Millar 1992). Well over four million children (33 per cent of all children) live in poor families (defined as those living below 50 per cent of average income after housing costs), particularly in families where there is no full-time paid worker.

The HBAI figures also provide a picture of growing economic divides. They show that between 1979 and 1992–3 average income overall rose by 38 per cent. The richest in society (the top 10 per cent) did particularly well during this period: their real income rose by 62 per cent. However, the poorest (the bottom 10 per cent) fared dramatically worse: their real income actually fell by 14 per cent between 1979 and 1990–1, and by 17 per cent between 1979 and 1992–3 (DSS 1995e). Examining such data Goodman and Webb (1994), and Jenkins (1994), reveal that increases in income inequality over the previous 15 years had left the poorest tenth of the population no better off than in the late 1960s. However, these conclusions have been rejected as 'flawed' by right wing think tanks and politicians, among others (see for example Pryke 1995). Peter Lilley has argued that, by focusing on *spending* patterns rather than *income*, it can be seen that people on lowest income are able to purchase far more luxuries and consumer durables than in the past. He suggests that the *expenditure* of the bottom 10 per cent, rather than falling, has actually risen by around 14 per cent (Lilley 1996, DSS 1996c). Moreover, the bottom quintile of the income distribution is a mobile, not a static, group – between a quarter and a half move up and out of this group, to be replaced by others (Lilley 1996, Webb 1995). Lilley argues that this lowest income group is certainly not poorer than in 1979, indeed it has done very well under the Conservatives. However, Lilley's argument is challenged by evidence from the government's Family Expenditure Survey. Low income families may spend more than they receive in benefits, but their lifestyle is very much more restricted than high income or even average income families. A much higher pro-portion of spending of low income families goes on basics such as food and heating, not consumer durables or luxuries.

Unravelling the meaning of these figures and the HBAI data is a political and academic minefield. The evidence that the poor have got 'absolutely' poorer under the Conservatives is perhaps less convincing than it was in the early 1990s, although the evidence that they have got relatively poorer remains compelling (Timmins 1996: 9). The findings of those involved in budget standard work confirm that those living on half average income or less will experience exclusion from social participation; these levels of income, irrespective of differing family structures, fall short of enabling claimants to have a 'low cost' or 'modest but adequate' standard of living (Bradshaw 1993, Oldfield and Yu 1993, Middleton, Ashworth and Walker 1994). The cumulative evidence suggests that a 'poverty line' (defined as the income level at which people only just have the minimum socially defined necessities) is somewhere around two-thirds (not half) of average incomes in the UK (Veit-Wilson 1994: 25).

In conclusion, the Low Income Families and HBAI figures provide two proxy, and controversial, poverty lines. That they can be considered to be measures of 'poverty' is reinforced by budget standard work, other academic poverty research, and the voices of poor people them-selves. Together, these confirm that income support levels, and half average income levels, are too low to allow people to participate fully in society. Both measures show that poverty in Britain is widespread, with about a quarter of the population being counted as 'poor'. The number of poor people has increased significantly during the 1980s and 1990s. This is quite a different picture to that proposed by others, particularly those on the right, who maintain that there is no such thing as 'real' poverty in Britain today.

Academics, poverty research and the media

Academic research has, by and large, failed to quell the level of ideo-logical and political disagreement as to the definition and measurement of poverty, or for that matter, its solution. Indeed, to a large extent, many academics have added to the confusion and controversy, as researchers and think tanks from different political persuasions and with competing agendas have put poor people under the social sciences microscope. The 'individualisation' of poverty (chapter 1) has also been a dominant characteristic of much poverty-related research, and particularly the media reporting of poverty, since the so-called 'rediscovery' of poverty in the 1960s. To a large extent the focus on the characteristics and lifestyles of the poor (as opposed to a sustained analysis of the structures and policy context of poverty) was a necessary factor in bringing about the growing awareness of poverty in the UK. The earlier studies by Abel-Smith and Townsend (1965), by Coates and Silburn (1970), and the many others since then, have helped to shape our awareness of poverty, who the poor are, the extent of poverty, and why some people are more vulnerable to poverty than others. Following three decades of extensive poverty research, including a decade-long programme of work on transmitted deprivation (Brown and Madge 1982), it has become harder for researchers in the 1990s to produce new findings about poverty or the poor. We have all become more aware of poverty, and its consequences and effects, as a result of exposure to case studies and human interest stories generated both by academics and the media. Almost every conceivable aspect of the lives of the poor has been scrutinised, dissected and laid open to public view. It appears that there is very little that we do not know. Silburn argues:

we know a great deal about the subject. We know why they are in poverty; we can describe their personal characteristics and their family circumstances; we can document their experiences and anatomise their attitudes ... We have debated the concept of poverty, the economics and politics of poverty, the psychology and philosophy of poverty ... We suffer in short from a combination of over-exposure and exhaustion. It has all been said before, many times. There is little or nothing to say on the subject that is new; there are no new insights around, no breakthroughs to report, and very little by way of policy recommendation that has not already been recycled more than once.

(Silburn 1994: 122)

And yet, if academics and others have provided so many of the answers, then why is it that governments have failed to eradicate poverty and the fear of poverty? The answer to this question draws us back into the politics of poverty: the ideological and political disagreements as to what constitutes poverty, how widespread it is and what needs to be done about it. While there is a broader political consensus that welfare needs reforming (see chapter 1), there is still very little agreement about the means and ends to eradicate poverty itself. Moreover, the fact that poverty and the fear of poverty have not been abolished in the UK, despite decades of academic study and media interest, a multitude of local and other initiatives, and the testaments of the poor themselves, supports a thesis that poverty is somehow functional in modern capitalist states (Spicker 1993), and that the *costs* of eradicating poverty, particularly the implications for social expenditure, would be too great for any 'sensible' government to contemplate seriously. Consequently: 'Governments have sought to manage poverty by controlling the amount of resources available *to alleviate its worst effects, not by preventing it*' (Walker 1993: 15–6, my emphasis).

Many academics, researchers and anti-poverty campaigners, fuelled by a moral commitment to act on poverty, and knowing that there is little new to report, have changed their focus from 'what still needs to be said' to 'how best to say it'. The concern has shifted more explicitly to how to influence the political and policy-making process. Researchers have made new alliances with journalists and others in the media and elsewhere, as academics have become more conscious of the need to disseminate their findings to wider audiences, to influence social attitudes and the climate in which policies are formulated and implemented. For example, the children's charity, National Children's Homes (NCH 1994) thought it had a new way to communicate poverty when it published a report which claimed that 1.5 million families were so poor that they could not afford the diet of an 1876 workhouse. Following a barrage of criticism concerning its methodology and calculations, the director of policy at the charity conceded that: 'By itself, poverty is not particularly attractive. In order to attract journalists, one has to have a good line, and the workhouse diet is a good line' (Dent, quoted in the *Sunday Times* 1994a). It seems that poverty can be made 'attractive' to a wider audience, and perhaps have greater policy influence, when it personalises and individualises poverty, and when it refers to the tragedy or human face of poor individuals, families or communities. The *Guardian*, in a 1994 series 'Stories from the streets', revealed the tragedy of 'Britain's underbelly' with stories of the 'destruction of [children's] personalities by a childhood spent in poverty' (see for example, *Guardian* 1994e). In 1995 the *Guardian* ran a further series, 'At the front line', from the 'pressured points of our fractured society', highlighting the pain and despair of the poor and poorest (*Guardian* 1995c, d, e, f). Such media images construct the poor as victims, suffering in poverty and despair. *Guardian* stories of the 'underbelly', and *Sunday Times* stories of the 'underclass', help to sell newspapers and, to an extent, make poverty 'attractive' to diverse readerships of different political persuasions. Whether they will have an influence on social attitudes towards poverty and the poor, and on the political and policy process, remains to be seen.

Images of the poor as victims, and as villains, have existed for decades but there has been relatively little change in how the poor have been defined and treated by politicians, policy makers or the public during the 1980s and 1990s. While the wilder excesses of the Poor Law may have been replaced, British social attitudes and social policy still maintains, indeed legitimates, arrangements for the control and exclusion of the poor, particularly those seen as 'undeserving' (Novak 1988, Squires 1990). The discussion of poverty in the 1990s, especially in some academic and media circles, has often become repetitive, voyeuristic and competitive: who has the best story to tell, who can produce the best 'sound-bite', what new angle is there to make poverty 'attractive'? Meanwhile, economic divisions have increased, and the number of people living in poverty, according to data reviewed earlier in this chapter, has escalated to around a quarter of the population.

Successive governments during the 1980s and 1990s have attempted to 'neutralise' or suppress the publication of some academic research, or have attempted to discredit reports which are out of line with their own thinking on poverty and the poor. In the 1980s, Prime Minister Thatcher, encouraged by the 1980 Rayner Scrutiny of government, imposed tight controls on what data were collected and published. In particular she promoted the collection of data that she thought were directly relevant to the activities of government, rather than to the wider democratic debate or public interest. Since then, poverty reports have been given little attention by politicians, and consequently by policy makers, if they do not confirm the chosen analysis or preferred policy options. Reports which are critical of government but which have received widespread media coverage are harder to ignore, hence a need by governments to counter their analysis or findings, either privately or out in the open. For example, the children's charity, Barnardo's, the publisher of a high profile study on child poverty (Wilkinson 1994), received a private letter from Virginia Bottomley, the then Health Secretary, reprimanding them for publishing the document, which also led to the charity delaying the publication of a follow-up report on inequalities (*Guardian* 1995a). Other examples are available where the government has attempted to suppress the publication of social policy-related reports when the analysis or findings have been politically unfavourable (see Craig 1995 for a review of some of these incidents). The report of the Rowntree Foundation Inquiry into income and wealth (Barclay 1995) could not be suppressed or ignored (every paper and news programme carried a feature on it), but ministers and others tried hard to discredit it. In the House of Commons the Social Security Secretary, Peter Lilley, accused the principal Rowntree author, John Hills, of left-wing bias. The right-wing press, and some right of centre think-tanks, also suggested that the report was methodologically 'unsound' and ideologically biased (Cooper and Nye 1995, Beresford and Green 1996).

Why should governments want to ignore, suppress or discredit some research on poverty and the poor? One answer may be related to political self-interest. Politicians may feel the need, supported by allies in the media and similar-thinking academics, to discredit the findings of reports that show poverty has worsened under that government, or as a consequence of government policies (see for example Pryke 1995, Cooper and Nye 1995). There is evidence to suggest that during the 1980s and 1990s governments have attempted deliberately to keep the discussion of poverty, and the policy options, rooted in 'common sense' rather than being research-driven.

The effects of poverty: the dominance of ideology over 'facts'

Battles of ideology, understanding and interpretation are especially fought out with regard to some of the 'big issues'. For example, is poverty linked to crime and ill health? Some say yes, others say no, and then there are those who argue for variations in between. What all sides have in common is their well-presented, well-researched and well-argued positions, and the belief that their position is the only one that is correct. Some of the protagonists may be willing to accept a link between poverty and ill health, or between poverty and wrong-doing, but would be reluctant to accept that poverty is the *cause*. To accept poverty in such a way, and crime or ill health as the *effect*, would require new political responses and ways of dealing with, and talking about, criminals, sick people and the poor themselves. It would challenge some of the most deep-seated assumptions, beliefs and prejudices of British society, many of which locate the cause of illness, crime and poverty – and other forms of deviancy or difference – as a personal, rather than a social construct or social problem.

The Thatcher and Major governments have persistently argued that there is no direct causal link between criminal behaviour and living in poverty, despite research evidence to the contrary (Kempson *et al.* 1994, Benyon 1994, NACRO 1995). In the 1980s, despite the riots in deprived inner cities and the findings of the Scarman Committee (Scarman 1982), the government still rejected any poverty-related influences on crime and disorder. More recently, a Conservative Home Secretary, Michael Howard, confirmed that 'We should have no truck with trendy theories that try to explain away crime by blaming socio-economic factors' (Howard, quoted in *The Independent* 1994a). Prime Minister John Major has also declared that: 'There is no excuse for crime. Just because you're poor, you are not likely to become a criminal … ' (Major, quoted in the *Guardian* 1994g). The government has argued that, rather than poverty causing crime, in fact crime and delinquency are largely the consequences of bad parenting and family conflicts (see also Utting, Bright and Henricson 1993). The right wing media have been quick to draw on this type of argument:

> Instead of blaming economic conditions, it should help to focus attention on the real origins of such behaviour. One of the primary factors leading to criminal tendencies has been identified as the quality of parenting, and this in turn relates to the stability of family life … Sometimes crime rises and sometimes it falls, and the same goes for unemployment and poverty. But they do not rise and fall together, as they would if they were cause and effect.
>
> (*Daily Telegraph* 1995b)

Others on the right have argued that it is the welfare state itself, not poverty, which has encouraged a growth in lawlessness. Marsland (1994), for example, suggests that welfare benefits and services inflict moral and psychological harm by sapping people of their independence and commitment to hard work: 'It is turning estates and neighbourhoods right across Britain into factories of crime and arbitrary violence' (Marsland, quoted in *The Times* 1994a).

The debate over poverty and ill health is another battleground where ideology and politics have ruled over research 'evidence' and 'facts'. The view that poverty is associated with, let alone causes, ill-health has been especially hard to accept for Conservative governments in the 1980s and 1990s. When Sir Douglas Black produced his famous report on the subject (Black 1980), the then Social Services Secretary, Patrick Jenkin, refused to publish it. Since then there have been a number of other important assessments of the links between ill health and poverty, confirming the causal association (Whitehead 1987, Townsend, Davidson and Whitehead 1992, Benzeval, Judge and Whitehead 1995, Bartley, Blane and Davey Smith 1996). Up to 42,000 deaths a year could be prevented if the health of the poorest in Britain reached the levels of the richest (Phillimore, Beattie and Townsend 1994). Despite the evidence, the Major government has refused to accept the causal link. In 1992 it published its 'Health of the Nation' strategy, which effectively denied any association between poverty and ill health (Cole-Hamilton 1991, Root 1995).

These disagreements over the association between cause and effect – in crime and ill health – are sometimes concerned with the measurement, analysis and interpretation of complex sets of data, but they are most often ideological and political. It is not surprising therefore that there is little movement to eradicate the social determinants of crime, inequalities in health, and poverty itself, when there is so much disagreement as to definitions, measures, causes and effects. The dominant paradigm locates the cause of crime, ill health and poverty on to the individual and family unit. The consequence of this medical-pathology model is to redefine social problems as individual, private matters. The plethora of academic studies from the 1970s onwards, and media attention, have not led to the eradication of poverty, or even to a reduction in the number of people living in poverty. Indeed, the evidence suggests that there are more people living in poverty in the 1990s than in the 1960s – when poverty was 'rediscovered'. Academics continue to research and publish on poverty and some have made direct alliances with politicians and political parties in order to have more influence on the policy-making process. Their ideas have influenced in particular Labour's Social Justice Commission and the 1995 Rowntree Inquiry into Income and Wealth, to name but a few. There does appear to be a greater commitment among academics and research sponsors to influence policy formulation and implementation as it relates to poor people. As Piachaud asserts: 'If the term poverty carries with it the implication of moral imperative that something should be done about it, then the study of poverty is only ultimately justifiable if it influences individual and social attitudes and actions' (Piachaud 1987: 161). Academic studies and media coverage have made us all more aware of, but – as exposure has increased – perhaps less angry and concerned about, the existence and condition of poverty. The developing alliances between academics, researchers and the media, concerned with disseminating findings and influencing the policy agenda, is important in ensuring that alternative analyses are forthcoming and open, and that the government does not wholly control the climate of ideas, beliefs and attitudes in which poverty and the poor are constructed, and in which responses are formulated and implemented.

There are some, however, who have questioned the dominant approach to anti-poverty campaigning during the 1980s and 1990s, with its emphasis on research and the collection of 'facts' and 'evidence' by academic 'experts'. Beresford and Croft assert:

Modern anti-poverty campaigning has emphasised measurement and the production of evidence of poverty. To secure support and provide ammunition for reform, campaigners have offered apparently incontrovertible data to show increasing inequality and the worsening scale and nature of poverty. But government and the political right – key players in poverty debates and developments – have so far had little difficulty in dismissing or neutralising these arguments.

(Beresford and Croft 1995: 12)

There is a movement, growing in voice and influence during the mid-1990s, and paralleling the earlier achievements of the disability movement, to shift the parameters of the debate on poverty away from the academic and professional domain, to one which gives greater power and resources to enable poor people to speak out for themselves. However, as will be shown in the remaining chapters of this book, these voices have gone largely unheard in the spheres of cash and care, as ideology and politics have dominated the policy agenda, and poor people have borne the cost.

CHAPTER 3

Cash, care and welfare: continuity and change in historical perspective

Introduction

This chapter examines the human need for welfare, particularly among poor people, and charts the changing balance between the major sources of 'cash' and 'care', namely the informal, independent and state sectors. It provides a historical overview of some of the main concerns and policy developments in the fields of cash and care, with especial focus on the state's role and responsibilities with regards to social security and personal social services, including social work and community care. The contemporary structure of benefits and social care services, and the existing balance between the main providers of cash and care, need to be understood as the latest, but certainly not the last, phase in a broader, historical continuum, of twists and turns in the relationships between the family, the state and the markets. In particular, social security and social services have developed primarily as state responses to the growing awareness of poverty and the poor, to 'difference' more generally, and from the political need to be seen to regulate and control the behaviour of those defined as 'undeserving' or 'dangerous'. The balance between state provision and other sources of welfare is in constant flux; in the future the private sector and families are likely to take greater responsibility, as they have done in the past, for meeting the welfare needs of citizens, including the poorest. The underlying concern here, and in subsequent chapters, is with the consequences of these shifts in policy and politics for poor people. It is these citizens who make heaviest use of state provision, in particular social security and social services, and it is they who will also bear a disproportionate cost, in terms of life chances and exclusion from social participation, as the balance between the state, the markets and the family continues to change, and as the state retracts, adapts and takes on new responsibilities and functions.

Meeting needs for welfare: the importance of cash and care

As citizens, we all have basic needs for cash and care, just as we need food, drink and shelter (Doyal and Gough 1991). Money enables us to purchase the goods and services that we require as individuals, families or communities; it enables us to go about our daily life, make choices, live our life with decency. At other times, though, our need is not so much for 'cash' as it is for 'care': services that support and enable us to live with as much independence and dignity as is possible. Our needs for cash and care are inherently interlinked. Sometimes cash empowers us to buy care. Other times care is provided without the need for a direct cash transaction between the receiver and the provider. Often we need just one or the other, but it is a certainty that all of us will need both at some time in our life, and that many people will require cash *and* care frequently and intensively. So, for example, people with physical impairments, elderly people, those with mental health problems or learning difficulties, may require care services – in the community or within institutions – at particular stages in the life cycle, or when others are not available to provide care for them from within their own family networks. Their cash and care needs may be complex and multifaceted. Many people in these groups also face a particular vulnerability to poverty. Whether care services are provided for them, or whether they are given the cash to purchase such services, is a hotly debated issue (see chapter 6). Either way, their needs for cash and care are inseparable, although the ultimate balance between the two will depend on a complex range of factors, not least the availability of alternatives from within, and outside, the family. Adequate cash and care are the necessary foundations for welfare, citizenship, dignity and freedom from poverty.

The notion of 'welfare' refers to the well-being of citizens and the satisfaction of their needs (George and Page 1995: 1). Moreover, the *source* of that welfare is of importance both to individuals and to society, not least for reasons of security, reliability and cost, but also because different sources carry different social labels (George and Page 1995: 2). A wage from paid employment is the main source of cash income in capitalist systems and accords perhaps the greatest status. Sixty-one per cent of gross household income in Great Britain during 1994–5 came from wages and salaries (Government Statistical Service 1996). Income from work is a key mode of empowerment because it enables people to make choices about their life, about consumption, lifestyles, priorities, futures and opportunities. All the main political parties now consider the best route out of poverty is through paid employment and benefit-to-work programmes (chapter 1). People outside the labour market (for example because of their caring responsibilities, because they are sick, disabled or have retired) are generally excluded from receiving direct income from paid employment. People on low wages are also denied an income which is adequate to provide choice, dignity and freedom from poverty. Depending on accumulated savings, wealth or other financial resources, low income families may require additional income to enable them to continue to function and live their lives with some decency and independence. In post-war Britain, the main vehicle for income replacement, or for topping up low levels of income in or out of work, is the state's social security system. In the mid-1990s, eight out of ten households received at least one social security benefit; 18 per cent of gross household income came from benefits (Government Statistical Service 1994, 1996).

The term 'social security' is commonly used in Britain to refer to all cash benefits, including insurance transfers (for example, benefits for the unemployed such as unemployment benefit/jobseekers allowance, old age pensions), means-tested social assistance (income support) and universal benefits (for example, child benefit). All citizens will use social security at one time or another, and many will make extensive use of it throughout the life cycle. The majority of people who use it will have limited or restricted incomes from elsewhere, and many of these people will be among the poorest in society. Three-quarters of all social security spending goes on people with below average incomes and 25 per cent of the population are in receipt of means-tested benefits (DSS 1992, 1995b, 1995e). In the 1980s and 1990s many people 'opted out' of the state's social security system and attempted to maximise their replacement incomes during periods of sickness, disability, unemployment and old age, through occupational work-based schemes or through private means, including personal pensions and private insurance. The expectation that the state could or should be the only provider of social security was eroded; there is an acknowledgement, across the political spectrum, that other sources can provide cash, as well as care. The social security system, and its relationships with poverty and the poor, are the focus of chapter 4.

Social care services are also provided through a number of sources, including family and friends (the 'informal' sector), private, voluntary and charitable organisations (the 'independent' sector), and through the state itself. The state's responsibility for the delivery of social care in England and Wales now rests with local authority social services departments; with social work departments in Scotland; and with health and social services boards in Northern Ireland. These departments provide, or arrange provision, of personal care services for vulnerable people, including those with special needs because of old age, mental or physical impairment; their carers; children in need of care and protection; and families. The main users of personal social services are the same groups who are the main beneficiaries of social security expenditure (HMSO 1995: Figure 5.1). They are also among the poorest in society. Nine out of ten users of social work services are claimants, and around half of these are in receipt of means-tested social assistance reserved for the poorest (Becker and MacPherson 1986). Only about one in ten social work users are in paid employment and many of these receive or are eligible for a benefit 'top-up' because they are in low paid work (Becker and MacPherson 1986, Becker and Silburn 1990). Users of social services are among the most marginal people in society: 'the recipients of social work services are people whose lack of resources, vulnerability and behaviour cannot be adequately met and dealt with by their own social networks or privately purchased alternatives' (Davis 1991: 84). The relationships between social services, social work and poverty are the focus of chapter 5.

The balance, interrelationships and interdependencies between state, independent and informal providers of cash and social care will vary at different times, depending on the ideology, politics and approaches of governments, prevailing social attitudes, beliefs about the role and responsibilities of the state in relation to individual and collective need, and so on. So, for example, in the nineteenth century private organisations and charities were major sources of social care and welfare; private organisations supported those who could afford to buy help while charities assisted those who could not afford to take out insurance or buy services directly. From the mid-twentieth century the state took on major responsibilities for meeting needs by providing both cash *and* care. During the 1970s, and particularly the 1980s and 1990s, there has been a shift back to a greater role for the informal and independent sectors, particularly for 'market' arrangements with private organisations providing services or insurance, and for internal markets within the fields of health and social care. As patterns of human need change, and as ways of meeting need also change, so too have the relationships between the different sources of welfare and the relationships between the individual, the state and the markets. As discussed in chapter 1, the balance at any one period in time is influenced strongly by the ideological and political values and beliefs of those commanding influence and those exerting power. The emphasis on *who* should meet needs – the individual or the state – has also fluctuated over time. The post-war Beveridge settlement, as shall be shown later, marked the start of a distinct period of state welfare collectivism, while the 1980s and 1990s represent a shift to the dominance, again, of the ideology of individualism. All political parties in the 1990s, despite differences of emphasis and detail, are agreed that it should be the individual's prime responsibility for meeting their needs and those of their family, and that 'welfare' will be best guaranteed and secured through a 'mixed economy' – the combination of informal, independent and state – working in partnership, *and* in competition, to provide and promote the well-being of all citizens, including the poorest.

Concerns and developments in cash and care: a historical perspective

To understand the importance of cash and care to poor people, particularly the centrality of the state's provision of social security and personal social services, we need to have some knowledge of historical concerns and policy developments in these fields. We also need to understand how the balance between the different sources of cash and care – informal, statutory and independent sectors – have changed over time. Focusing on state provision enables us to explore the changing boundaries between the state and other sources of welfare, and between cash and care themselves. Moreover, it helps us identify the consequences of change on poor and vulnerable people.

Early mixed economies of welfare and the growing awareness of poverty and 'difference'

The oldest social welfare institution in Britain, as elsewhere, is the family (Kamerman and Kahn 1978, Ungerson 1990, Jani-Le Bris 1993). Throughout history, family members and relatives, and close friends or neighbours, have been the main providers of care and support – including financial support – to those who are sick, disabled, elderly, young, frail or have other special needs. This support has almost always been provided free of charge, as part of a sense of family duty or social obligation. At times, where there are no family or friends available, willing or able to provide cash or care, others have sometimes stepped in to protect individuals or groups, to avert suffering or death, to change behaviour, to make a profit from the enterprise, or for a combination of reasons and motives. These providers of care and support have included religious orders, charities, philanthropic organisations, voluntary groups, friendly societies, private (for profit) organisations, local government bodies, central government agencies and so on. The 'mixed economy of welfare' has existed for centuries. Whatever the balance between the private sector, voluntary groups and public authorities; between individuals and the state; and between individuals, the state and the markets, it has been the institution of the family – with all its strengths and weaknesses – which has continued throughout history to be the main provider of social welfare. The 1990s discourse and rhetoric concerned with the importance of the family places informal carers centre-stage in the delivery of social care and community care, and puts the emphasis on to the individual, rather than the state, for taking responsibility to meet personal and family needs.

Some of the earliest welfare services provided from *outside* the family were supplied by religious orders 'augmented in medieval times by the manor houses and merchant and craft guilds, which assumed as part of their duties and responsibilities the care of the sick and the destitute' (HMSO 1995: 2). However, this practice fell into disuse with the dissolution of the monasteries and the decay of the feudal system. Some replacement was needed to deal with the vulnerable sick, disabled and others who could not always help themselves, whose families needed assistance, or for those who did not have any family available to help with cash or care. From the middle ages, the old Poor Law provided help to poor, disabled and elderly people at parish level. Issues around the care of disabled and other vulnerable people were closely linked to a wider concern to protect society from the perceived social and economic burden, and threat to morality, represented by the 'undeserving' poor. The 1601 Poor Relief Act gave local authorities in England and

Wales the duty to provide from local taxation for the sick, the needy and the homeless (similar duties had been passed in Scotland in 1579) (HMSO 1995: 2). The Act sought to distinguish between the 'infirm' and the 'idle' poor. The infirm were to be given relief; the idle were to be punished (Golding and Middleton 1982: 10). Under this system each parish in England and Wales was obliged to support its own elderly and disabled poor and to ensure that the 'idle' – the able-bodied poor – were engaged in work (Digby 1989, J. Scott 1994).

By the early nineteenth century the cost of Poor Law rates and the growing concern that population growth would outstrip the resources available to meet need, led to the reform of the Poor Law and the establishment of workhouses (Rose 1971, Thane 1982, Novak 1988, Digby 1989, Squires 1990). In the 1834 Poor Law, an important distinction was made between 'indoor' and 'outdoor' relief. The workhouse was to provide basic indoor shelter for the idle and 'undeserving' poor. This was to be intentionally unattractive and stigmatising, so as to support and promote the 'principle of less eligibility', namely that the conditions imposed for the receipt of such poor relief should always be less attractive than undertaking the worst paid labour. If the workhouse test was too easy and lenient, and there was no stigma attached, it was believed that the principle would be undermined (the 'idle' and 'undeserving' would positively seek out the workhouse rather than take low paid work). This approach, segregating the 'idle' and 'undeserving' from the 'deserving' poor, has underpinned much social security and personal social services policy ever since. It also provides the historical antecedents to residential care and treatment or correction within institutions.

For the deserving poor, infirm, elderly and physically impaired people, whose needs were more for care than for control, some financial and care support was provided by charities, charitable giving, and voluntary organisations outside the confines of the local workhouse and in a less stigmatising manner. In the nineteenth century, social services and social work (as they were to become) were almost exclusively the province of charity and philanthropy (Woodroofe 1962, Jones 1991). The support of the deserving poor, those with physical impairments and elderly people, was both a humanitarian gesture as well as a religious and moral crusade for the bodies, souls and minds of the poor, deprived and infirm. However, for some groups, particularly people with mental health problems (mental illness) or learning difficulties (mental handicap), the solution to their needs was often viewed in terms of social control rather than cash or social care. It was widely accepted that these groups required incarceration in an asylum or other institution, where their threat to society could be isolated, regulated and controlled. The 1845 Lunatics Act made the building of asylums for the mentally ill compulsory. The 1886 Idiots Act confirmed the need for residential treatment for people with learning difficulties (Korman and Glennerster 1990). The nineteenth century solution to the poverty of the idle and 'undeserving' poor, and the dominant response to the difference and 'dangerousness' of the mentally ill and people with learning difficulties, was institutional segregation in work-houses, asylums or long-stay hospitals, rather than cash and care in the community.

The combination of industrialisation (the growth of the factory sys-tem of production) and urbanisation (the movement of people from the country to the towns in search of employment) had a particular effect on reshaping patterns of social need and the conditions under which such needs might be met (Clarke 1993: 5). In the mid-nineteenth century a programme of sanitation reform was developed as a response to the intensification of sanitary problems associated with the rapid growth of towns. The 1848 Public Health Act established for the first time a com-prehensive public health system under unified control, and laid down minimum standards for its services. The 1875 Public Health Act devel-oped and consolidated the system and all subsequent health legislation is based upon this (HMSO 1995: 3).

The policy of institutionalising the mentally ill and those with learn-ing difficulties was reinforced by the growth of the eugenics movement in the latter part of the nineteenth and early part of the twentieth cen-turies. The movement expressed concern that the quality of the population stock was being corrupted by people with disabilities, whose 'menace' needed to be tightly regulated and controlled, using methods such as euthanasia, sterilisation, marriage regulation and segregation (Searle 1976, Macnicol 1989). The eugenics movement became increasingly vociferous, particularly in the early twentieth century, when it called for the government to implement some of the recommen-dations of the 1908 Royal Commission on the Care and Control of the Feeble Minded. The resulting 1913 Mental Deficiency Bill, concerned with 'idiots, imbeciles, feeble minded and moral imbeciles', endorsed the approach that they should be sent or placed in an institution for 'defectives' or placed under guardianship. The birth of an illegitimate child was considered proof of 'moral weakness' and consequently feeble mindedness. Many women, particularly those already receiving poor relief, were incarcerated in asylums and other institutions because, as unmarried mothers, they had shown themselves to be 'mentally defective'.

Meanwhile, the pace of 'legislative innovation' quickened (George and Page 1995: 6). The provision of health services began to improve rapidly as a result of medical progress and the wider availability of treatment. The National Health Insurance Act 1911 introduced a scheme whereby people on lower earnings were entitled to general practitioner services in return for regular contributions made by them-selves and their employers to certain insurance organisations ('approved societies'): 'The scheme came to cover most of the poorer half of the population while the rest were dependent for their medical care either on paying fees as private patients, or on a certain number of voluntary sick clubs (a form of voluntary insurance whereby people paid the doctor a few pence a week)' (HMSO 1995: 3). Voluntary hospitals expanded their own free services for the poor, helped by public donations and fees from other patients.

More legislation was introduced which maintained the strong regulation and segregation of the mentally ill and those with learning difficulties. The 1914 Education Act required local authorities to provide separate schools for the 'educable mental defective'; the 1927 Mental Deficiency Bill, despite the protestations of critics such as Josiah Wedgwood, widened the definition of 'defective' to include people who became mentally defective after birth but before the age of 18 (Jones 1972). Calls for the sterilisation of people with learning difficulties came to the fore in the early 1930s with the formation of a Ministry of Health departmental committee on the issue. The committee's report recommended sterilisation of females with learning difficulties (Jones 1972, Macnicol 1989). Although compulsory sterilisation was not implemented in Britain, it did become law in Germany in the early 1930s (Jones 1972, Scheerenberger 1983). The Nazis sent tens of thousands of 'incurables', people with mental illness and learning difficulties, directly to their death or to an uncertain future in concentration camps, justifying it by the need to maintain the purity and integrity of the race, and the general benefit of humanity (Scheerenberger 1983).

The legacy of the eugenics movement in Britain has endured throughout the post-war years and remains an influence on attitudes toward people with learning difficulties, and the poor. In 1972, for example, the then Secretary of State for Social Services, Keith Joseph, expressed alarm at the persistence of poverty and deprivation in society despite economic advance and the growth of personal social services. His concern was that deprivation was transmitted through poor families, from parents to children, and through them to future generations. One way to stop this cycle was to improve family planning among poorer households: '... an understanding use of family planning could reduce the numbers afflicted by deprivation' (Joseph, reproduced in Butterworth and Holman 1975: 390). In the 1980s the issue of sterilisation reappeared on the social policy agenda, amidst concerns about the sexual activities of young women with learning difficulties (Stainton 1992). However, as an overt force the eugenics movement in Britain declined for a number of reasons. Not least was its failure to make a scientifically convincing case for the hereditary transmission of mental illness or learning difficulties. Additionally, as shall be explored in more detail later in this chapter, the anti-institution critique and case for community care were becoming more forceful and persuasive. Of most significance, though, was the experience and legacy of the Second World War itself, which not only changed the welfare expectations of politicians and the public, but also served to expose the ultimate logic and horror of eugenics as a mass-scale 'final solution'.

Beveridge and beyond: the evolution of state responsibility for cash and care

The Second World War precipitated major reforms in cash and care (Addison 1975). To deal with people wounded in war the emergency hospitals service was developed within existing organisations; welfare food was introduced for mothers; school meals and industrial canteens were expanded. The inter-departmental committee chaired by Sir William (later Lord) Beveridge surveyed the existing national schemes of social insurance and allied services to make recommendations on the way that social services should be reconstructed after the war. The Beveridge Report, published in 1942, recommended extensive changes, including the extension of health, social security and personal social services. Two years later the government published their first plan for a comprehensive national health service, later embodied in the National Health Service Act 1946. The NHS came into operation in July 1948, providing a complete general practitioner and hospital service for all.

The 1948 National Assistance Act also finally brought to an end the Poor Law, while introducing a national social security system and an expanded role for local authorities in delivering social welfare. The administration of the Poor Law had earlier been transferred from Boards of Guardians to Public Assistance Committees of local authorities under the 1929 Local Government Act, and the 1930 Poor Law Act had renamed Poor Law relief as 'public assistance'. The 1948 National Assistance Act consolidated this, giving local authorities a greater direct role in the provision and management of social welfare. Personal social services, as caring organisations, were to be organised, administered and delivered locally, responsive to the expressed wishes and assessed needs of the individual, and delivered by face-to-face contact between service provider and client. Professional social work, as it has evolved for the past 50 years, is deeply rooted in this local, decentralised and individualised perspective. Meanwhile, policies of income maintenance were to be the responsibility of central government, which would finance and administer nationwide programmes of social security (Becker and Silburn 1990: chapter 1).

At the core of Beveridge's proposals was the extension of the national insurance scheme. Beveridge envisaged that almost everyone would pay flat rate national insurance contributions which would then entitle them to flat rate benefits, so covering them against loss of earnings due to old age, sickness, unemployment and other contingencies. These benefits would be sufficient for subsistence – enough to live on but little more. For those 'outside' the national insurance system, a means-tested safety net, national assistance, would be available. To be viable the whole system relied on the continuation of full employment and 'standard' family structures. In the event, a growing number of people found themselves outside the insurance scheme for long periods of time, mostly because of unemployment, lone parenthood, disability, poor health and caring responsibilities. Beveridge's scheme included no specific provision for many of these groups; it was not until the 1970s, for example, that benefits were introduced to meet some of the extra costs arising from disability. Many of the individuals outside the national insurance scheme had therefore to rely on the means-tested safety net to meet their immediate, and long-term, cash needs. However, the levels of insurance-related benefits were themselves never high enough to allow a clear distinction between insurance and means-tested benefits: 'assistance benefits were paid at a higher rate than the corresponding insurance benefits in the majority of cases' (Deacon 1995: 77). Consequently, many of those receiving insurance benefits would need to apply for additional money (means-tested national assistance) unless they had other sources. The numbers claiming means-tested benefits, rather than declining and withering away, grew and grew. Over time this was to challenge the whole viability of the state social security system and precipitated a series of reviews and reforms, particularly in the late 1970s, and throughout the 1980s and 1990s (chapter 4).

Meanwhile, in the field of social care, the 1948 Children Act provided the legislative framework for the welfare needs of children. It established that each local authority must have a separate children's committee. The responsibility for other welfare functions, largely determined by the framework of the National Assistance Act, was divided between health and welfare committees and between housing and education committees. Children's committees were responsible for children and families; welfare departments helped to look after older people, people with disabilities and the homeless; health departments were concerned with people with mental health problems and learning difficulties (Langan 1993: 48). All these committees were served by separate departments and different professional groups, which 'inevitably impaired the co-ordination of policy ... It also led, in the implementation of policy, to a multiplicity of visits to those in need by a succession of officials, each concerned with only one specialist aspect of care' (Lowe 1993: 263). From the outset there was an in-built problem of co-ordination and fragmentation in policy formulation, and implementation, in social care.

The new welfare consensus, best illustrated by the popularity of the Beveridge Report and post-war settlement, and the newly evolved welfare state, were to change the way in which the poor, and physically and mentally impaired people, would be treated by the state (Beveridge 1942, Vincent 1991, Silburn 1995). Stevenson refers to the 'pervasive sense of optimism' of the times: 'We believed that the foundations of a welfare state had been laid which were rock-solid, in the NHS, social security, education. We had a lot to do, but things could only get better' (Stevenson 1995: 2). Elderly people, the sick, disabled, unemployed and poor would now, as of right, be able to secure health care, cash benefits and care services, in principle from cradle to grave (Timmins 1995, Sullivan 1996). Social security would go hand in hand with a new

National Health Service, new rights to education, to housing and to social care.

Beveridge believed that the voluntary sector should play an important role in providing housing for older people and helping to overcome their loneliness, given that the state had taken over comprehensive and universal coverage to deal with the five 'giant evils' (Want, Disease, Ignorance, Squalor and Idleness) (Beveridge 1942, 1948, Mess 1948, Woodroofe 1962, Timmins 1995). Charities and philanthropy had a continued role to play, but this was now seen more in terms of filling the gaps in state provision and meeting the special needs of vulnerable people, rather than the widescale and widespread coverage of the past. The post-war years saw an immediate and far greater direct involvement in cash and care provision by the state, both at central and local level: 'it came to be generally accepted that the state should be the main provider of welfare, either directly through the provision of services or indirectly through the maintenance of full employment ... it is difficult not to conclude that collectivism had ousted individualism as the guiding principle in state affairs during this period – a truly remarkable trend in historical terms'(George and Page 1995: 7–8, see also Butcher 1995: 1). It was not surprising therefore that voluntary organisations and charities had to redefine their own specific role in relation both to the poor and to disabled people, and that they would need to do this again in the 1990s following a further period of rapid change (Commission on the Future of the Voluntary Sector 1996).

As time went on, however, the cost of direct state provision of cash and care grew inextricably as the Beveridge assumptions were shown to be out of date. Between 1949–50 and 1992–3, real expenditure on social security (at 1992–3 prices) rose from £10.3 billion (4.7 per cent of GDP) to £74.1 billion (12. 3 per cent of GDP) (DSS 1993a). By the end of the 1970s the cost of social security expenditure (then standing at £44.9 billion or 9 per cent of GDP) was a prime concern for the incoming Conservatives under Margaret Thatcher. By the 1990s it was a concern for *all* political parties, as the case for welfare reform and cost curtailment became a key objective – perhaps *the* key objective – for social policy (see chapter 1).

The growth in social security, and its changing composition (with a shift towards greater use of means-tested benefits) was driven by a number of factors during the post-war period, and from the mid-1970s in particular. These included demographic changes (for example, an ageing population which required retirement pensions and social assistance); economic changes (for example, the growth in unemployment, whereby more and more people required insurance-based benefits or social assistance if they had insufficient contributions); policy changes (for example, the trend towards deinstitutionalisation/community care, the introduction of new benefits such as non-contributory benefits for disabled people, or changes in other spheres – such as housing or personal social services – which have a knock-on effect upon social security); and social changes (for example, changing family structures and reconstituted families, increasing numbers of lone-parent families, many requiring social assistance because they had an inadequate contributions record) (Hills 1993, Lowe 1993, Sullivan 1996). The independent sector (especially the markets), and informal carers would re-emerge in the 1980s and 1990s, particularly in political rhetoric, as allies or 'partners' in the solution to a welfare state being defined increasingly as too costly, ineffective and misdirected, a welfare state in 'crisis' (O'Connor 1973, Gough 1979, Mishra 1984). New Right ideology, coupled with the rejection of Keynesian economics and the advent of monetarism, helped to reassert the doctrine of individualism over the policies of collectivism (Marquand and Seldon 1996).

The cost of social care also rose during this period. Real expenditure on personal social services, which had remained relatively static during the 1950s, doubled between 1960 and 1968, but the rate of growth slowed down again in the 1970s (Lowe 1993: 266, Langan 1993: 54). Social work as an activity, and social workers as a professional group, become more powerful during the 1950s, 1960s and early 1970s; indeed, they owed their very existence and status as 'experts' to the 'power of the state' (Clarke 1993: 15). Within the profession, and outside, there was growing concern that the workings of the 1948 Children Act and National Assistance Act were denying many families and vulnerable individuals, including those with physical and mental impairments, the care and support that they needed. Services were fragmented and poorly coordinated. The 1965 Seebohm Committee, charged with reviewing the organisation and responsibilities of local authority personal social services, widened its remit 'to consider what changes are desirable to secure an effective family service' (Lowe 1993: 266). Seebohm's vision was to establish a progressive universal service to 'reach far beyond the discovery and rescue of social casualties' and to 'enable the greatest possible number of individuals to act reciprocally, giving and receiving service for the well-being of the whole community' (Seebohm 1968: para. 2). However, there was a contradiction at the heart of the Seebohm Report which worked against the attainment of this vision:

On the one hand, [Seebohm] proclaimed a universal approach, aiming to transcend the stigmatising selective approach of much of the existing welfare services. On the other hand, the individualistic character of social work intervention and the continuing preoccupation of the social services with 'problem families' and 'difficult personalities' meant that, in practice, social work retained its focus on a particular section of the community ... new departments could never escape the selectivist legacy of the Poor Law.

(Langan 1993: 50–51, see also Webb 1980: 279)

This legacy is critical in understanding the operation and practice of contemporary social services, especially in the areas of social work and community care. Personal social services have developed from two separate (and sometimes conflicting) traditions (Payne 1979). One is the social work tradition, which has its origins in nineteenth century charities, especially Christian ones, and was subsequently influenced by psycho-dynamic theories concerned with individual growth and self-determination. The second tradition is of local authority welfare services, which had their origins in the Poor Law of 1834, and which were concerned with providing services and accommodation for the poor as required by law (Payne 1979, Woodroofe 1962). Modern social work has developed from a dual base of caring for and controlling poor people. Its Poor Law legacy has created 'stigma by association' (Gladstone 1995: 164).

Some of the Seebohm Report recommendations were implemented in the 1970 Local Authority Social Services Act, which established that each local authority should have an enlarged social services department, not a 'family service'. This department would: 'unite the various social work professions, co-ordinate fieldwork (so that both the "total requirements" of clients could be identified and the service made more "accessible and comprehensible") and pack sufficient political weight to attract adequate resources ...' (Lowe 1993: 267). The intention was, as far as possible, to ensure that families or individuals in need of care or protection should be served by a single social worker. However, the Seebohm Report and the subsequent changes failed to effect an immediate revolution in the personal social services similar to that achieved in social insurance by the Beveridge Report: 'This was perhaps inevitable because – despite its traditions stretching back to the nineteenth century – social work lacked the basic infrastructure, the tried methods and, above all, the universal appeal of social security' (Lowe 1993: 270). Local government reorganisation shortly afterwards led to increased numbers of social workers, but nonetheless damaged the reputation of social work and personal social services, as professional divisions became more transparent and as resources were diverted away from some 'respectable' areas such as child care to other spheres such as 'social action'. The 1970s saw the birth of the radical social work movement (Bailey and Brake 1975, Brake and Bailey 1980), the Community Development Programme and other initiatives which led to greater conflict with central government and funding bodies. The 'generic' social worker was a brief phenomenon. Social workers specialised increasingly in terms of their skills, approaches or client groups. Many social workers, influenced by the so-called 'rediscovery of poverty' and new academic thinking on its relative nature, questioned the casework approach to their work, of managing people rather than changing structures (Corrigan and Leonard 1978).

Some of the academics central to the rediscovery of poverty also had their own vision for the role of social services and social security. Peter Townsend, while supporting broadly the Seebohm recommendations, argued at the time that they did not go far enough. He suggested that a great opportunity had been missed to launch a new family and community welfare service whose aim should be to equalise resources, reduce social isolation, increase family support and enhance community integration (Townsend 1970). While these views had limited impact upon the new organisation of social services departments they did have an influence on the thinking of some social workers, particularly the 'radical' movement. Townsend's work, and that of the emerging poverty lobby and disability movement, challenged the very basis and function of social work in a capitalist, unequal, unjust, society (Corrigan and Leonard 1978, Bolger *et al.* 1981).

The debate over aims, objectives and methods raged within social work education and practice for much of the 1970s. Some questioned whether social work could actually survive as a profession (Brewer and Lait 1980). However, financial stringency, rather than professional concerns, was to have the decisive impact on the organisation of social services and the practice of social work. In 1974, the government issued a circular to social services departments urging them to concentrate their effort mainly on those in the most acute and immediate need: children at risk of ill treatment, the very old and severely handicapped in urgent need of care, and individuals and families at risk of imminent breakdown (Langan 1993: 54).

The next major examination of the roles and tasks of social workers was conducted less than a decade later, under the chairmanship of Peter (now Sir) Barclay. The Barclay Report (or more accurately the main report) argued that social workers should be involved in social care planning and community social work, to support existing family and community structures of care (Barclay 1982). These recommendations were not acceptable to some members of the committee, and two alternative strategies were proposed, one based on neighbourhood or 'patch-based' social work, the other on a traditional casework approach (Brown, Hadley and White 1982, Pinker 1982). Barclay did little to distil the tensions within the profession, indeed, many of the divisions within the Report were indicative of the continued crisis in social work as to the purpose and future of the profession.

It was the 1986 Griffiths Report on community care, and the NHS and Community Care Act 1990, which were to have far more radical implications for personal social services, social care and social work:

> The Seebohm Report, the Barclay Report ... have endorsed a broader view of social work than prevailed in the 1960s. But what Griffiths has endorsed is the philosophy and values of social services departments, not the primacy of social work in delivering community services. Indeed, while never making explicit his perception of the social work role, Griffiths may have provided a means of resolving the long-running debate within social work by providing clues to a new structural response to community needs, one which can utilise the categorisation of informal care.
>
> (Bamford 1990: 161)

Many departments in the 1990s split their organisation and operations between children's and adult services, propelled by the Griffiths Report and subsequent legislation, and by the 1989 Children Act. The contemporary structure of personal social services owes far more to Griffiths than to Seebohm or Barclay. And it was family carers who, once again, were to be acknowledged and promoted as the main providers of social welfare, rather than personal social services or professional social workers. The implications of these changes for poor people are the focus of chapter 6.

The anti-institution critique and the case for community care

A critique of the 'failure of institutions' has featured heavily in many of the social policy developments outlined above. This critique was especially important in developing thinking and policy about community care for vulnerable, poor people. Despite public hostility towards the 'undeserving' poor, and fear of the mentally ill and those with learning difficulties, some commentators in the nineteenth and early twentieth centuries attacked the ideology and policy of segregation, control and correction within institutions. The Webbs were vocal in their condemnation of workhouses for the poor at the same time as Josiah Wedgwood was critical of the new mental deficiency legislation. But it was only from the 1950s that this critique had a more powerful influence on the shape of contemporary social policy in relation to cash and care in the community.

Just a few years after the establishment of the post-war welfare settlement, in 1950, Bevan wrote, in a memorandum to the Cabinet, that 'Most of the hospitals fall far short of any proper standard ... indeed some of the mental hospitals are very near to a public scandal and we are lucky that they have not so far attracted more limelight and publicity' (quoted in Klein 1989: 36). At the same time, the National Council for Civil Liberties argued that 50,000 people with learning difficulties were deprived of their civil and social rights because they were incarcerated in institutions (Alaszewski 1988, Korman and Glennerster 1990). Evidence to the 1954–57 Royal Commission of Law Relating to Mental Illness and Mental Deficiency highlighted the tyranny, degradation and inhumanity of the current institutional approach (HMSO 1957).

Others went on to develop the critique in more depth. Just as the poor were seen to be 'pauperised' and have a 'spoiled identity' through their receipt of poor relief and welfare support, the mentally ill, people with learning difficulties and the elderly were increasingly seen to develop 'institutional neurosis', becoming dependent on institutions which, rather than being part of the solution, were increasingly defined as part of the problem (Goffman 1961, Townsend 1962, Morris 1969). A number of high profile scandals, particularly one in 1967 concerning the ill treatment of residents at Ely Hospital (a former Poor Law institution) housing 600 people with learning difficulties, helped to discredit the policy of institutional care even further (HMSO 1969, Martin 1984, Klein 1989). Anthony Crossman used the scandal to raise and maintain public awareness of the issues. Within a few years a number of government reports were published which attempted to establish a framework for developing better services for vulnerable groups, including those with mental illness and learning difficulties, based upon a community-oriented approach (DHSS 1971, 1975, 1979).

A growing awareness of the damage of institutions was also taking place in the new professional sphere of social work. The 1948 Children Act had enshrined the principle that children 'in care' should be entitled to the same treatment as 'ordinary' children in families. The developing anti-institution critique was beginning to affect perceptions of the appropriateness or otherwise of the residential care of children, although it was not until the 1980s that real advances were made in this respect. Olive Stevenson, the first social work adviser to the Supplementary Benefits Commission and later a professor of social work studies, recollects her feelings on becoming a social worker in the mid-1950s:

I was optimistic, enthusiastic and totally committed to the improvement of child welfare provision. I felt part of a 'movement'; true, there was a lot to be done, but the direction of change seemed clear. For example, we needed to close as many residential nurseries as possible, being utterly convinced of the damage to very young children by institutional processes. We needed to individualise, per-sonalise, the lives of children in care.

(Stevenson 1995: 1)

She goes on to recollect her feelings about institutions:

I find myself remembering the weight of evidence during the 1950s and 1960s of the negative effects of institutional life on thousands of people and of the ter-ror (not too strong a word) of the workhouse which many elderly people, post workhouse and post-war, had inherited from their parents. I remember the recurrent scandals of the treatment of mentally handicapped people and, more recently, of mentally ill people in secure hospitals ...

(Stevenson 1995: 5)

Such scandals, especially in the residential care of children and elderly people, continue to this day. Throughout the 1980s and 1990s one inquiry after another was initiated to stamp out and prevent the contin-ued abuse of vulnerable people in institutional care. Indeed, so serious was the concern that, in 1996, the Social Services Secretary, Stephen Dorrell, warned directors of social services that the very future of local authority social services was at stake if they could not guarantee to pro-tect vulnerable people in their care (Dorrell 1996).

Redefining 'difference': new paradigms and the movement for independent living

The anti-institution critique was supported by the 'anti-psychiatry debate' of the 1960s and 1970s, which reconstructed mental illness as a social rather than a medical issue, and which helped to dislodge some of the dominant thinking and traditional responses to mental health problems (Laing 1959, Schur 1971, Bean 1980). Mental illness, rather than being defined as a pathological individual problem requiring institutional segregation and containment, was re-defined by some as a rational response to the tension and stress associated with modern day living, including the complex pattern of relationships between patients, their families and the wider community. Some queried the very existence of 'mental illness', arguing that those with mental health problems had been labelled as deviant by so-called experts, leading to their segregation and exclusion (Szasz 1972).

If the anti-psychiatry movement was to offer new ways of looking at and understanding mental ill health, the concept of normalisation was to provide new ways of understanding the experiences and position of people with learning difficulties and other 'devalued' groups. The problems of those with learning difficulties, as with the mentally ill, were increasingly being defined as the consequence of social attitudes which labelled them as different and deviant, and which excluded them from full participation in society. Rather than segregation and exclusion within institutions, normalisation promoted integration and citizenship in the community. Policies in both cash and care, and organisational structures, should enable people to live an 'ordinary life' (Wolfensberger 1972, Bank-Mikklesen 1980, O'Brien and Tyne 1981, Towell 1988). This model (or ideology, as some have thought of it – see Brown and Smith 1992) has had an important influence on the way in which many people with impairments present themselves.

It has been the 'social model of disability', however, which has had the most significant impact on thinking concerned with disability, exclusion and independence. As shall be discussed in chapter 7, this model also provides a framework for understanding, and responding to, the continued exclusion of poor people. From the 1970s, a 'new social movement' (Oliver 1990: 118) of disabled people has attempted to reconstruct the concept of 'disability' and provide a new social model (Glendinning 1991, Torkelson, Lynch and Thomas 1994, Schaff 1993, Swain *et al.* 1993). This paradigm challenges the view that disability is an individual or medical problem requiring physical or mental rehabilitation (Oliver 1990, L. Silburn 1993, Schaff 1993, Weitz 1994). Oliver distinguishes between 'impairment' ('lacking part of or all of a limb, or having a defective limb, organism or mechanism of the body'), and 'disability': 'the disadvantage or restriction of activity caused by a contemporary social organisation which takes no or little account of people who have physical impairments and thus excludes them from the mainstream of social activities' (Oliver 1990: 11).

The social model casts doubt on the legitimacy and effectiveness of almost every aspect of contemporary policy and practice with disabled people. For example, notions of 'independence' need to be re-evaluated in the light of the model. Brisdenen (1986) has observed that the term 'independence' does not refer to those who can do everything for themselves, but refers to people who have taken control of their lives and are choosing how those lives are led. The most important factor is not the number of physical tasks people can perform in their everyday routines. The degree of impairment does not determine the amount of independence achieved. Morris, for example, suggests that: 'It's not the inability to walk which disables someone, but the steps into the building' (Morris 1991: 10, see also Morris 1993). Independence is achieved if disabled people are empowered with choice, responsibility and resources, and when the barriers to disabled people achieving these powers are removed. Many disabled people do not have this power or control. They experience discrimination, poverty and exclusion (Martin and White 1988, Thompson, Lavery and Curtice 1990). Barnes suggests that there are two explanations for the disproportionate economic and social disadvantages of disabled people:

One is the traditional individual approach which suggests that impairment has such a traumatic physical and psychological effect on individuals that they cannot achieve a reasonable standard of living by themselves ... The other, developed by disabled people and their organisations and fast becoming the new orthodoxy, argues that a wide range of discriminatory economic and social barriers prevent disabled people from securing an acceptable quality of life by their own efforts. Therefore, the deprivations which accompany impairment are the result of discrimination. In this context discrimination is not just a question of individual prejudice, it is institutionalised in the very fabric of our society.

(Barnes 1992: 3)

The social model of disability rejects the individualisation, subordination and devaluing of physical difference. It attempts to reconstruct disability as a consequence of social structures and processes which regulate and restrict the life chances, opportunities and civil rights of people with impairments. The model also rejects collusion with notions that disabled people are 'victims'. Disabled people have sometimes been seen as victims of complex processes that maintain their exclusion and partial citizenship. As such, social policy has attempted to help or compensate them as 'deserving victims', encouraging a paternalism in much social policy and state welfare throughout the 1950s to 1970s: 'Social services set up during the social democratic era tended to be bureaucratic and paternalistic; they were relatively large-scale organisations which made unilateral decisions about people's needs, and dispensed their services according to their own criteria' (Jordan 1984: 134). In the 1980s many 'disadvantaged' groups, including Black people, disabled people and family carers, sought to distance themselves from the 'victims' position and promote their own cause for equality of opportunity, civil rights, citizenship, participation and integration, rejecting the welfare paternalism approach (Vaux and Devine 1988, Oliver 1990, Pitkeathley 1989). In the context of difference and poverty this has shown itself in a new discourse concerned with the 'agency' of the poor, disabled and other groups, and in the language of 'participation' and 'empowerment'.

The importance of these paradigms, of anti-psychiatry, normalisation, and the social model of disability, is in the extent to which, taken separately and together, they challenge the dominant attitudes and social policy approaches to the problems and needs of 'different' and relatively disadvantaged groups, including the poorest. The underlying common element throughout is that the medical-pathology model of difference, and poverty (see chapter 1), cannot be sustained in a society which genuinely wants to promote equality of opportunity, civil rights, participation and social citizenship for all. In their attack on the dominant orthodoxy, these critiques have served to cast doubt on the value of segregation and control within institutions – the ultimate embodiment of 'social exclusion' – and on the adequacy of benefits and services in the community. They question whether cash and care are sufficient to enable vulnerable and poor people to live 'an ordinary life', similar to their fellow, non-poor, citizens. This would require benefits to be set at levels which enable social participation, and personal social services to be structured and delivered in such a way as to be empowering and non-stigmatising. The dominant orthodoxy, at the heart of most social policy throughout the nineteenth and twentieth centuries, by segregating and excluding the poor and the physically and mentally impaired, has served to disable, disadvantage and impoverish them. The moral and political force of the critique comes not just from the efficacy of the analysis, but from the impetus and contribution that disabled people have made in intellectualising and articulating the effects that disabling attitudes, disabling barriers and discriminatory policies in cash and care have had, and continue to have, on vulnerable people.

During the 1980s and 1990s the state has attempted to retreat from direct provision of cash and care and to shift the mantle of responsibility for income maintenance and social care onto others, especially the independent and informal sectors, including private organisations and private insurance (Johnson 1990, Hill 1990, Deacon 1991). All the main political parties are committed to maintaining, if not accelerating, this strategy and direction of change. The shift to greater individualism, a growing role for the private sector, and the promotion of the family as the cornerstone of social care is set to have profound implications for poor people, many of whom will bear a heavy cost of the gradual, but radical, transformation of the welfare state, and many of whom will be left behind as the better off, and those on 'average' incomes, seek alternatives to state support. Both the social security system and personal social services, in this scenario, will become increasingly residualised, state providers of 'last resort' poor relief. A historical perspective, however, teaches us that where there is change there is also continuity. The current balance between the individual, state and the markets is only the latest phase in a historical and policy continuum. Seebohm's vision for universal, non-pauperising personal social services, and Beveridge's vision for social insurance and social security from cradle to grave may have been lost in the late 1990s, but this does not mean that they can't be found at some later time.

CHAPTER 4

Regulating the poor: the politics of social security

Introduction

This chapter is concerned with understanding the functions and purposes of social security, in particular its relationship to people on low income or living in poverty. As a means of understanding these functions, the politics and policy of social security during the Thatcher and Major administrations are examined, with a particular focus on the 1990s. The concern is especially with the key political debates, themes, ideas and concerns that have helped to shape policy formulation, implementation and change. The chapter concludes with a discussion of the prospects for future social security policy and delivery, and the implications for the poorest citizens on benefits.

The costs and structure of social security

Social security in Britain today can be classed as increasingly 'liberal' in nature, characterised by a growing role for means-tested benefits, a reduction in the importance of insurance-related benefits, and financial incentives and rewards for those who contract out of the state system (Esping-Anderson 1990, Clasen 1994a). As was shown in the previous chapter, the Beveridge ideal – that most citizens would be entitled to insurance-related benefits – has been undermined by economic, social and labour market restructuring, and demographic changes. Elderly people are now the largest single group of beneficiaries, accounting for 45 per cent of benefit expenditure, followed by long-term sick and disabled people (21 per cent) (HMSO 1995: 85). As noted in chapter 3, most social security expenditure goes to people with below average incomes.

Social security expenditure by the mid-1990s exceeded £85 billion per year. This accounts for nearly a third of all government spending – twice as much as the total expenditure on health, and more than 11 times as much as on education (DSS 1993a). In 1993, every working person paid on average £12 each day to finance social security payments (DSS 1993a). By 1994 the figure was £15 per day (Lilley 1994). Because social security expenditure is mostly demand-led (discretionary social fund payments being the exception), and because expenditure is so high, other spending departments cannot finalise their annual budget with the Treasury until expenditure on social security has been agreed.

The British social security system makes four different types of payment: contributory, non-contributory, universal and means-tested benefits. The type and amount of benefit a claimant (or 'customer') receives will depend on a number of interrelated factors, including their (paid) employment history, their contribution record, the level of other income, savings or capital, their family structure and their needs. This structure provides a complex matrix of benefits. So, for example, claimants who are receiving an insurance-related contributory benefit, or a non-contributory benefit, may also receive means-tested social assistance (income support) to 'top up' their income to a minimum level defined each year by Parliament as necessary to meet basic needs. Workers in low paid employment may receive, in addition to their wages, some family credit or earnings top-up if their income from work is below a defined minimum level. Each type of benefit is briefly examined.

Contributory benefits

It is these benefits which are at the core of the Beveridge social insurance scheme which has so dominated the shape of British social security provision for the last 50 years (see chapter 3). Entitlement to contributory benefits depends on a national insurance contribution record. These benefits provide the claimant with an income to cover such contingencies as unemployment, sickness and retirement. In 1995–6, for example, there were more than 10 million people receiving retirement pensions at a cost of almost £28 billion and over one million people receiving incapacity benefit, at a cost of £6 billion (DSS 1995c). In total, spending on contributory benefits accounts for about half of all social security expenditure. The dominance of contributory benefits has, however, been declining as a proportion of all benefits expenditure, particularly since 1978–9. The use of non-contributory and means-tested benefits has grown considerably under the Conservatives, as more people have found themselves outside or excluded from the national insurance scheme (through unemployment, long-term incapacity, etc.), and as more people have needs which cannot be met by the current structure of insurance-related benefits (Barr and Coulter 1990, Piachaud 1996).

Non-contributory benefits

These benefits are awarded to people whose circumstances are such that they have additional demands on their income – for example, because they have some physical or mental impairment – and as income replacement to people not covered by contributions. Examples of non-contributory benefits include attendance allowance, disability living allowance, invalid care allowance, severe disablement allowance, industrial injuries benefit. Many non-contributory benefits include a 'care' element in the amount of benefit paid to claimants. For example, the disability living allowance (DLA) introduced in 1992 is paid to people under 65 who need help with personal care or with mobility. There are different rates of benefit depending on the intensity of their personal care and mobility needs.

Total expenditure on non-contributory benefits in 1992–3 was £6 billion and accounted for 13 per cent of all benefits expenditure. Non-contributory benefits expenditure has grown very much faster than spending on contributory benefits since 1978–9. Three-quarters of the increase in total social security expenditure between 1978–9 and 1992–3 has arisen from the growth in non-contributory benefits (DSS 1993a). Again, this has arisen largely because many frail, sick or disabled people have found themselves outside the national insurance system.

Universal benefits

An example of a universal benefit is child benefit. It is paid, irrespective of income or need, for all children, via a parent or guardian. In 1995–6, nearly 13 million children, living in 7 million families, received child benefit, at a cost of more than £6 billion (DSS 1995c). Expenditure on child benefit accounted for about 12 per cent of all social security spending.

Means-tested benefits

These benefits (or 'income-related benefits', as the government prefers to call them) are available to people whose income falls below a certain level (defined each year by Parliament), depending on their individual and family circumstances. They are benefits 'reserved for the poorest'. Eighty-six per cent of spending on means-tested benefits goes to those in the bottom 40 per cent of the income distribution (DSS 1994). Capital as well as income is taken into account in the calculation of entitlement to these benefits. There has been a substantial increase in the use of means testing during the 1980s and 1990s (Piachaud 1996).

One quarter of all expenditure on social security – £24 billion in 1992–3 – was in the form of means-tested benefits. So, for example, over four million people on low income received housing benefit to help them with their rent, at a cost of over £7 billion per year, with a weekly average payment of about £34 in 1994 (DSS 1995a). The principal means-tested benefit is income support (formerly supplementary benefit, national assistance). Expenditure on income support was £14.5 billion in 1992–3 (DSS 1993a). The living standards and opportunities of 10 million people are almost wholly determined by the level of this one benefit – the safety net within the British social security system. The average weekly payment of income support in 1995 was just over

£55. Three-fifths of housing benefit recipients are also on income support (Kemp 1992).

While social security is not intended exclusively for the poor it has been poorer people who have become the main beneficiaries of the social security system, and in particular of means-tested benefits. By 1992–3, 14.2 million people claimed means-tested benefits in Britain (DSS 1995a). However, as discussed in chapter 2, many people fail to claim all the means-tested benefits to which they are entitled. It is estimated that between £1.6 billion to £3.2 billion of means-tested benefits went unclaimed by poorer people in 1993–4, compared to the £24 billion received (DSS 1995e).

The functions of social security

Promoting social cohesion, solidarity and citizenship

Social security policy in post-war Britain has had a number of functions, some of which are complementary, others of which are contradictory. A fundamental principle underlying social security is that of collective responsibility or solidarity. A key function of benefits is to provide citizens with security against risks such as unemployment, and against contingencies such as old age. It ensures that responsibility for meeting needs are shared between generations and the wider community. This involves some redistribution from one group to another, for example from rich to poor, from healthy to sick, from waged to unwaged, from men to women; but it also involves redistribution over the life cycle, as citizens make greater use of social security in particular times of need. A key function of social security is therefore to prevent poverty by promoting collective responsibility, rather than just the relief of poverty once it has occurred (Lister 1986, Becker and Bennett 1991).

The relief of poverty and income replacement

Despite the function of collective responsibility, the principle of poverty alleviation or poor relief, rather than the prevention of poverty or the maintenance of earning levels, has characterised British social security policy since the Second World War (Clasen 1994a, 1994b).

A key function has been the need to provide citizens with a replacement income across the life cycle, especially during periods of sickness, frailty, unemployment and old age, to meet their needs for cash and to promote their welfare (see chapter 3). This has also involved the redistribution of income from better-off individuals and groups to those who have lower or restricted incomes. For many millions of people in Britain, social security makes the difference between having no income at all, and having some income, no matter how limited this might be.

For some claimants this income will enable them to participate in some of society's norms, traditions and customs; it gives them some sense of belonging or 'inclusion'. But, as was seen in chapter 2, low levels of benefit restrict or curtail levels of social participation, serve to deprive and exclude citizens, label them as 'outsiders', and can impoverish them. While social security provides an invaluable income to many, relieves the poverty of some and prevents the poverty of others, it also contributes to the poverty of millions, particularly the poorest on means-tested income support.

Labelling and regulating the 'deserving' and 'undeserving' poor

A further function of social security is to endorse the position of certain groups, by labelling them as 'vulnerable' and defining them as 'favoured', 'deserving', and as people in 'greatest need'. Policy then seeks to 'target' benefits on them, rather than on others. An example of this includes elderly people, widely regarded, by virtue of their age, their contribution to society, and their national insurance contribution record, as a vulnerable and deserving group, who have built up their entitlement to state support, and who deserve to be treated with dignity and respect, and as a priority group. Another group constructed in a similar way are disabled people who, by being defined as vulnerable, have also been viewed by ministers and other policy makers in the last decade or so as a deserving, priority group (Glendinning 1992b: 90).

The other side of this coin is the need to regulate and control the behaviour of less vulnerable, less favoured groups, by labelling them as 'less deserving' or 'undeserving' and restricting their access to benefits through means tests, conditions of eligibility and other systems designed and implemented to exclude rather than to include. The attack on benefit fraud (see later in this chapter) is a key part of this process. People who are homeless, lone parents, asylum seekers and foreigners, and others have also been viewed and constructed as less vulnerable, less deserving, or even 'undeserving'. Many have received harsh treatment by politicians, policy makers, the social security system and benefits bureaucracy. The label of 'deserving' or 'undeserving' is assigned to members of the group irrespective of their own personal attributes or qualities, and irrespective of the fact that individual 'contributions', in cash or through good deeds and behaviour, may be more mythical and imagined than real. So, for example, there is no necessary actuarial link between an individual's contributions paid to the national insurance fund and that person's future level and length of benefit entitlement, even though these contributions are widely seen by the public as bestowing individual, personal entitlement and are regarded by all political parties, and much of the poverty lobby, as a key way forward for future benefits policy (see, for example, Harker 1996) [Document 9].

Labels of 'vulnerability', 'deservingness' and 'undeservingness' define a status, justifying and legitimising a way of responding to, and treating, individuals within different social groups. One contemporary example of this is the use of client-based 'premiums' on means-tested income support. Certain groups of claimants, including elderly people, disabled people and carers, are given additional income ('premiums') over and above their basic income support entitlement ('applicable amount') by virtue of their membership of that particular group, rather than based on their own unique needs. Other groups, however, including young people under 25, homeless people and unemployed people, are not given additions, and some (lone parents for example) have received a premium in the past, but this has been threatened as concern and panic over lone parents 'married to the state' have helped redefine the policy response (see chapter 1). These premiums 'reward' certain groups by recognising the legitimacy of their need for extra cash.

There is a debate as to whether or not the social security system should be used as a mechanism for changing the 'undesired' behaviour of certain claimant groups or individuals. Benefit-to-work strategies are one attempt at changing the behaviour of the 'able-bodied' unemployed/jobseeker. Despite governments maintaining that social security should not be used to encourage or reinforce 'respectable' behaviour, the reality is that the structure of benefits, and the conditions of receipt, encourage the institution of paid employment, and low paid work in particular. In the future we may see more developments of this kind, for example attempts to restrict the length of time for which a claimant can receive benefits, perhaps to two years in any one period, or to five years in a lifetime – similar to proposals to be implemented in the United States as it radically restructures its welfare provision in 1996–7.

Meeting the extra needs of the 'vulnerable'

The social security system also meets some of the extra costs associated with ill health, disability and other impairments, and some of the costs of providing care to other family members. Some of these extra costs are met through the income support scheme, others through the non-contributory system when claimants are unable to receive insurance-related benefits adequate for their needs. Under the supplementary benefit system which existed until 1988, for example, claimants could receive extra weekly income because of their unique additional requirements (because they were disabled, needed kidney dialysis, extra heating and so on).

People with physical impairments can claim a number of non-contributory benefits which compensate for some (but certainly not all) of the additional costs of disability. Family carers can also claim invalid care allowance in specific circumstances, although the level of all these benefits could not be considered 'generous'. Other groups with specific needs for extra cash are not accorded this status, for example there are no non-contributory benefits available to compensate for the extra costs associated with lone parenthood or long-term unemployment.

Benefits enable policy makers and administrators to reward claimants who are defined, either through rules of entitlement or through the application of discretion, as 'vulnerable' and in need of extra financial support. Those defined as less vulnerable and less needy are excluded. The terms 'needy' and 'vulnerable' have become modern shorthand and alternatives to the phrase 'deserving'. They have become acceptable and popular partly because they appear to be less moralising and judgemental than describing someone as 'deserving' or 'undeserving'. However, the effect of the label is still to exclude some and to include others. Social security is concerned with categorising claimants, labelling and influencing behaviour, particularly the lifestyles of the poorest on social assistance, and those who rely on benefits for long periods of time. Social security is simultaneously concerned to care, and regulate, claimants, especially the poor (see also Novak 1988, Squires 1990, Andrews and Jacobs 1990, Alcock 1993). In a climate of financial restraint on public expenditure, particularly on social programmes, politicians and policy makers are involved in a series of ongoing judgements, revising and refining notions of vulnerability and deservingness, and determining whose benefits can be curtailed or cut and whose benefits cannot be touched, for the moment at least. This is the politics of social security.

To understand the origin and maintenance of these functions we need to understand the historical context of social security and its roots in the relief of poverty (see chapter 3). We also need to locate these functions in the context of broader social attitudes toward claimants and the poor (see chapter 1), as well as the political values, ideologies, themes and debates that influence social security policy formulation and implementation in any given period. There is a general contempt for, and fear of, many claimants, particularly those labelled as 'undeserving'. Images of the poor infuse and inform attitudes, responses and policies towards poverty and towards welfare; they form the foundation to the harsh treatment and regulation of some claimant groups and individuals. This treatment is maintained, and legitimised, by a political rhetoric which recasts social security as a mistargeted system – one which regards many claimants as 'undeserving' at best or fraudsters at worst.

To understand this process in operation this chapter will focus later on the ideas and concerns of key politicians and the major policy themes of the 1990s. First, however, social security politics, policy and delivery in the 1980s are briefly examined.

Politics and policy: review and reform in social security during the 1980s

During the 1980s and 1990s there were three distinct periods of reform in British social security policy. The first period, largely piecemeal and incremental, took place from 1980 until about 1983–4. It was a period of considerable, even fundamental, change in social security policy, but without being prefaced by a process of public review and debate. Within a year of her becoming Prime Minister, Margaret Thatcher's first government had introduced a number of social security changes which, to a large extent, heralded her particular style and approach to government in general and to social policy in particular. Thatcher believed that it was important to be guided by political conviction rather than public dialogue and consultation, the notion that 'there is no alternative' to her chosen path (Young 1989, Timmins 1995). The first Social Security Act in 1980 broke the link between average earnings, pensions and other long-term benefits, widening the gap between the elderly and others on benefits and those in paid employment. Exceptional needs payments – discretionary additions paid to people on supplementary benefit who required extra money – were abolished and replaced with single payment grants, based on the application of strict rules of entitlement (see, for example, Hill 1990, Savage and Robins 1990, Johnson 1990). The 1980 Budget and second Social Security Act removed earnings-related supplements which had been payable for the first six months of sickness, unemployment, maternity or widowhood, and some benefits were increased at a rate 5 per cent below the level of inflation.

These changes, particularly the 1980 Budget and social security reforms, signalled a major 'watershed', a political and policy shift in the way that claimants, particularly the poorest ones, could expect to be treated by the state under the new Conservative administration (Donnison 1982: 206, Lister 1989, Deacon 1995, Sullivan 1996). The break between average earnings and benefits has had a particularly harsh impact on poorer people, whose living standards 'have moved too far away from the living standards of those in work' (Bradshaw and Lynes 1995: 53). Indeed, had the link between earnings and the indexation of benefits not been broken, many of today's claimants would have the extra money needed to avoid real hardship (Kempson 1996).

The Fowler review

The second distinct period of reform was the government-initiated review of welfare and social security expenditure, which took place between 1984 and 1986 and culminated in the publication of the 1986 Social Security Act, implemented in April 1988. The 'Fowler review' (as it was referred to, after the then Secretary of State for Social Services), and the subsequent reforms, were heralded as the answer to a social security system that 'had lost its way' (DHSS 1985a: para. 1.1). Many issues concerned the government, not least some of the unintended consequences of its earlier reforms. The government was concerned increasingly with the rising cost of 'single payment' grants, a policy only introduced in 1980. These grants, paid to those on supplementary benefit for items not covered by weekly benefit, including clothing and footwear, cookers and essential house repairs, were based upon the application of detailed regulations, governed by volumes of rules. The cost of these payments rose from £48 million in 1980–81 to reach £335 million by 1986–7 (Becker and Silburn 1989). In particular, the government was alarmed at the fact that 80 per cent of single payment expenditure was going to only 17 per cent of eligible claimants (DSS 1989). This was seen as evidence of abuse rather than of effective targeting of benefits. Spending on single payments was relatively small change in the context of the social security budget overall, but, even at this early stage in the Conservative government's period of office, the concern with fraud and abuse played a strong role in influencing the shape, tone and content of social security policy and delivery.

The government was also alarmed at the sheer cost and complexity of the social security system and the characteristics and composition of those relying on supplementary benefit in particular, notably the high proportion of lone-parent families. The principles on which reform was to be based were made explicit at the outset of the Fowler review. Social security was to be viewed not as a function of the state alone, nor should it discourage self-reliance or individual provision (DHSS 1985a: paras. 1.5/1.7). Rather, social security was to be seen as a partnership between the individual, the state and the private sector. The objectives for change were also made clear. These were to target benefits to those in most need; to create a social security system consistent with the government's overall objectives for the economy; to create a simpler system; to reduce administrative problems; and to reform at no extra cost (DHSS 1985a: para. 1.12).

The reforms, introduced as a 'big bang' on 11 April 1988, were presented as 'the most important changes in the safety net of support provided by the state since the 1930s' (DHSS 1985a). Some even viewed them as a 'New Beveridge' (DHSS 1985a). Supplementary benefit was replaced by income support, family income supplement was replaced by family credit. The weekly, individually tailored cash 'extras' that supplementary benefit claimants could receive because of their individual, unique needs ('additional requirements' as they were then called) were replaced by client-based premiums. Other changes included reductions in entitlements to the state earnings-related pension; the encouragement, through financial incentives, for people to take out private pensions; a new housing benefit scheme; and greater alignment of assessment rules for means-tested benefits.

The old single payment scheme, which had become 'unacceptably cumbersome and expensive' and 'subject to complex regulations and instructions as a result of which help is often dependent more on intricacies of interpretation than on a genuine assessment of need', was replaced by the social fund, perhaps the most controversial part of the government's package of reforms (DHSS 1985a: para. 9.8, SSAC 1987, 1990). Some years later, the government-funded review of the social fund suggested that those who were given payments were in no greater need than those who were refused help (Walker, Dix and Huby 1992, Huby and Dix 1992). This was the same criticism the government had raised about the old single payment scheme and which had led to its abolition and replacement by the social fund itself.

The social fund was introduced as a scheme to help people on low income with 'exceptional expenses' which are difficult to meet from regular income. Payments are made from two funds: a regulation-based social fund which deals with the situations of birth, death and cold weather; and payments from a discretionary social fund, which are used as a response to exceptional needs – such as those arising in an emergency or crisis – or for community care. In its first eight years the fund provided more than 11.5 million grants and loans, worth over £2.1 billion, to people on low income. During this period there were many changes to the regulations and guidance concerning payments, although the basic principles that have governed the scheme have remained the same, despite considerable criticism from many quarters.

The social fund's importance to the discussion of social security and poverty stems from the unique characteristics of the discretionary part of the fund and its function *vis à vis* those in poverty or on low levels of income. Essentially, 'applicants' (as they are called) to the discretionary fund have no rights or entitlements. It is up to the officer assessing applications (the 'social fund officer') to decide who gets a payment from the fund, and what amount they will receive. The use of discretion is at the heart of the policy:

In handling the special difficulties of a minority of claimants, the scheme needs a degree of flexibility that is only possible with discretion.

(DHSS 1985b: para. 2.109)

Social Fund Officers are thus able to decide cases with flexibility and sensitivity using discretion to target the available money on those in greatest need.

(DSS 1989: para. 3.3)

The use of discretion for allocating scarce resources to applicants is certainly not new. In the 1970s discretion played a strong part in the allocation of exceptional needs payments (ENPs) to people on supplementary benefit requiring extra money. These payments, as discussed earlier, were replaced by single payment grants in 1980, based on rights and entitlements, and in 1988 single payments were themselves replaced by the social fund. Administrative discretion, seen as a part of the problem in 1980, had by 1988 become part of the solution (Becker and Silburn 1989: 26).

A number of other characteristics of the discretionary fund, however, give it its unique place in British social security policy. These include the fund's use of loans and cash limits. While the discretionary social fund does provide grants to promote community care, the bulk of the available cash is given in the form of loans, to be repaid by an applicant from their future income or benefit. This is the first time in post-war British social security policy that the poorest claimants have been expected to repay money given to them to meet their exceptional needs. As a consequence, many are forced to live below income support levels.

The final factor that so distinguishes the social fund is its cash-limited nature. From the Second World War until 1988, the administration of discretionary additions was demand-led and there was, at least in theory, no predetermined limit to the amount of money which might have to be devoted to meeting those needs. From 1988 it was supply-led, driven not by the volume of need but by the size of the budget, which was to be predetermined by ministers rather than claimants. The policy now concerning exceptional needs was to meet as much need as possible within a cash-limited budget. Applications for social fund grants or loans would be determined by social fund officers following detailed guidelines, exercising discretionary powers, and aided in speed and accuracy by monthly budget profiles and computer technology which would maintain continuous budgetary monitoring. This new 'process of considered decision-making' would enable, in theory at least, cash-limited resources to be targeted on the most vulnerable or deserving – those in greatest need (Becker and Silburn 1989).

This was also a process that, by the early 1990s, had come to dominate decision making in local authority personal social services as well, as social workers and care managers came to grapple with the policy and practical implications of having to meet needs for 'care' from within government-determined, cash-limited, community care budgets (Becker 1990). The 1988 social security reforms were introduced at the same time as the publication of the Griffiths Report on community care. His review of care in the community policy, and the subsequent reforms (examined in chapter 6), required tight regulation of public expenditure on care needs (particularly the care needs of those who could not afford to pay for themselves), just as the social security reforms, and the social fund, had required tight control of expenditure on 'cash' needs, particularly the 'exceptional' needs of the poorest claimants. The precedent had been set by the social fund, and the policy of cash limits, heralded by ministers on numerous occasions as a 'great success', had obvious applications to community care and other spheres of welfare policy. Despite the fact that much of the research on the social fund – including government-funded work – indicated that the fund was failing to meet its specified objectives of targeting help to those in 'greatest' need, the government 'found no evidence to alter our belief that the basic principles of the discretionary scheme are right' (quoted in Huby 1996: 9). From the point of view of economic efficiency and effectiveness, the social fund was successful in controlling public expenditure on the exceptional needs of the poorest (Becker and Silburn 1989, 1990, Huby 1996). This was to become the model, and intention, for community care policy from 1993, and for later changes to legal aid funding.

These reforms, in cash and care, need to be understood in the context of changing political views on the role of the state and the functions of welfare. As discussed earlier, the opposition parties from the early 1990s moved closer to the Conservative welfare model, with a greater emphasis on individualism, selectivity and private insurance for future cash and care needs, even though there are important differences in approach and detail between the parties. The next section focuses on the political themes and debates that helped shape social security policy and delivery in the 1990s, and which also helped to bring about a greater political convergence in thinking on welfare reform.

Politics and policy in the 1990s

The objectives for social security policy for the 1990s were outlined clearly by the Secretary of State for Social Security, Peter Lilley, in his speech to the 1992 Conservative Party Conference. Lilley stated that there were six principles to guide future policy: to focus benefits on the most needy; to restore incentives to work; to encourage personal responsibility; to simplify the system; to adapt it to the needs of beneficiaries, not bureaucrats; and to crack down on fraud (Lilley 1992). These objectives continued to drive, indeed dominate, social security policy and delivery up to the 1997 general election. A comparison of Lilley's six objectives for the 1990s, with the objectives for the 1988 reforms of social security, also outlined above, show a strong overlap. The objectives are essentially the same except that, for the 1990s, there is more explicit emphasis on tackling fraud and abuse of social security, a theme which has become increasingly popular to those on the left as well as those on the right (Field 1995).

The government justified its concern with tackling benefit fraud and targeting benefits on the most needy by referring to an impending 'crisis'. It alleged that social security expenditure was becoming 'outstripped by the taxpayer's ability to fund it'. Figures presented by the government 'to stimulate an informed debate on the reform of social security' (Lilley 1993a) seemed to show the crisis was deepening – with projected costs reaching £93 billion by the turn of the century. The underlying causes of this situation, according to the government, were the ageing population, and social and labour market restructuring (DSS 1993a, 1993b).

The Portillo/Lilley review

The concern with the escalating costs of public expenditure and social security heralded the third major period of review and reform in social security policy, from 1993 to 1997. In 1993, the then Chief Secretary to the Treasury, Michael Portillo, announced to the House of Commons a 'sweeping' public spending review reminiscent of the Fowler exercise of the 1980s. The purpose of the new review was to 'identify areas where better targeting can be achieved or from which the public sector can withdraw altogether' (*Guardian* 1993a). The first four departments to be examined were to be Social Security, Health, Education and the Home Office – together accounting for almost two-thirds of all public spending. The review was to be conducted within the context of a stated government aim of curbing the *increase* in public borrowing, already at a level of £1 billion per week. The size of the social security budget, as mentioned earlier, far outweighs the other welfare spending departments, and gave the greatest scope for cuts. It was, according to Portillo, the 'cuckoo in the nest' (*Guardian* 1993c). Three years after the review was initiated it became apparent that social security was the only one of these areas in which substantial savings were achieved. There was little withdrawal by the state in expenditure on health, education or the Home Office. In social security, despite the rising cost of benefit expenditure in real terms, the *rate* of increase actually slowed down, following the introduction of a series of benefit changes outlined later in this chapter. By 1997–8, the real average annual growth of benefit expenditure was expected to be 1.3 per cent, with an underlying rate of 2.1 per cent from then until the end of the millennium. This was considerably less than the 3.3 per cent growth forecasted by the government in 1993 and significantly less than the 4.6 per cent average rate of growth since 1949–50 (DSS 1995c). Additional savings, amounting to billions of pounds, were also to be achieved by a series of anti-fraud measures and changes to the delivery of benefits introduced during this period.

Between 1993 and the 1997 general election, social security was to become one of the key political issues, as the Conservatives, and then the opposition parties, engaged in a debate as to the future of welfare and social security in particular (see also chapter 1). Throughout this period ministers emphasised that any reforms would be implemented on an incremental 'benefit-by-benefit' basis, rather than the big bang 'revolution' that had characterised the 1988 reforms. From 1992–3 the government introduced a series of social security changes whose combined effect on the structure and delivery of benefits was to a large extent far more significant and far-reaching than the 1988 package of reforms. So, for example, benefits for disabled people were reformed radically in 1992 after many disabled people had 'lost out' considerably in the 1988 reforms (Glendinning 1992b); the Child Support Agency was introduced in 1993; social security arrangements for community care and residential care were radically restructured in 1993; invalidity benefits were reformed in 1995; housing benefit was reformed during 1995–6; unemployment benefit was abolished and replaced by the jobseekers allowance in 1996; benefits for asylum seekers and young people under 25 were restricted in 1996; statutory sick pay was reformed in 1997, among other changes. This so-called 'gradual' approach to social security reform, introduced benefit-by-benefit over a period of four years, seemed to disguise what in effect was a radical restructuring of benefits – a 'permanent revolution' (Lister 1996b) – the implications of which would stretch well into the next millennium.

Review and reform: chronology and dominant themes

Portillo's 1993 announcement that a new welfare debate was to take place opened the door to numerous proposals for reform, from many different sectors. Within a week the Social Security Secretary, Peter Lilley, had indicated that he was prepared to see a fundamental shift towards private provision of social security benefits. 'At the very least,' he said, 'we must curb the long-term growth in spending' (*Guardian* 1993c). Within days the right-wing Adam Smith Institute called upon the government to provide inducements such as tax incentives or bonds, for more people to opt out of state benefits, including the basic pension, by taking out private insurance (Pirie 1993). By April 1993, Peter Lilley and his ministers, civil servants and political advisers needed 'time out' to consider the suggestions and options available to them. They retreated for two days to the sanctuary of the Foreign Secretary's country mansion in Kent, where they considered a number of strategic approaches to reduce social security expenditure (*Observer* 1993). It is only with hindsight that we know how important this meeting was in determining the shape of social security policy for the next three to four years.

Within a few days of his return to London, it was reported by the media that Lilley had put his officials to work drawing up two separate strategies to cap the rise in social security spending (*Guardian* 1993b). One set of options was concerned with a more radical overhaul of the contributory benefits system, including steps to encourage the better off to contract out of unemployment benefit and the state pension. However, the political implications of this strategy were potentially so explosive that decisions on some of these matters would need to be deferred beyond the next election. A second set of options – which could be implemented in the short term – included reform of sickness and invalidity benefits, the shifting of certain statutory payments to employers, and reducing the time period for which unemployment benefit is paid. It was this second set of proposals which were to be implemented in a series of reforms which took effect from 1995 onwards. For example, in March 1995 invalidity benefit – costing £7 billion per year and going to 1.7 million claimants – was replaced by incapacity benefit. The intention was that this would cut the numbers claiming by a quarter of a million people in the first two years, and cut expenditure by £410 million in 1995–6, rising to £1.5 billion per year from 1997–8, and rising to savings of £2.3 billion a year in the longer term (DSS press release 1995a). However, it soon became clear that the new incapacity benefit was not remotely close to achieving the predicted savings. Only 5,000 people had been disqualified from receiving the new benefit in the first four months (*Financial Times* 1995b), rising to 76,000 disqualified in the first year (*Financial Times* 1996).

Strategies to cut the time period for which unemployment benefit was payable were also identified in 1993. The jobseekers allowance (JSA) which replaced unemployment benefit and income support in 1996 cut the period of non-means-tested entitlement from one year to six months, with anticipated savings of about £500 million a year. Lilley made it clear that the allowance should 'help the jobseeker and motivate the job-shy' (*The Independent* 1994b). The jobseekers agreement, which each jobseeker must sign, sets out a plan for each claimant to find work. It specifies the kinds of activity which claimants must do to 'actively seek work', including making themselves 'acceptable' to employers. Claimants can be issued with a directive to undertake courses, and breaches can result in loss of benefit for specified periods. Reacting to the jobseekers allowance proposals, the TUC described them as a 'nasty and vindictive measure'. General Secretary John Monks commented that the allowance was 'based on the wholly false view that the unemployed are work-shy shirkers that need to be forced back to work by the heavy hand of state control' (*Financial Times* 1994c). The Jobseekers Act also introduced a power to pilot future benefit changes locally before national implementation – a theme returned to later in this chapter.

Analysis of the chronology and main themes of the new review, and the way in which ideas and concerns were communicated by politicians to a wider audience, help us to understand the political context of social security policy making and implementation. It also reveals a considerable amount about the politics of poverty. During 1993 to 1997 there appeared very little interest or consideration of issues concerned explicitly with poverty, particularly how to adapt the social security system to more effectively relieve poverty, prevent it or redistribute income between the better off and lower income groups. Rather, the agenda was dominated by measures to cut costs and expenditure by greater and more efficient targeting of benefits on the most vulnerable and deserving; to get claimants off benefits and back into paid work; to tackle social security fraud; and to reform the system. However, getting people off benefits and back to work, and targeting cash at the most vulnerable, were not necessarily compatible objectives. Many people would be unable to come off benefits and enter paid employment because of their sickness, disability, caring responsibilities, or because there were few jobs available; many of these people would also be defined as 'vulnerable' and in greatest need of cash, and care. The strategy of getting people back into work could not be as applicable to all groups; some would require long-term support on benefits while others required some help – a carrot, stick or both – in leaving benefits to enter, or re-enter, the labour market.

Communicating policy and the role of the media

The public face of the Portillo/Lilley review was played out in the daily columns of the quality newspapers and in the media more generally. The review was not so much a debate as a series of leaks of one policy option after another. Many options were front page news. In May 1993, for example, *The Times* (1993) announced that John Major had signalled that welfare benefits and free state services for the middle-class were under threat. In June, *The Independent* (1993) warned that the 'complete dismantling of the welfare state' was being considered by ministers. Privatisation of benefits and compulsory insurance were back on the agenda. Days later, the *Guardian* (1993c) declared that housing benefit, invalidity and sickness benefits were under the spotlight by a 'special unit of civil servants reporting directly to Peter Lilley'. Fundamental changes to these benefits, including the taxation of invalidity benefit, appeared certain. The leaks appeared to be a 'softening-up' exercise to test public reaction to far-reaching changes in invalidity benefit and housing benefit, introduced later in 1995, and to changes in unemployment benefit, introduced in 1996.

The debate – or rather the leaks – and the policy prescriptions for reform were being rehearsed within closely determined boundaries. Only certain ideas and particular proposals were allowed onto the government's reforming agenda. The Conservative Party's distrust of state involvement was paramount. Lilley observed: 'If the provision of welfare is effectively monopolised by the state, people will have less reason to work, strive and save. People will only make second rate effort for second order needs' (DSS press release 1993). The outcomes for the review were already determined: the rise in public expenditure had to be controlled and the rate of increase curtailed, and the direct involvement of the state in welfare matters had to be restricted and reduced. Individuals would need to take greater responsibility for protecting themselves and their families against unemployment, sickness, old age, poverty. The details of the strategy would be announced in the November 1993 Unified Budget. However, in his 1993 Mais Lecture Lilley was happy to make public the principles that would govern any future changes in social security, including the need to cut and target benefits to fewer people; and to encourage more people to opt out of the state system and take out private insurance for such benefits as pensions. Lilley declared: 'There is no escaping the need for structural reforms of the social security system. Any effective structural reform must involve either better targeting or more self provision, or both' (Lilley 1993a).

While reform would continue to be introduced benefit by benefit, the policy intention was increasingly defined as 'structural reform'. Within two weeks of the Mais Lecture, the Thatcherite 'No Turning Back Group' – which counts Peter Lilley and Michael Portillo among its membership – had its draft plans for the radical overhaul of the welfare state leaked to *The Times*. Their proposals, developing on from some of those announced by Lilley just a fortnight earlier, included scrapping child benefit, means testing on a points-scoring basis, a gradual end to the state pension for the middle classes and incentives to take out private pension schemes (No Turning Back Group of Conservative MPs 1993). Policy papers leaked to the *Guardian* (1993e) also suggested that Whitehall was drawing up plans to shift £1.4 billion of the social security bill, in statutory sick pay, from the state to employers. Meanwhile,

David Willetts, Tory MP for Havant and an influential right-wing thinker on welfare policy, made other proposals (Willetts 1993), including one that pensioners should be encouraged to sell their assets or refinance their home to provide for their retirement (see also *Independent on Sunday* 1993a). As will be seen in chapter 6, this suggestion evolved into a policy of sorts, if somewhat by stealth. Tens of thousands of elderly people requiring residential or nursing home care were forced to sell their homes, or put the value of their assets towards their residential or nursing home costs, as social services took responsibility for community care from 1993. The government later responded to the ensuing public outcry by introducing proposals to protect the capital of elderly people requiring residential social care (see chapter 6).

The Labour Party's Commission for Social Justice published a number of important reports on welfare issues, but not surprisingly these made little headway onto the government's reforming agenda for social security. Moreover, they did not make much headway onto Labour's agenda either. Within a year or so of their publication Labour's leader, Tony Blair, initiated a new internal review of social security policy, as we have seen in chapter 1. The Liberal Democrat Dahrendorf Commission and the Rowntree Foundation Report into Income and Wealth also made proposals for change, but many did not strike the right chord with government, and were ignored or 'rubbished' by some politicians, right-wing media and others (see chapter 2).

There were others who suggested that the government's whole welfare debate had been one-sided, and had involved a misreading of certain key facts (Hills 1993). Similarly, the Child Poverty Action Group's response to the new review of social security questioned the 'alarmist' discussion of 'crisis' and the hidden, private nature of the whole debate, arguing that it fostered a myth of unsustainable spending, laying the ground for cuts in benefits. The Group outlined what they considered to be the key points to underpin a genuine review of social security, and went on to detail their policies (Oppenheim 1993b, Harker 1996). The government's own social security watchdog, the Social Security Advisory Committee, also observed that 'ways of containing growth by better targeting is a legitimate aim but we do not subscribe to the view, expressed in the media and elsewhere, that social security is out of control' (SSAC 1993: 57).

The 1993 Unified Budget and beyond

While the 1980 Budget was a watershed for the new Thatcher government and its policies on social security (Donnison 1982), Chancellor Kenneth Clarke's first Unified Budget on 30 November 1993 was of strategic importance for the Major government. It established the framework for the reform – or restructuring – of benefits that was to take place between then and the 1997 general election. Peter Lilley's social security statement, the day after the Unified Budget, finally confirmed the policies that many were already aware of through the series of leaks to the media. Lilley announced the package of changes that would 'take Britain's social security system into the next millennium'. His priorities were clear: '... To nurture economic growth we have to curb borrowing and make sure that the social security system does not outstrip or undermine the nation's ability to pay for it' (Lilley 1993b). The reforms to be implemented included raising the pension age for women to 65; reforming statutory sick pay (SSP) and abolishing the government's reimbursement of SSP to large firms; replacing invalidity and sickness benefits with a new incapacity benefit that would be subject to a tougher medical test and that would be taxable from 1995; abolishing unemployment benefit and replacing it with a jobseekers allowance, with a cut in the period of entitlement from a year to six months; help with child care costs for certain families on low income benefits; and establishing a Fraud Board to crack down on benefit cheats. Lilley concluded: 'All the reforms I have announced are intended to strengthen our welfare state, to adapt it to modern needs, and to make it affordable into the next century' (Lilley 1993b).

There were few surprises in this package, and, as discussed earlier, many of the proposals were implemented in a series of benefit-by-benefit changes introduced thereafter. The *Independent on Sunday* (1993b) was one of the few papers to recognise that the media had been manipulated by ministers to prepare voters 'for what was once unthinkable'. As a consequence, there was little public outcry towards the proposals put forward by Chancellor Kenneth Clarke or by Peter Lilley, despite the revelations by the Institute for Fiscal Studies that middle earners and the poor would be the greatest losers in the budget/social security changes, and by the Labour Party that 95 per cent of all families would be poorer. Many would have to pay higher national insurance contributions and indirect taxes, including VAT on fuel.

The 'restructuring' agenda had been set. Despite opening a debate on the future of social security – a debate which was still ongoing – the government had committed itself to implementing a series of reforms, benefit by benefit. The objective of these changes was structural reform, itself determined by the political imperative of controlling both the rate of increase in social security expenditure and restricting direct government involvement in welfare. As Michael Portillo stated: 'the State now seeks to do only the things that it alone can do, or that it does best at least for the time being. Competition and value for money are watchwords' (Portillo 1994) [Document 4].

Other proposals for reform continued to be made. The Adam Smith Institute (Bell *et al.* 1994) published further recommendations to privatise the welfare state, which it sent to Lilley and Portillo in February 1994 (*The Times* 1994a). Two months later the Thatcherite group, Conservative Way Forward (CWF), argued for a 'welfare revolution' and proposed the abolition of child benefit and the state earnings-related pension, as well as drastic cuts in housing benefit (CWF 1994).

However, there was little open discussion of these proposals as Lilley had already pledged his commitment to child benefit and the state pension. In public at least, ministers attempted to keep their distance from the more radical suggestions for welfare reform. Lilley maintained that he could not envisage a big bang overhaul of benefits while the Chancellor, Kenneth Clarke, made it clear to his officials on a number of occasions that he had no intention of dismantling the welfare state, describing his own approach to welfare reform as 'pragmatic' and cautioning against the 'overnight' slashing of social security, which could lead to civil unrest (see for example *The Independent* 1996a).

Lilley's commitment to get people off benefits and back into work showed itself in his 1994 announcement to introduce a 'back-to-work bonus' (which came into effect in October 1996), whereby a lump sum would be paid to people who returned to full-time work after part-time employment. Further proposals were announced in the November 1994 social security statement. In this, Lilley prefaced his proposals for reform with the observation that: '... social security on average now costs every working person £15 every working day. I am therefore announcing today further measures to curb the growth of expenditure and to help people off benefit' (Lilley 1994). His new package of reforms included allowing formerly unemployed people to keep housing benefit and council tax benefit for four weeks after taking up a job; giving a full national insurance rebate for up to 12 months to employers who took on a long-term unemployed person; speeding up the processing of family credit to five days; and a 'radical innovation in social policy' – piloting a family credit type benefit for in-work couples and single people without children (DSS press release 1994f).

The government's strategy to strengthen work incentives through the benefit system became fully operational during 1995 and 1996, when all of Lilley's proposals were introduced. The aims of the reforms were to encourage people into work, to remove uncertainty at the point of moving into work by easing gaps in income, to speed up the payment of benefits, and to encourage employers to look more favourably on the long-term unemployed (DSS press release 1996f). The government's benefits watchdog, the Social Security Advisory Committee, set out its own ideas on the review of social security in a series of three publications during 1994 and 1995. In one, the SSAC made it clear that, in its view, state benefits had to remain the major source of provision for unemployment and longer term sickness and disability. The SSAC saw only limited scope for further development of private sector alternatives:

The state should remain the major provider of benefits for long-term sickness, disability and unemployment. The universal coverage of the state scheme is its great virtue and is essential for the protection of the most vulnerable who might find private cover difficult to afford or even to obtain, if they represented a high risk.

(SSAC 1994: 21) [Document 8]

However, as will be seen later in this and subsequent chapters, attention was focused increasingly on proposals for private insurance as a basis for future entitlement to cash *and* care.

Reforming housing benefit

The housing benefit budget appeared to offer some new opportunities for cuts in social security. Expenditure on housing benefit had grown from £4.2 billion in 1983–4 to about £9 billion a decade later, with projections that expenditure would reach between £10.3 billion and £11.9 billion by 1999–2000 (SSAC 1995a: 7). In March 1994 there was discussion among ministers about ways of setting maximum housing benefit rates for different parts of the country (*Guardian* 1994b). A month later it was reported that plans were being drawn up to reduce housing benefit expenditure and mortgage interest payments for low income groups (*Financial Times* 1994a). By June it was official, as Alistair Burt, then Parliamentary Secretary for Social Security 'placed the need for the review of Housing Benefit expenditure in the context of the Government's long-term social security expenditure review'. Burt, echoing so many other ministers, declared: 'We must ensure the benefits system is meeting its objectives and that its growth does not outstrip the nation's ability to pay for it ... The review is being conducted on a sector by sector basis. There will be no big bang' (DSS press release 1994b).

By July 1994, detailed plans were being considered to reduce expenditure on mortgage interest (*Sunday Times* 1994b). By August, Peter Lilley was signalling that housing benefit reform was likely. Within weeks he had commissioned a study of overseas housing benefit systems to see whether there were any lessons to be learnt for cost-cutting in Britain (*Daily Telegraph* 1994a), and a month later the then Treasury Secretary, Jonathan Aitken, had added his weight to the attack on housing benefit: 'If you look closely at housing benefit, you will find that quite a lot of people on housing benefit are living in houses which are too big for them ... '(*Guardian* 1994f). However, there is little evidence that people decide deliberately to move up-market to take advantage of the availability of housing benefit, and there is no evidence of tenants seeking to move to accommodation that was 'over-large' for their needs (Kemp *et al.* 1994).

By the end of 1994 it was reported in the media that Lilley was playing down speculation about cuts. Only 'cosmetic' changes to the housing benefit programme were likely because of the pressure of other cost cutting projects (*Financial Times* 1994b). Immediately, Lilley announced such a cosmetic change, with plans to end the practice of using housing benefit to meet prisoners' rent for up to a year when they were in prison (DSS press release 1994e). The next month the Cabinet agreed to limit overall expenditure on housing benefit, in an effort to stop spiralling costs (*The Independent* 1994c). However, in the November 1994 social security statement, Lilley seemed to move away from 'cosmetic' changes when he announced: '... far reaching plans to limit the cost of support for housing. The aim is to stem the growth of public expenditure on Housing Benefit and Mortgage Interest Payments, which is set to rise to £15 billion in 1997–98' (DSS press release 1994h). His proposals included restricting benefit for rents above the average for the area; limiting the time that tenants absent from home can have rents paid through housing benefit; withdrawing income support for mortgage interest for the first nine months of a claim for new home owners; limiting mortgage interest payments for existing borrowers during the first six months; reducing the ceiling to £100,000 on which mortgage interest payments will be available. Lilley commented: 'I want to ensure people have an incentive to make responsible and informed choices ... when people pay for accommodation themselves, they choose what they can afford. It is only right to ask people to make similar choices when the taxpayer foots the bill' (DSS press release 1994h).

In the event, most of these proposals and other reforms, including limiting housing benefit for some single people under 25, were implemented in a series of benefit changes introduced in 1995 and 1996, designed to cut expenditure on housing benefit and income support mortgage payments by restricting access to these benefits; by cutting the period for which benefit is payable; and by limiting the amount of money available for people considered to be living in properties too expensive or too big for their needs. Some of the earlier 'radical' proposals for social security restructuring from groups such as Conservative Way Forward and the Adam Smith Institute had finally been implemented despite forewarnings from the government's Social Security Advisory Committee that housing benefit 'is important to the fabric of society [and] that it should continue to be a prime part of social security provision. The increasing cost of the scheme is a measure of its importance in protecting low paid and unemployed people ... Radical changes or drastic cuts would be likely to increase poverty ... ' (SSAC 1995a: 39).

The attack on fraud and 'abuse'

Attacking benefit fraud and 'abuse' offered another, high profile means of reducing social security expenditure and ensuring that those not entitled to state support should be excluded from receiving benefits. The Benefits Agency employs 3,700 out of nearly 70,000 staff on individual fraud work, and 270 staff on organised fraud work, and reported that it saved taxpayers £654 million and uncovered 312,000 cases of people cheating the system in 1992 (Benefits Agency 1994). In April 1996 another 100 Employment Service fraud investigators were transferred to the Benefits Agency to form the Benefit Fraud Investigation Service in readiness for the introduction of the jobseekers allowance.

Early figures presented by Whitehall officials investigating social security abuse suggested that more than £5 billion a year was being lost through fraudulent benefit claims (*Financial Times* 1993) although a series of 'fraud reviews', initiated in 1995 benefit by benefit, provided, perhaps, more reliable estimates (see Sainsbury 1996 for a challenge to the methodology and findings). The first major survey of fraud in income support and unemployment benefit put the figure at £1.4 billion per year (Benefits Agency/Employment Service 1995). According to Peter Lilley, almost one in five lone parents and one in ten unemployed people were making a fraudulent claim (*Guardian* 1995b). The first official survey into the extent of housing benefit fraud indicated that almost one billion pounds a year was fraudulently claimed (DSS press release 1996a), although the Commons Social Security Committee has suggested that the figure may be closer to £2 billion per year, equivalent to 1.5 pence on the basic rate of income tax (Social Security Committee 1996). The government, however, rejected the Select Committee's figures as a gross over-estimate (DSS 1996b). In a heated Commons debate on fraud Lilley stated: 'I have no incentive to overstate the amount of fraud ... By contrast, Labour now has every incentive to exaggerate. It wants to appear tougher than the Government, so as to con people that it is no longer soft on fraud. Above all, it needs to conjure up imaginary "savings" to offset the real cost of its spending plans' (*Commons Hansard* 18 June 1996: col. 704).

While the attack on fraud has been on successive Conservative governments' agendas for more than a decade, it was during the 1990s that they actively pursued substantial public expenditure savings by combating social security 'abuse'. In his 1992 speech to the Conservative Party conference, for example, Peter Lilley made it clear that he would be clamping down on fraud and abuse when he attacked the 'something-for-nothing society' (Lilley 1992, see also Document 5). In February 1994 he announced plans to halt 'benefit tourism', whereby foreigners allegedly came to Britain to claim social security. Lilley stated that: 'This proposal is part of a process of concentrating benefits on those who genuinely need support. The Government will stop abuse of benefits by a minority and ensure social security expenditure does not outstrip the taxpayer's ability to fund it' (DSS press release 1994a). In July 1994, Lilley laid regulations whereby claimants would have to establish that they are habitually resident in Britain before key benefits could be paid. He declared that: 'In recent summers we have seen a growing number of European nationals taking advantage of the accessibility of our benefit system to spend a few months in Britain at the taxpayer's expense. These people have no history of work in this country and obviously no intention of getting a job and paying taxes towards the cost of our benefits' (DSS press release 1994c).

While presented as a response to growing abuse, the motivation behind the habitually resident test also appeared to be related to reducing benefit expenditure as a whole. A leaked note to the government's Social Security Advisory Committee revealed that 'The proposal is part of a process of narrowing access to benefit for people the taxpayer should not be asked to support' (*Guardian* 1994a). At the end of 1994 Lilley announced a £300 million 'boost to the fight against fraud' – a three-year programme to include the introduction of benefit payment cards, more checks on new claims, and increased reviews of existing claims. Lilley observed: 'The fight against benefit fraud remains a top priority ... we plan to make even greater savings next year' (DSS press release 1994g). Five companies, including BT and IBM, were short-listed to develop proposals to automate post offices and the benefit payment system in the fight against abuse (DSS press release 1994i).

By 1995, attacking benefit fraud and 'abuse' was a major priority for *all* the political parties. Lilley declared: 'My intention is to shift the focus from detecting fraud to preventing it happening in the first place' (Benefits Agency 1995). The new strategy would include the introduction of benefit payment cards, more targeted checks – including home visits – more cross-checking of information, a major investment in IT, rewards to vigilant post office staff, a 24-hour freephone fraud hotline and other measures to attack housing benefit fraud (DSS press release 1996a). The package of anti-fraud measures would save, Lilley suggested, £600 million in 1996–7, rising to £1.5 billion in 1997–8 and £2.5 billion in 1998–9 (*The Times* 1995d). In 1996, further measures were announced to combat fraud, including the high profile 'Spotlight on Benefit Cheats' campaign, with its anti-fraud drive in major urban areas throughout Great Britain, and an attack on organised benefit fraud (DSS press release 1996e). The government also restricted severely the rights of asylum seekers to claim and receive benefits, in an effort to stop their alleged 'abuse' of the system. Against the backdrop of this concerted campaign to attack fraud and 'abuse', it has been suggested that: 'the amount and type of smaller-scale fraud that takes place could be taken as an indication that social security is not adequately responding to the needs of many people forced to be reliant on benefits. If as much is admitted, we can begin to ask sensible questions about the adequacy of benefit levels ...' (Sainsbury 1996: 20).

Private insurance

While the government restricted access to a range of benefits in its 1994–6 reforms it simultaneously encouraged citizens to take out private insurance to protect their income and cover their cash and care needs during times of unemployment, sickness and old age. Restricting mortgage interest payments for those on income support was just one example where the government took away existing rights and encouraged claimants to use the private sector to secure future entitlements. Social security minister, Roger Evans commented: 'We believe the package of measures [restricting mortgage interest] ... will ensure that private insurance and Income Support mesh together to provide more comprehensive cover for borrowers who lose their income' (DSS press release 1995b).

The government's intention was that insurance companies and building societies would be more likely to sell cover to their 10.5 million mortgage borrowers if there was no help available from the state for the first nine months of loss of income. However, evidence suggests that these types of insurance-based payment protection schemes fail to meet the needs of those most requiring cash protection (Bennett 1995).

Within the field of personal pensions the government had achieved what it regarded as considerable success in shifting responsibility from the state and back onto individuals and private insurance. Between 1988 and 1993–4, 5.7 million people had become members of an appropriate personal pension scheme introduced as an alternative to the state earnings-related pension (SERPS) under the 1988 reforms, although the cost to the National Insurance Fund for the rebates rose to £16 billion between 1988 and 1994 (DSS 1995d). The 1995 Pensions Act also extended the scope of personal pensions. Lilley declared: 'The new Act will provide a solid foundation for the further growth of funded private pension provision into the next century' (DSS press release 1995c). As an example of the 'success' of the private insurance strategy in personal pensions, Peter Lilley reported that OECD predictions showed that only the UK would avoid the mounting debt problems faced by other OECD countries as a result of the growing cost of pension provision. By encouraging people to opt out of the state scheme by taking out private or occupational pensions, so reducing the demand on public expenditure, Britain's 'system and foresight are the envy of the world and now our approach is belatedly being copied elsewhere' (DSS press release 1995e). The value of British private pension funding rose to nearly £600 billion by 1995–6 – more than the pension funds in the rest of the EC put together, and an increase of £100 billion from the previous year (DSS press release 1996b).

The government continued to promote the private pension industry with its pilot campaign, 'What are you doing after work?', to ensure that young workers would think about, and provide for, their retirement (DSS press release 1996c). However, others have suggested an alternative scenario: 'The [Pensions] Act will boost insurance companies' flagging profits. By the turn of the century SERPS will be down to a quarter of what was intended at its inception in 1975 – with nothing in its place except private provision' (Ward 1996: 12). Bennett points out that the private insurance market is fraught with problems, particularly for poor citizens and those who have the greatest needs:

People who represent 'bad risks' are more likely to take out insurance cover; good risks ... are less likely to, because the premiums will not represent good value for money. Insurance companies may try to exclude the worst risks completely – often the most vulnerable groups in society – or, in schemes with differentiated premium levels, may instead charge them a much higher price for insurance cover. Private insurance schemes therefore often end up exacerbating existing inequalities in income and labour market position, rather than compensating for them.

(Bennett 1996: 11–12)

Assessment: past and future policy – continuities and change

This final section considers some of the main issues and concerns that are likely to dominate policy formulation and implementation in social security during the last few years of the twentieth century and the early years of the twenty-first. In particular, it is concerned to identify some of the main implications of past and future social security policy for poor people.

Simplifying the system and the adequacy of benefits

The structure of benefits outlined in this chapter is both complex and confusing for administrators and claimants alike. A dominant concern throughout the 1980s and 1990s has been to simplify the system and target benefits at those in greatest need. Furthermore, the system is increasingly costly, even though the rate of growth has slowed down, and it is increasingly exclusive: more and more people are excluded from receiving national insurance-related benefits; more people are having to rely on means-tested benefits (with all their associated problems, including high rates of non-take up); more and more are becoming poor, according to the proxy indicators of poverty reviewed in chapter 2. Moreover, evidence presented in chapter 2 about the levels of social assistance in Britain, in particular the amounts provided for children, indicate that they are far from adequate to provide for subsistence, never mind social participation. That politicians should choose to pay income support at these levels, without recourse to scientific data or information about the level of minimum income required to allow people to take part in ordinary social life and keep them out of poverty, must be a source of continued concern. The budget standards approach outlined in chapter 2 provides information on minimum standards and minimum income levels but is not 'officially' sanctioned. Nonetheless, it provides one of the few firm standpoints from which to make judgements about 'adequacy' (see, for example, Piachaud 1979, Bradshaw 1993, Oldfield and Yu 1993, Middleton, Ashworth and Walker 1994). The consequences of low levels of benefits are the continued deprivation, exclusion and poverty of millions of citizens. There is no evidence to suggest that any of the political parties are willing to engage in discussion, or action, to combat poverty through increasing the level of benefits to make them adequate for ordinary social life, thus preventing poverty. The emphasis – as this chapter shows – has been, and will continue to be, on simplification of the system, encouraging claimants to return to work, and cutting the costs of state support.

Containing costs and regulating behaviour

As discussed earlier, social security is also very much about control and regulation – of public expenditure and the lifestyles of the poor. The

1988 reforms, and the debate about the future of welfare that so dominated the 1990s, are predominantly about containing the costs of social
expenditure. Reviewing his reforms, for example, Peter Lilley has
observed that: 'Over the past three years I have carried through a widespread programme of reform, and as a result I have reduced the planned
growth of the welfare budget to little more than 1 per cent a year. That
is half the underlying growth of the economy, and will allow scope for
lower taxes, lower burdens on employers and more job creation'
(*Commons Hansard* 20 February 1996: col. 193). In an analysis of the
distributional and other effects of the changes to means-tested benefits
introduced since April 1988, Evans, Piachaud and Hunter (1994) show
that the immediate effect was to redistribute incomes *within* the poorest
two-fifths of the population, rather than between better off and poorer
people. Controlling expenditure on benefits, in effect, seemed to
involve redistributing the available money among the poorest, to secure
lower taxes for the better off. In addition, it has involved regulating the
behaviour and lifestyles of the poor. One policy after another has been
designed to bring about personal change, particularly the promotion
of the work ethic and sense of individual responsibility (for example
the actively seeking work test, restrictions of benefits to young people
aged 16 and 17, the incapacity for work bill, the jobseekers contract,
benefit changes for lone-parent families, and so on). Reviewing the
Conservative record on social security and means-testing, Piachaud
suggest that 'It is hard to avoid the conclusion that the more politically
vulnerable and expendable have been more harshly treated in order to
restrain public expenditure' (Piachaud 1996: 8).

The apparent 'crisis' in spending has legitimised a government and
opposition rhetoric which has been directed increasingly towards the
promotion of private insurance and family responsibility, and against
the 'undeserving' and the benefit fraudster. This has been coupled with
a concerted attack on the dangers of state intervention and the limitations of social policy – dangers that extend beyond their apparent cost
and economic implications – to a consideration of the moral degeneracy
cultivated by 'dependency' on welfare and social security benefits.
Despite no rigorous evidence to support the thesis that welfare spending
'crowds out' economic growth or creates and sustains mass dependency, political attention, and social security policy formulation and
delivery, has focused increasingly on the problems generated for society
(usually referred to as the 'taxpayer') by specific *groups* of the population who are most likely to be claimants (lone parents, for example), or
who 'abuse' the benefits system. This concern has traditionally been
directed at 'scroungers' and other villains, including the 'underclass',
but others, including homeless people, foreigners, asylum seekers and
sick people have also become targets for vilification, control and regulation in the 1980s and 1990s (see also chapter 1). It is not a coincidence
that 'benefit dependency', lone parenthood and the 'underclass' should
become hotly debated issues in Britain during this period. This is a

debate the government and the opposition parties want to have out in the open. It fosters and sustains public ambivalence and hostility towards certain welfare groups; it legitimates policies for restricting access to, and levels of, benefits. In the future we will see more emphasis on benefits to work strategies and in-work benefits, even though there is little evidence to suggest that they actually get people off benefits and back into work. Family credit, for example, is more effective in helping people stay in low paid work rather than getting people off benefits and back into work (Bryson and Marsh 1996).

Localisation of benefits

We should also expect more emphasis on the 'localisation' of benefit delivery. Peter Lilley's 1995 speech to the Social Market Foundation included a discussion of this theme. Lilley asked:

Whether all social security benefits should be uniform nationally and centrally administered. A national system ... has many advantages – economies of scale, avoiding disparities and inequities, and preventing internal benefit tourism. But it means local provision cannot be tailored to local circumstances. It becomes harder to bring local knowledge to bear on the delivery of benefit. It is harder to mobilise local pride to generate positive alternatives to welfare dependency ... I do not conclude that the whole benefit system should be localised. But whenever changes are made in future I will consider cautiously whether some greater degree of localisation could bring improvements.

(Lilley 1995b)

Within the field of social care and community care, local variation – in the range of services available, the quality and cost – is very much the order of the day. But within income maintenance, local variation was replaced by a national scheme of social security as part of the Beveridge settlement (see chapter 3). Some have feared that what Lilley intends is a return to localised rates of benefits – a return to the Poor Law tradition of local variation rather than a national unified benefits system.

There is some evidence of 'creeping' localisation in social security. Changes to housing benefit in 1996 established local ceilings on rents for which housing benefit would be payable, with local authorities having a discretionary fund to pay above the ceiling for those defined as vulnerable (for example sick or disabled people and families with children). The introduction in October 1996 of the pilot 'earnings top-up' benefit, aimed at encouraging young people back to work, was implemented in eight areas across Britain, on a three-year trial basis. The aim is to support low paid people in work rather than paying them benefit on condition that they do not work. It is expected to increase the income of participants in the chosen areas by up to £56 a week for couples and up to £28 a week for single people without dependent children (DSS press release 1996h). By piloting a new benefit locally before national implementation, the government effectively established local variations. People outside the pilot areas will live on lower levels of income even though they will have the same underlying entitlement to benefits. The Labour Party proposals for 'flexible benefits' (Labour Party 1996, Document 2), even though the rates of benefits are to be determined nationally, would also introduce local variation in the amount of money claimants could receive because of the flexible use of training and benefits money.

Withdrawing rights

Other ways to reduce social expenditure have included 'defining-out' of their entitlement some potential claimants, or 'delaying' the time at which people will receive benefits. For example, those who have paid national insurance contributions, bestowing rights to unemployment benefit, will find that from 1996 their rights will have been restricted by the introduction of the jobseekers allowance. Additionally, many women who planned to retire at 60 will find that they can only receive benefit at 65. We are likely to see further examples of the withdrawing and redrawing of the boundaries of legitimacy and entitlement: some people, and some types of need, will be placed outside the boundaries of entitlement, even though these rights may have been secured previously through contributions or proof of entitlement. The shift to greater selectivity is also taking place in other spheres of social welfare, including community care and social care, as will be seen in chapter 6. The social contract between the individual and the state, symbolised through contributions of national insurance and personal labour, is being redrawn. The impact for the poorest, who cannot afford to pay for their social care or pay for private insurance to secure future income replacement or protection, is as yet uncertain. However, we can speculate that the poor will experience greater marginalisation and exclusion, and more reliance on a residual, and second class, welfare state.

Improving efficiency in delivery: privatising benefits

We should also expect further measures to improve efficiency and reduce costs of delivering social security benefits. In 1994, Peter Lilley announced a review of the work of the Benefits Agency and invited views on ways to improve the delivery of benefits 'to establish what future way of organising it will best support the cost-effective delivery of social security benefits; serve the needs of those who use the benefits system; and improve value for money and security (in terms of both improved accuracy and fraud)'. Lilley made it absolutely clear what the review was not about: 'It is not about social security benefit levels or entitlement' (DSS press release 1994d). The outcome of that review was that the Benefits Agency would not be abolished or privatised, although it would be required to make greater efficiencies.

In 1996, under pressure from the Treasury, Lilley announced that further efficiencies would have to be found in the DSS, which would have to cut its operating costs significantly to save around £3 billion before the end of the millennium. To achieve this, Lilley announced a fundamental review of the legal basis of all social security decision making and appeals as well as a programme of cost cutting and efficiency measures (DSS press release 1996d). The 'Change Programme' (as it is called) is aimed at reducing operating and administrative costs by a quarter [Document 6]. In the first instance the national freephone advice service, used by three million callers a year, was abolished in July 1996, to cries from the Labour Party that: ' ... by closing the advice line, the Right Hon. Gentleman [Lilley] is not only again ignoring the needs of the poor, but trying to ignore their very existence' (*Hansard* Oral Answers 23 April 1996: col. 185). Further measures included the closing down of satellite benefit offices in mostly rural areas and the scrapping of the emergency out-of-hours service – used primarily by poor people who suddenly faced an emergency or crisis such as destitution. The aim of these measures was to cut £200 million in operating costs in 1996–7 (*The Independent* 1996b).

More substantial savings would need to come from more radical changes. Despite his 1994 Benefits Agency review opting against the privatisation of the Agency, Lilley now proposed the introduction, as in the government's health and social care reforms, of internal markets and the greater use of the private sector in administering benefits – in effect the privatisation of the delivery of benefits [Document 7]. A 'mixed economy' of cash already exists within the social security system, with large numbers of people making use of private insurance to meet their future income needs. However, the government proposed to expand the role of the private sector beyond the role of private insurance to include administration and delivery of the national benefits system itself. The private sector has been responsible for developing the benefit payment cards which will replace order books and giros. In addition, under the government's Private Finance Initiative (PFI), private sector money can be used for major public capital projects, with the transfer of risk going to the private sector.

A private company won the contract to develop the DSS accommodation in Newcastle, housing 13,000 people (DSS press release 1996i). A week after the Newcastle announcement, the Government confirmed that the ownership and management of *all* the DSS's premises would be transferred to the private sector under the PFI. This will be one of the largest and most complicated property transactions ever conducted in the UK and will provide the DSS with serviced accommodation over a period of 20 years. The transaction should be completed by the end of 1997 (DSS press release 1996j). Moreover, the government has announced that child benefit will be administered by the private sector, and that other benefits will follow (DSS press release 1996k). The Change Programme, by privatising the delivery of benefits and introducing a purchaser–provider split, is likely to have profound implications for the restructuring of social security, and for the poor, just as the introduction of the purchaser–provider split in community care has done for poor, vulnerable people requiring social care (chapter 6).

The privatisation of social security is also taking place by increasing numbers of people contracting out of the state system to take out private insurance, to provide income replacement in times of sickness, disability, unemployment and old age. However, not all those who contract out will necessarily be better off in private schemes. Of the 5.7 million people who contracted out of SERPS, about a quarter of a million people – mainly lower paid workers whose working lives have been interrupted – are likely to be worse off than they would be had they stayed in the state system. Many millions of people, however, will be denied access to these private insurance schemes – schemes that will increasingly characterise Britain's pluralist, mixed economy of welfare. As the SSAC has commented:

> Universal coverage regardless of risk is the great strength of the state scheme and unless this can be replicated by the insurance industry, at affordable cost, we could see little prospect of private provision supplanting state benefits for the vast majority of the population, and for high risk, vulnerable groups in particular … our principal concern is for the many people – those with low life-time earnings (especially women), the long-term unemployed and others with interrupted work patterns, and sick and disabled people – who are unable to benefit from the expansion in private provision … .
>
> (SSAC 1995b: 57)

It will be poor people who are excluded from making use of private insurance-related schemes and the state's national insurance structure. It will be they who will have to rely on an increasingly residualised, means-tested, state system – in both cash and care.

Which way forward?

These changes, proposed in varying degrees by all the main political parties and becoming the new orthodoxy of social security policy, fail to recognise the empowering and socially cohesive nature of social security – its potential to foster and promote solidarity, freedom from poverty and freedom from the fear of poverty (Becker and Bennett 1991). The SSAC commented in their ninth report that:

> What we consider to be more important in any review of social security is that the system should be adequate and that there should be a balance and sense of fairness in the way the budget is spent. We feel strongly that our social security system is a reflection of the underlying values which society places on its care for fellow citizens in time of need. It is therefore a vital element in the social cohesion of the nation.
>
> (SSAC 1993: 50–51)

This vision does not appear prominently on the policy agenda of any of the main political parties. What is clear, however, is the extent to which the Conservatives and New Labour are committed to the reform and restructuring of social security, to control rising expenditure. The British welfare state is at a crossroads. The key political question that all parties are now asking is 'who should pay for welfare in general and social security in particular?'. Amidst the technical complexities the policy choices are relatively simple. Should the state carry communal responsibility, through national insurance and taxation, for its citizens' cash needs, from cradle to grave? Or should social security be paid for on a personalised basis, by citizens themselves, through payments to private insurance or other forms of group personalised accounts, including occupational schemes, group personal pensions or revitalised friendly societies? Or should we move forward with a combination of both – a partnership – with the state providing a minimum level of income in times of need, to enable citizens to participate in ordinary social life and stay out of poverty, supplemented by secondary tier provision from private, occupational or other sources? All the main political parties are now asking, if not addressing these questions. How they respond, in power and in opposition, will determine the future direction of the welfare state and the prospects for Britain's poorest citizens. As the pace of welfare reform quickens, the poor may well be left behind. The prevention of poverty, even its relief, has ceased to be a major concern of the social security system. Indeed, labour market restructuring and social security are largely responsible for the increasing incidence and experience of poverty, deprivation and exclusion from social participation for millions of citizens.

CHAPTER 5

Managing the poor: social services and social work with poor families and children

Introduction

Social services policy formulation, at national and local level, and implementation, has largely ignored the single characteristic which most users of social services and social work have in common, namely their receipt of social security benefits. Nine out of ten users of social work services are claimants of benefits, and the majority are on means-tested benefits reserved for the poorest. Social services departments, and social workers in particular, have been uneasy about their role and responsibilities *vis à vis* people on low incomes or in poverty, and have found it difficult to come to terms with policy, procedural and practice issues around money, income maintenance, welfare rights and anti-poverty initiatives. This is perhaps more surprising as many of the skills and techniques that are now the essence of professional social work were originally evolved within nineteenth century agencies such as the Charity Organisation Society, for which the relief of poverty was a fundamental concern (see chapter 3). Today, many social services employees, social workers, managers and educators, are reluctant to acknowledge the inescapably close professional contact they have with some of the poorest people in society.

Chapter 3 described how, throughout the last few centuries, there has been a mixed economy of welfare, incorporating the state, family and independent sectors, which have provided care, support, control or protection to vulnerable people in times of need. The focus was on some of the historical policy developments that helped shape the structure and delivery of the state's provision of personal social services, particularly social services departments, social work and community care. Here, the growing awareness of poverty by social services departments and social workers during the 1980s and 1990s is examined. The evidence is reviewed on the association between poverty and the use of social services, especially social work, by vulnerable people, particularly low income families with children, and the question is raised as to why this evidence, or 'poverty dynamic', has failed to make a more significant influence on policy and practice within social services and professional social work. The types of responses, including direct financial payments, casework and other approaches, that social workers and departments have adopted as responses to the needs of their users, are considered and their appropriateness as responses to poverty is assessed. The evidence indicates that, far from empowering poor families and enabling them to secure independence and dignity, social work has labelled poor families as 'problem families' and has managed them as such. For many poor families, use of social services and social work has become fraught with danger – part of the problem of daily living, rather than part of the solution.

The cost and structure of social services in Britain today

Local authority social services are now regarded widely as the 'fourth arm' of the welfare state, alongside the health service, social security and education. Social services departments (SSDs) accounted for 12.5 per cent of all local authority staffing and 9 per cent of all local authority spending in 1990–91. In total, 237,750 people were employed in SSDs in 1994, an increase of almost a quarter since 1978–9 (HMSO 1995: 61, Department of Health 1995c). Expenditure on SSDs nationally was £6.9 billion in 1995–6. This figure has two components: £5.1 billion for existing responsibilities; and £1.8 billion for community care – of which £648 million was ring-fenced money (Department of the Environment 1992, Department of Health press release 1995a). Expenditure on social services has increased tenfold over the last 25 years, although it is still less than a tenth of what is spent on social security (chapter 4).

Most social services provision is provided within a statutory framework (Vernon 1993). So, for example, the Chronically Sick and Disabled Persons Act 1970 is a primary piece of legislation to enable and encourage disabled people to live reasonably independent lives in their own homes; the Children Act 1989 recasts the legislative framework for children's services, care and protection into a single coherent structure, while the NHS and Community Care Act 1990 provides the framework for the provision and delivery of health and social care services. A few examples of the type of services provided by SSDs include:

Residential care Many vulnerable people, including those with physical or mental impairments, elderly people, children and others, may not be able to live at home on their own, or with family, because they are frail, need care or protection, need control, or have no one else available to care for them. Social services departments provide residential care for such groups, including residential care homes and children's homes. By 1994, however, local authorities provided only a quarter of the total residential care for adults, compared with 55 per cent 10 years earlier. This change has arisen because of the increasing role of the private and voluntary sectors in the mixed economy of care (see chapters 3 and 6). The number of children in children's homes has also declined from about 18,000 in 1984, to 11,000 in 1991, and to 8,000 by 1994 (Chief Inspector of Social Services 1995). A third of all SSD staff, about 72,000 people, work in residential care establishments (Chief Inspector of Social Services 1993). Only a small minority of residential staff are professionally qualified – a situation which has generated calls for all heads of children's homes to have appropriate qualifications by the mid-1990s (Utting 1991).

Day care Nationally, SSDs provide 1,500 day centres for up to 60,111 elderly people, people with mental illness or physical disability. They also provide a further 56,700 places in special day provision for people with learning difficulties. As the independent sector grows, particularly private provision, it is anticipated that social services will provide less day care of their own.

Home helps and personal carers Many vulnerable people living at home receive domestic and other personal assistance. There were 540,000 households receiving home care in 1994. Twenty-four per cent of these households received six or more visits a week, compared to 16 per cent of households in 1992. Home helps and personal carers provided a 24 per cent increase in contact hours in 1994 compared to 1993, as a consequence of the 1993 policy shift to care in the community (Chief Inspector of Social Services 1995). One quarter of all social services staff are home helps.

Meals on wheels In 1994, over 300,000 people a week received meals on wheels (Chief Inspector of Social Services 1995). In total, more than 45 million meals on wheels were delivered to vulnerable people in the community, of which 32 million were delivered to the recipient's home and 13 million elsewhere (for example, to luncheon clubs).

Welfare rights services Many SSDs now employ specialist welfare rights advisers to advise local people, and other SSD staff, about benefits and other welfare entitlements (services in kind as well as cash), and help them to secure their rights.

Field social work Only 13 per cent of SSD staff are field social workers. They provide help and support to, and also social control of, many different groups of people defined as in need of care or protection (protection from themselves or from others). So, for example, social workers will be involved in assessing and responding to cases of child abuse and neglect, compulsory detention of people with mental health problems where they are a danger to themselves or others, arranging fostering and adoption services for children in need, counselling people with trauma, and many more activities.

Social work and social workers

Social workers are often viewed as the 'professional' side of personal social services. Most field social workers have a professional qualification gained from a university course accredited to the Central Council for Education and Training in Social Work (CCETSW). Moreover, social work practice is largely governed by a framework of legislation – social workers fulfil statutory requirements under children and adult legislation: 'For social workers to act outside their powers is illegal, while to fail in their duties is liable to put them in peril of a public inquiry, an Ombudsman investigation for maladministration or a prosecution' (Cooper 1993: 59, Document 10). However, despite the legal framework, much social work practice is discretionary, based upon professional judgement: 'The exercise of legal duties and discretionary powers leaves social work in an equivocal position' (Cooper 1993: 59). Social workers are the most powerful group within personal social services, indeed, many people confuse 'social work' with 'personal social services' – seeing the two as being the same thing. In fact, social work – as a service – is only a small part of what SSDs actually provide, although social work does receive most of the publicity, particularly in those cases where vulnerable children and adults require care and protection.

From the 1990s much of the work of SSDs, and social workers, can be categorised under two broad headings. First, there are those services that are concerned with families with children, including child protection services, children's homes, secure units, fostering and adoption (substitute family care), family work, young offenders work, work with disabled children, guardian *ad litem* work, and so on. Much of this activity, and many of these services, are provided within the legislative context of the 1989 Children Act and consequent guidance. Services for children accounted for £1.7 billion, or 31 per cent of all personal social services spending in 1992–3 (Department of Health 1995e: 6).

Second, there are those services concerned with adults – which now relate predominantly to community care. These services include residential care homes for elderly and other vulnerable people, day care for elderly people and those with physical or learning difficulties, alcohol and drug misuse services, community care assessments of vulnerable service users and family carers, care management, inspection and complaints work and direct service provision (for example meals on wheels, community care assistance/home helps, etc.). The legislative context for much of this work is provided by the NHS and Community Care Act 1990 (finally implemented in 1993), the Carers (Recognition and Services) Act 1995 (implemented in 1996) and other pieces of legislation concerning the needs of disabled people, those with mental health problems, and other vulnerable groups. In the first full year of community care implementation (1993–4), just under 2,500 formally designated 'care manager' posts were established in SSDs to assess the needs of vulnerable people (and their carers) requiring support under the new community care arrangements (Department of Health 1995c). Services for adults accounted for £3.8 billion, or 68 per cent of all personal social services spending, in 1992–3. Of this, £2.4 billion was spent specifically on services for elderly people (Department of Health 1995e: 5). Community care is discussed in chapter 6.

Some services cut across children's and community care boundaries, and also cut across health care boundaries (for example in the area of 'continuing care' of the elderly). Social services complaints and inspection units have functions with regard to both children and adults. However, the distinction between children's services and adult/community care services has led to many SSDs reorganising themselves, in terms of policy, administration and organisational structure, to deliver, or arrange the delivery by others, of services based upon this two-fold distinction.

Social services departments also work closely with other sectors to deliver social care. Voluntary organisations, including charities, have traditionally been central to identifying and responding to human need (see also chapter 3). Voluntary groups often fill gaps in state and private service provision; they draw upon the expertise and agency of local people and local communities in delivering care. They have a tradition of being creative and preventative whereas 'policy developments in the personal social services are almost always reactive and spasmodic' (Baldock 1994: 189). Social services departments may work in partnership with voluntary organisations – departments may also fund them to provide a service to specific groups – rather than the SSD providing services directly themselves. In the future, SSDs will also have to forge new relationships and sustain new interdependencies with the private sector. Community care legislation and policy requires SSDs to help develop the private market in social care; funding arrangements require SSDs to spend a high proportion of community care monies on the private sector (see chapter 6). Up to one million people are in paid employment in the mixed economy of social care (a quarter of whom are in social services). This figure excludes the millions of unpaid family carers and relatives (the 'informal' sector) who provide the main bulk of care for other family members (Twigg, Atkin and Perring 1990, Glendinning 1992a).

While local authority social services departments have to implement central government policies in the field of personal care, particularly community care, they still have considerable power to determine their own priorities based on their own local profile of needs. Priorities and policies are determined by local politicians; implementation is through paid officers – welfare professionals such as social workers, care managers, home helps and so on. However, professional judgements influence political decisions, and vice versa. The intermeshing of national with local politics and policy is critical to understanding the operation and delivery of personal social services in Britain. In the climate of financial stringency there is growing debate about who should receive social services, including social work, and under which conditions. This debate includes discussions about the appropriate role of charities, voluntary and private organisations, and the family in the provision of care. There is a parallel debate within the field of social security, as was seen in the previous chapter.

The 1980s and the growing awareness of poverty

Many social workers have distanced themselves traditionally from the material and cash problems of their clients, which, if they are acknowledged at all, are seen as the proper responsibility of other agencies, particularly the social security bureaucracies, or other specialists such as welfare rights advisers (for a detailed discussion of these issues see Becker and MacPherson 1986, 1988). Traditionally, while many social work users are claimants of social security, and many are also poor, this did not translate itself into prescriptions for social services policy or social work practice. It was as if social workers and their organisations had failed to recognise the importance of this shared experience of many of their clients, in effect they had little 'poverty awareness' (Becker 1988). Perhaps this should come as little surprise given the lack of recognition of poverty within the wider society. The growing awareness of the extent, nature and impact of poverty among social services' clients parallels the growing awareness of the existence of poverty amidst affluence within British society more generally. The so-called 'rediscovery of poverty' from the 1960s marked a period of academic and policy interest in the issue and experience of poverty and deprivation (see chapter 2). This also coincided with the publication of the 1968 Seebohm Report which paved the way for a major reorganisation of the personal social services in 1971, an area in which Peter Townsend and others, particularly the Fabians, had a keen interest (chapter 3). Seebohm had estimated that 60 per cent of referrals to the new social services departments would be requests for advice on income maintenance or housing (Sinfield 1969: 34), although in the years following reorganisation there was very little monitoring of this or any real consideration of what such a statistic, if it were accurate, might mean for clients, social workers or their departments.

At the time of the Seebohm reorganisation and the creation of the new social services departments, and the short-lived 'generic' social worker, there were those who did see these developments as an opportunity to do something about poverty, in particular about preventing poverty among vulnerable families with children (Holman 1996: 25). The first Secretary of State for Social Services, Sir Keith Joseph, referred to the new directors of social services as 'powerful advocates for the poor' (quoted in D. Townsend 1996: 26), and there was serious consideration of poverty issues during the 1970 election, particularly the outgoing Labour government's record on the poor (Timmins 1995). However, the commitment by the new directors of social services and the new social work profession to do something about poverty was quickly overtaken by international events outside their control, including the 1973 oil crisis which 'dealt a mortal blow to public spending' (D. Townsend 1996: 26), and other developments within social services themselves, including the growing recognition of child abuse and neglect. As Parsloe states: 'In 1971, child protection was unknown'

(1996: 24); by 1974 the Maria Colwell case had changed all that: 'it led to an emphasis on child protection away from other client groups, such as elderly people, that is only being redressed now with the advent of community care and care management' (Clode 1996: 22).

While the zeal of the new departments to engage with poverty slipped off the organisational and professional social work agenda within a few years, it was still a period in which interest in poverty *outside* social services burgeoned. Throughout the mid-1970s and early 1980s one report after another was published on the issue of transmitted deprivation and cycles of disadvantage, a programme of work initiated by Sir Keith Joseph (Coffield, Robinson and Sarsby 1980, Brown and Madge 1982, Ashley 1983, Fuller and Stevenson 1983). As more research on poverty was sponsored, particularly by the then Social Sciences Research Council, more academics, policy makers and others, including the media, engaged with the issues (see chapter 2).

To an extent, the study of Social Policy and Administration as an area of academic interest arose partly out of these developments in the late 1960s and early 1970s. However, in the context of the new social services departments and the new social work profession, the realisation of poverty's importance to their work was a much slower process. It took about a decade from the establishment of the unified social services departments in 1971 before poverty became identified as an area of concern for personal social services. Some early studies had identified associations between being a user of personal social services and being on low income. In the late 1970s, for example, Goldberg and Warburton observed that 'high use of social work services is still very much associated with low socio-economic status, above average unemployment, large families and poor housing conditions' (1979: 57). In 1981 a *New Society* poll conducted with the National Institute for Social Work discovered that 'poor workers and people on state benefits were more likely to be clients' (Weir 1981: 216), while a number of other surveys found that unemployed people made disproportionate use of social services (Nash 1983, Murray 1983). Shortly after, work by the Policy Studies Institute on the reform of supplementary benefit revealed that, in 1982, 20 per cent of all supplementary benefit claimants (843,000) were in contact with a social worker, and of these, 30 per cent had contacted the social worker for benefit advice only (see Becker and MacPherson 1986 for a full review of these earlier studies).

In the early 1980s a small number of social policy and social work academics and others began to research and examine the associations between poverty, personal social services and social work, complementing the wider academic interest in poverty and deprivation (CPAG 1982, McGrail 1983, Silburn, MacPherson and Becker 1984, Fimister 1984, Becker and MacPherson 1985a, 1985b). This specialist interest in poverty and social services followed shortly after a new government-initiated review of the roles and tasks of social workers, the Barclay Inquiry. This reported in 1982 and acknowledged the value of neighbourhood and community approaches to meeting the needs of vulnerable people, many of whom would have financial difficulties (see also chapter 3). But, perhaps of more significance, this academic interest was fuelled by a broader concern with the Thatcher government's record on poverty and the poor, the developing field of study around 'Thatcherism' and social policy, and concern about the newly announced review of social security, the Fowler Review, which raised profound implications for millions of people on benefits, the poor, social services and social work (Stewart and Stewart 1986).

A year or two later, the Association of Metropolitan Authorities found that, of all referrals to social workers, 92 per cent were from 'economically inactive' people or the unemployed (AMA 1985). At the same time, in 1985, the Polytechnic of the South Bank published a report on the implications of unemployment for health and social services (Popay and Dhooge 1985), which led to the development of a training programme aimed at improving social work with unemployed people, funded by a number of organisations, including CCETSW and the Health Education Council (Dhooge 1985, Dhooge with Becker 1989). In the same year a report from Strathclyde Regional Council showed that 88 per cent of all people making a referral to their social workers had a welfare benefit as the main source of income, and that 46 per cent of referrals were from the poorest people, those on supplementary benefit (Strathclyde Regional Council 1985). The evidence showed that it was poor people who made heaviest use, willingly or unwillingly, of social services and social work:

It is not that those with higher incomes do not suffer the problems that the personal social services are formally there to help with ... They do, but the chances that they will seek or obtain help from local authority social services departments is slight. The fundamental, but largely unwritten, rationing rule applied by the services is that those who can pay for help elsewhere should do so.

(Baldock 1994: 169)

Other reports around this time revealed the kinds of responses that poor people could expect from social workers. Many showed that social workers were often ineffective in maximising the income of their clients on state benefits. Many vulnerable people were not receiving their full entitlements despite being in contact with a social worker (Smith 1982, Corden 1983, Blunn and Small 1984, Silburn, MacPherson and Becker 1984, Fimister 1984, Becker and MacPherson 1985a, 1985b, Hill 1985). Social workers seemed ill-prepared for the task of maximising the welfare rights of users, especially income maximisation. Consequently, a growing number of local authorities joined the few that had already established specialist welfare rights services to provide advice and advocacy on benefits and income-related matters. By 1986, 65 local authorities had welfare rights officers. Many of these officers were employed in Labour controlled authorities and worked in urban areas, although there were some notable exceptions. Sixty per cent of all welfare rights officers were based within social services and social work departments (Berthoud, Benson and Williams 1986).

The original impetus for setting up specialist welfare rights teams 'had come from the post-Seebohm social services departments general responsibility for promoting welfare' and the growth of the 'entitlement' view of social security (Berthoud *et al.* 1986: 12, 20). The first welfare rights officer was employed as early as 1972, but the real expansion of welfare rights work took place a decade later, in the 1980s. This expansion (or 'second wave' as Berthoud and colleagues call it) arose for a number of reasons, not least the growing tension between national and local government and Labour controlled authorities' view that welfare rights work offered a low cost and effective way of tackling poverty and disadvantage; the huge growth in unemployment from one to three million between 1980 and 1982; and the revision of the supplementary benefit scheme which took effect at the end of 1980, with the move towards rights and entitlements, and the introduction of single payment grants.

In 1986, the Benefits Research Unit (BRU) at the University of Nottingham published the first comprehensive review of the available data on the association between poverty, social security and personal social services (Becker and MacPherson 1986). The authors argued that 'claimants are poor before they become [social work] clients, but more and more are becoming clients because they are poor' (1986: 1). Quantitative analysis of Strathclyde and other referral data (concerning more than 73,000 people) found that 88 per cent of new referrals to social workers were from people on social security benefits and that two-thirds of all referrals were to do with financial and housing problems, a figure consistent with earlier, Seebohm, projections. The BRU also discovered that a large proportion of referrals, 52 per cent of the total, were from people on the lowest income, then supplementary benefit (now income support). A later analysis of Strathclyde referral data showed that, between 1985 and 1987, nearly two-thirds of poverty-related problems were brought to social workers by women. Indeed, 93 per cent of all women using Strathclyde social work department were claimants of social security and nearly half were in receipt of supplementary benefit (Becker 1989a, 1989b). Clearly, as in the wider understanding that poverty had a gendered dimension (sometimes referred to as the 'feminisation' of poverty), there was a parallel issue of gender to be addressed in the sphere of personal social services and the poor. The BRU report also identified some of the main implications for social services departments, social workers and their poorer clients of the proposed changes in social security that formed part of the Fowler Review, particularly the implications of the discretionary social fund.

The politics of the social fund

These reports on poverty, social services and income-related issues were being published five to six years after the Conservatives had taken power in 1979. The government's first phase of social security reform, from 1980 to 1983, had introduced a number of fundamental social security changes which had already reduced the income of many claimants and had changed the system of meeting exceptional needs. The second phase of reform, the Fowler Review, was also well under way (see chapter 4). The Fowler Review was intended to be the most far-reaching examination of the social security system since the Beveridge Report, and was established to scrutinise every aspect of the system.

The proposals for the social fund were the most worrying to those in personal social services. The fund would abolish rights to single payment grants for the poorest, many of whom, it was then known, were also users of social work services (Becker and MacPherson 1986, Stewart and Stewart 1986). However, a number of other features generated particular concern. First, as discussed in chapter 4, the fund for loans and grants was to be cash-limited. Many in personal social services believed that they may become the next port of call for poor claimants in need of additional financial assistance.

Second, the fund was to be discretionary. Social fund officers would call upon others outside the income maintenance bureaucracies to provide additional information about claimants' needs. The Green Paper suggested that: 'There will need to be clear links with the work of social service and health professionals who may also be involved in helping the same person. The view of outside professionals may have a part to play in helping officers reach judgements on individual cases' (DHSS 1985b: para. 2.107). Social workers, the most powerful professional grouping within social services, feared that they would be drawn into an income maintenance role, one which would be in conflict with their own professional agendas and the interests of their clients. Many social services and social work departments were forced to consider, some for the first time, what the implications of the impending benefits changes might mean for their clients, for their own services and procedures, and for their own budgets. Departments were now more aware of the impoverished state of many of their service users. Many departments submitted evidence to the Fowler Review highlighting their concerns. In particular they expressed anxieties about the proposals for the discretionary social fund and the suggestion that professional social workers may have a part to play in the decision-making process relating to cash payments:

The expectation that social workers might be consulted by the social fund officer about individual applications to the fund, might become involved in the detailed exercise of discretion, might help to determine the priorities to be set in each local office, might even have the power in effect to endorse or veto an application, aroused the greatest apprehension. The professional relationship that a social worker tries to establish with a client is one of mutual trust and respect and the client must be confident that the social worker has the client's best interests at heart. It was feared that this relationship might be fatally compromised if it was suspected that the social worker was acting as the agent of another government department, or was colluding with social security officials to help decide which clients deserved financial support and which did not.

(Becker and Silburn 1990: 9)

While field social workers had professional anxieties of this kind, their managers had other worries. For many years, social services and social work departments had been able to make use of limited powers to make cash payments to some poor families with children. Section 1 payments (or Section 12 payments in Scotland) were aimed at providing modest financial support, at times of crisis, where there is a risk that a child may otherwise have to be brought into care. Managers were concerned that these budgets might be at risk if the cash-limited social fund budgets were quickly exhausted, or if whole categories of need were given a low priority and applications for loans and grants were turned down. Disappointed applicants might turn increasingly to social services and social work departments for financial, rather than social work, help – imposing new demands upon social workers' Section 1 or 12 budgets – and creating a situation in which local authorities came slowly but steadily to accept a *de facto* and unwelcome income maintenance role.

The package of proposed reforms provoked other alarms among departments, professional social work bodies and trade unions. Many social services clients, who had traditionally been able to secure the highest levels of supplementary benefit because of their physical or mental impairments, health problems or other circumstances, would be among the 'losers' when their weekly 'additional requirements' were abolished and replaced by income support premiums (Svenson and MacPherson 1988). There was a fear that claimants in general and poor clients in particular would face reductions in their benefits and the further erosion of their living standards, and that more would look to social services for financial support or advocacy. Departments were also concerned that claimants who had never before been in contact with social workers would be drawn into the net of personal social services for no other reason than poverty and low income. The proposed new benefit arrangements, in particular the social fund, and the thinking behind the reforms, seemed set to blur the 50-year-old dividing line between cash and care.

As a consequence, social services departments throughout the UK, supported by the local authority associations, unions and professional associations, entered into national and local discussions about how best to respond to the social security proposals. Some argued for a policy of strict non-cooperation, and urged a boycott of any connections at all with the social fund and its officers. Others, rather fewer of them, proposed a guarded and carefully controlled form of collaboration. The doctrine that emerged, and which became the recommended code of the then three local authority associations (the Association of County Councils, the Association of Metropolitan Authorities and the Confederation of Scottish Local Authorities) and of the British Association of Social

Workers, was that of 'determined advocacy'. The local authority organisations published a 'Policy Statement and Practice Guide' to determined
advocacy in 1988 which attempted to redefine an 'acceptable' boundary
between personal social services and social security. It emphasised that
while social work staff must do all that is reasonably possible to meet the
needs of their clients, advocates must not be drawn into prioritising
under the social fund (AMA/ACC/COSLA 1988).

Of all the issues affecting personal social services in the mid- to late
1980s, concern about the social fund was one of the most fiercely
debated. This interest was fuelled considerably by the growth in the
1980s of welfare rights services within social services departments; it
was welfare rights advisers who played a key role in determining and
drafting the local authority associations' joint strategy towards the
social fund, and the local authority associations continue to draw on the
expertise of welfare rights advisers when responding to any new proposals for social security reform. As far as the social fund was
concerned, social services and social work departments declared that
they were not to become agencies of income maintenance, and that their
services should not be used to support an inadequate income maintenance system. However, in some very small respects they were already
agencies of income maintenance through their own limited financial
powers (Section 1/12) to help poor families with children. Little did
they know that, in less than a decade, they would take on major income
maintenance responsibilities as they took control of 'direct payments' to
disabled people (see chapter 6).

Cash from care: Section 1 and 12 payments

As already seen, social services and social work departments had
powers to make limited cash payments to certain poor families with
children. Section 1 of the 1963 Children and Young Persons Act
(which later became Section 1 of the 1980 Child Care Act and then
Section 17 of the 1989 Children Act) empowered local authorities to
provide financial and material help to promote the welfare of children by
diminishing the need to receive, or keep them, in care. Similar powers
to Section 1 existed in Scotland and in Northern Ireland, although
the Scottish powers allow social workers to interpret 'in need' more
broadly. These payments are both important indicators of evolving patterns of financial need within communities and of social services'
perceptions and responses to those needs. But they also illustrate the
shifting boundaries between central and local agencies and their
respective responsibilities for cash and care. At the heart of the use of
these budgets has been a debate about *who* should be responsible for
providing extra cash to people who run out of money (for whatever
reason), and whether it is the responsibility of the social security system or social services departments.

Researchers have studied the use of these limited financial powers for some years. The earliest studies found that social workers were involved in a crisis response of grant giving in order to keep families in their homes, to provide food in emergencies or to provide other household necessities (Heywood and Allen 1971, Valencia and Jackson 1979). Later studies confirmed that the need for food was the most likely reason for social workers to make a payment (Hill 1985, Camden 1985, Southwark 1985, Nixon 1988, Leicestershire 1989, see Becker and MacPherson 1986 for a review of the earlier studies). Total expenditure on Section 1 payments rose considerably during the 1980s, from just under £1 million in 1981–2 to just under £13 million in 1987–8 (Becker and Silburn 1990: 40). The average level of expenditure per department in 1984–5 was £92,000 (Stewart and Stewart 1988: 77), although there is large variation between departments, particularly between metropolitan and county council authorities (Jones 1989). In the scale of both social security and social services expenditure, however, these payments are small-scale, but it is their overlapping nature with social security that has been at the centre of their controversial nature, and attraction, to many researchers.

Historically, Section 1/12 payments have always been made for some items and needs that are provided for under social assistance (supplementary benefit/income support). In the 1970s, a study revealed that half of all Section 1 payments went to families on supplementary benefit for needs which the supplementary benefit scheme was designed to cover (Lister and Emmett 1976). In the 1980s, about a quarter of payments were for items such as food, fuel, clothing – items which were supposed to be covered by either the basic weekly benefit or an additional single payment (Nixon 1988: 62). Many of these social services payments arose from administrative errors among social security personnel (Rainbow 1985), or were compensating for the breakdown in benefit delivery or the inadequacy of benefits (Stewart and Stewart 1988: 77).

During the months before the introduction of the social fund in April 1988, most social services and social work departments prepared individual policy documents and procedures along the lines of the local authority associations' formal response, although the Scottish authorities appeared to take a more non-cooperative stance with the social fund (Svenson 1988). The majority of these documents also referred to departments' own financial powers under Section 1 or 12. Some departments initiated new procedures specifically trying to clarify the boundary arrangements with the social fund. Guidelines were formulated to protect these budgets, social workers and clients, and to safeguard the principle that it was the Department of Social Security, not social services, which was responsible for income maintenance. Individual local authority reports, policy statements and practice guides, issued a couple of months before the introduction of the social fund, contained strongly worded statements about the separation of responsibilities between the

DSS and social services. These guidelines usually included a number of the following operational principles:

- Section 1/12 payments should only be made where they are clearly appropriate and are in line with the intention of the legislation;
- payments should only be made where the person requesting help cannot receive help from social security;
- payments should only be made where the urgent need of the person requesting help is such as to make an application to the social fund impractical, or where the person has already made an application to the social fund which has been unsuccessful;
- payments should only be made as part of an overall social work plan of intervention. Nonetheless they should still only be made in exceptional circumstances and generally be 'one off' payments;
- payments should only be made to those in greatest need. Some prioritising will be necessary, especially for departments that pre-limit their annual budgets;
- payment should only be made after all other alternatives have been explored, including family and friends, charitable and voluntary funds.

(Becker and Silburn 1990: 41–42)

These guidelines were to be used by social workers to help determine who should, and who should not, be given direct financial help from their own limited budgets, and what poor families must give in return. To a large extent they recreated both the ideology of the social fund itself, and the administrative mechanisms for selectivity, by establishing procedures whereby social workers needed to make judgements about the relative 'vulnerability' of the different people who sought help – between those who most needed financial support, and those who should, or could, be excluded.

Monitoring the impact of the social fund

Such was the concern over the social security and social fund proposals that about half the social services and social work departments in Britain participated in two research programmes to monitor the impact of the changes, in particular the social fund, on the operation and practice of social work, and on social work clients. One of these projects was co-ordinated by a group of academics, the Social Security Research Consortium (SSRC), working with 21 authorities. The other was organised by the Benefits Research Unit (BRU) and the Social Services Research Group, and included 27 social services and social work departments across England, Scotland and Wales.

These projects started collecting data in 1988, coinciding with the introduction of the social security changes, and continued to 1990–1. Between them they generated a considerable research literature on the boundaries between social security and personal social services, with associated lessons for the broader consideration of poverty and social work. The findings were widely disseminated by the projects and others, and this process included the publication of a regular supplement in *Community Care* magazine ('Fundamentals'), a newsletter (*Benefits Research*, later to become the journal *Benefits*) and a number of in-house and externally published reports and articles (for example, Becker and Silburn 1990, Stewart and Stewart 1991, SSRC 1991).

The findings of the research were broadly similar. They showed that many vulnerable people, including people with mental health problems, elderly people, disabled people, lone-parent families and young people were turning to social workers for help directly because of poverty, with benefits-related problems, or with lifestyle problems precipitated or exacerbated by poverty and low income. In the BRU study, for example, over 3,000 people with financial and social fund related problems were in contact with 87 participating social work teams during a series of week-long 'snapshots'. Many of these people (1,281) were existing social work cases with financial problems, but a larger number (1,853) were people who made a new referral to social workers during the designated snapshot weeks solely because of financial or social fund difficulties. People with the greatest likelihood of being, or coming into contact, with social workers because of financial and social fund problems (referred to as the 'new poor clients') were women (particularly lone parents on benefits), young people under 25, elderly people, those with mental health difficulties and those from minority ethnic groups (Becker and Silburn 1990). Nine out of ten of the 'new poor clients' were claimants of social security and over half were among the poorest, in receipt of income support. Only one in ten were in paid employment and of these nearly half received family credit because of low pay. Only one in seven owned their home. These characteristics not only defined the new poor clients but are common among many other people who would be considered to be especially vulnerable to poverty.

More than a quarter of the new poor clients were people who had made one or more applications to the social fund. At the time of the snapshots, 40 per cent of these were still waiting for a social fund decision and in many of these instances the waiting was itself generating problems and uncertainty. Of those who had been given a decision from social fund officers, the majority (56 per cent) had been turned down, even though many of these were considered to be in traditionally vulnerable groups, such as lone-parent families, those with mental health problems, and so on (Becker and Silburn 1990).

The monitoring of the social fund suggests that changes in one welfare system (social security) have an immediate impact on the operation, practice and clients of other welfare systems (in this case, social services and social work in particular). To a large extent this is because many users of welfare services have a coexisting need for cash *and* care (chapter 3). The social security reforms had an almost immediate knock-on effect upon the operation and practice of social services and social work, and on the kinds of demands that vulnerable people and others brought to departments and social workers (Becker and

Silburn 1990, SSRC 1991). There were a substantial number of new referrals to social workers for help or advice with a financial problem, many of whom had no earlier contact with the department, nor any other presenting problem. Similarly, many existing clients had fresh financial difficulties to cope with as well. Many required financial help from social services and social work departments' own limited financial budgets. In terms of demands for Section 1 and Section 12 payments, the BRU research showed that between 6 to 10 per cent of all new financial referrals made to social workers in the participating social work teams were requests for direct financial assistance. Indeed, just over one in ten of the new poor clients were helped by social workers through these budgets. Over 90 per cent of these payments were for less than £30 in value. Most payments and expenditure were to meet basic needs, including food and child care expenses, although there was considerable variation between authorities in the number and size of all payments, particularly between county council and metropolitan authorities (Becker and Silburn 1990: 42–50). In theory at least, food and other basic expenses are the very items of routine household expenditure that are covered by the weekly scale rates paid to claimants of income support. While not all applicants for Section 1/12 help are in receipt of income support the vast majority are claimants and many would be receiving or entitled to income support.

The degree of overlap between Section 1/12 payments and social security was considerable. Nearly half of all payments (one third of total expenditure) went on items covered by the income support basic scale rates. Another 4 per cent of payments (6 per cent of expenditure) went on items covered by housing benefit. A further 13 per cent of payments (15 per cent of expenditure) went on items that could be covered by the social fund. In all, two-thirds of all section 1/12 payments (and just over half of all expenditure) were for items covered by other social security benefits. The data indicate a situation in which social services were making financial payments to poor families most often as a direct income maintenance function. This pattern of payment was quite the opposite to the intention of departmental policy statements and guidelines, which attempted to exclude poor families from receiving cash help for items and needs covered by other social security benefits.

Just three years after the 1988 reform of social security, Section 1 payments were themselves replaced by Section 17 of the 1989 Children Act. The Act came into force in October 1991 and, among other things, provided social services departments with duties and powers to take action to protect children and support families. Section 17 gave local authorities a general duty to safeguard and promote the welfare of children in need and to promote the welfare of such children by their families (where this is in the child's interests) by providing a range and level of services appropriate to their needs (Tunstill 1995). Section 17 also allowed for payments by the local authority to meet immediate hardships where children are involved and to prevent reception into care. Tunstill suggests that 'the concept of family support has, over the period between the late 1980s and the present, come to be regarded by both politicians and practitioners as the dominant successor to the notion of preventing reception into care' (Tunstill 1995: 21). Such provisions have an important part to play in buffering the effects of stress, and poverty, on vulnerable families (Gibbons 1992: 3). Social services have discretion in how they use their funds, which may be given, for example, for household equipment, clothing and shoes, child care costs, and so on. Similar to Section 1 payments before them, Section 17 budgets, and their use, vary across Britain. Ninety-six per cent of local authorities surveyed by Aldgate and Tunstill said they made such payments, although there is little contemporary detail on what these payments cover, or their overlap with social security. However, there is no evidence to suggest that the overlap today will be any less significant than that suggested by Becker and Silburn (Aldgate and Tunstill 1994: 80, Tunstill 1995: 28, Becker and Silburn 1990).

Clearly, a critical issue to be addressed by social services departments and social workers is the extent to which poor families with children can be supported by these small-scale payments and other social work interventions in order to *prevent* family breakdown, rather than dealing with the crisis after it has occurred. Moreover, consideration must also be given to the significance of the levels of social security benefits that many families have to rely on, and the extent to which these levels actually precipitate family crisis, which then requires a social services or social work response.

Managing the poor

The fear that local social services and social work offices would become *overwhelmed* by increasing numbers of poor people in the late 1980s and early 1990s, as a consequence of the 1988 social security reforms, was largely misplaced. Social services have always been used predominantly by poorer people (see chapter 3) and the 1988 social security reforms confirmed and maintained this pattern. Social workers seemed to adjust to the additional demands on their time and budgets imposed by the initial changeover from one social security system to another. However, the ways in which they adjusted to, or coped with, the problems of poor people seeking help was not without some cost. First, the quality of service that many poor people could expect from social services seemed to be in doubt; in most cases clients were seen for very short periods of time by social workers, despite the complexities of their financial and material circumstances or needs. The evidence suggests that many social workers were still unable to maximise their clients' limited incomes, and many people with financial problems received a superficial response (Becker and Silburn 1990). The ambivalence held by social workers towards welfare rights work and issues concerned with money did not change, despite the attention given by social services to the monitoring of the social fund and the importance of a coordinated response.

Second, many people with poverty or financial problems were referred on from social services to other agencies or organisations, including charities, for support, money, advice or advocacy. The BRU reported that one in ten of all new poor clients were referred to charities, particularly for needs to do with clothing and furniture. The SSRC reported that 'one of the most worrying consequences of the social fund is the extent to which social workers are being forced to connive in the resurrection of private charity as a primary means of meeting basic needs' (SSRC 1991: 42). Evidence suggests that many charities found it hard to deal with the increased demand for their items and services. One of the main charities providing cash to poor people is the Family Welfare Association (FWA), which was established in 1869 as the Charity Organisation Society (the precursor to organised local authority social work). Indeed, the director of the FWA wrote in 1990 that charities were 'being conscripted, without any option, as so-called "partners" with the government in the struggle against poverty. Nobody asked us whether we wished to be partners or whether we had the resources to fill the gap ... the social fund stands convicted ... of causing a massive waste of social workers' valuable time and casting a hideous and disproportionate burden on charities without the means to meet it' (Morley 1990: 12–13).

By the mid-1990s the FWA and other charities were again raising concerns about the overlap between their grant-giving, social security payments and Section 17 payments from social services. The FWA suggests that there are strong indicators that charities are 'replacing government funding as one of the principle sources of assistance for families and individuals in need' (Hollins 1995: 1). Social workers and their clients often failed to make an application to the social fund or to Section 17 budgets before approaching the charity, whereas the charity's rules require such approaches before they will consider making a payment. Many social workers suggested that the social fund was too inflexible and applying was often 'a waste of time'.

Third, many local social services offices increasingly came to resemble the old-style DSS offices:

> The tackiness of the furniture, the torn magazines, the broken toys, the doors that can only be opened by tapping in a code-number, the separation of client and worker by partitions or glass screens, the increasing use of appointment systems, the air, even the smell, of drab, down at heel despair in the waiting rooms, this is now commonly encountered in many places, as though working with the new poor clients creates a poor working environment.
>
> (Becker and Silburn 1990: 81)

This poor environment in many local social services offices, which continues to this day, reinforces the stigma and feelings of failure that are now widely associated with using social services and social work in particular. In contrast, local social security offices, criticised in the 1980s by academics and the welfare rights movement for the poor quality of their environment, have attempted to upgrade their reception areas and facilities, making them more accessible and amenable to their 'customers'.

Finally, as already indicated, many social services and social work departments were able to regulate and manage the demands upon their financial budgets by preparing new guidelines on how such monies should be used. These recreated the ideology of the social fund itself, establishing operational principles and procedures for managing poor clients, to exclude particular kinds of people and categories of need, and to make demands on the behaviour of those successful in receiving cash support. These statements borrowed much of the language and principles of the social fund manual in their attempt to manage and 'target' cash-limited resources on meeting the exceptional needs of the most vulnerable and poorest families. In reality, however, payments continued to be made in many instances for basic income maintenance functions and needs already covered by social security benefits. Social services and social work departments had, in no small measure, moved into a phase where selectivity and rationing of their own limited cash budgets was commonplace. As shall be shown in the next chapter, the advent of 'care in the community' forced most, if not all of these departments, to manage their new larger scale, but nonetheless cash-limited community care budgets, by rationing access to, and charging for, social care.

The professional fear that social workers would be drawn into compromising complicity with social fund officers never materialised in the way that the local authority associations and others had envisaged. It was precisely to avoid social workers being drawn into the discretionary social fund decision-making that led to the strategy of determined advocacy. But even before the fund started, the DSS seemed to back off from its original concept, indicating that the great majority of applications would be determined on the basis of the written application form alone. The evidence suggests that rarely did social fund officers try to involve social workers in unacceptably compromising negotiations. Indeed, if anything, approaches were more likely to be made to social fund officers by social workers on behalf of clients and in pursuit of their applications. There was strong support among social work teams for liaison arrangements between them, the DSS and the social fund. Indeed, in many instances, clients were referred on by social workers to the social fund for help, particularly for community care needs (Becker and Silburn 1990, SSRC 1991).

The strategy of determined advocacy had always been a problematic one, forged out of anxiety and loathing of government plans, rather than a complete and well-considered approach. Much modern social work is concerned with liaison with other professional groups and organisations, indeed the Barclay inquiry into the roles and tasks of social workers

commended the networking approach of social work. It was always difficult, therefore, to see how social workers would have been able to
maintain a professional distance from one group of welfare bureaucrats,
social fund officers, especially given such a high proportion of social
security and income support claimants among social work clients. In the
event, many social workers evolved a working relationship with social
fund officers to their own satisfaction, which they construed to be in the
best interests of their clients, and which continues to this day.

Poverty, social services and social work in the 1990s

If the 1980s was a decade of increased awareness in social services and
social work as to the importance of poverty and social security on the
lives of many clients, the 1990s was characterised by a reluctance,
indeed a withdrawal, by social workers and their departments, from
doing anything substantial about these issues. The two major research
projects monitoring the impact of the social fund and other social security changes on the operation and practice of social work reported in
1990 and 1991, and little further research was conducted into these
issues thereafter. Indeed, the social fund itself failed to attract the intensity of attention, concern or feeling that had been so prominent in the
late 1980s. Many of the academic researchers involved with issues of
the social fund and social work moved on to other projects, while social
work's professional bodies and local authority associations also moved
on to new concerns and new agendas, not least the implementation of
the Children Act in 1991, and the community care reforms phased in
between 1991 and 1993. Between them these two pieces of legislation
led to fundamental changes in the organisation and operation of many
social services and social work departments: 'An unintended consequence of reforming children's services and community care at the
same time is that many [social services] departments have set up separate planning processes and some are reorganising into children and
adult divisions, rather than following the explicit recommendation of
the proposals that " … the full range of social services authority functions should continue to form a coherent whole"' (Smale *et al.* 1994:
para. 1.21). As a consequence of this separation, there has been a resur-
gence of old problems of lack of coordination (characteristic of the
immediate post-war period), the move away from a 'whole person'
approach, and an even greater shift away from the Seebohm ideal of
community development and preventive work, generic social workers
and the 'one door' philosophy.

Academics in social policy and social work, and researchers in social
services, were presented with so many research challenges in the early
1990s that ongoing monitoring of the social fund and social security
changes became increasingly unattractive and outdated. The under secretary responsible for the social fund had publicly commented in 1989

that 'the social fund is here to stay; it is here to stay' (Becker and Silburn 1990: 78), and it became clear to academics and others that, regardless of what they discovered about the shortcomings of the fund, the government had no intention of changing the scheme, even when further criticisms of its operation were made by the Social Security Advisory Committee and by the 'official' research team at the University of York (SSAC 1990: 51–2, Huby and Dix 1992). The 'big issues' in social security research had shifted from the social fund to the new disability benefit changes and the impending introduction of the Child Support Agency, while in social work the research focus turned to monitoring the Children Act and preparing for community care and its monitoring and evaluation.

Little has been published in the 1990s about the association between poverty, social security, personal social services and social work. Poverty has, to a large extent, slipped off the social work and social services agenda for both research and practice. Local authorities (as opposed to social services), however, did not lose interest in anti-poverty initiatives, and many joined one or other of the new networks of authorities committed to examining, and promoting, anti-poverty strategies (Balloch and Jones 1990, Pearson, Alcock and Craig 1996). There has been a substantial increase in the number of local authorities engaged in anti-poverty work between the late 1980s and mid-1990s, much of which, but certainly not all, centres around profiling poverty, welfare rights work (including take-up campaigns, income maximisation, advocacy etc.), and improving access to services through neighbourhood offices and one-stop shops. These activities are being built upon increasingly by other initiatives, including encouraging participation by poor people in planning services and setting local priorities; creating partnerships with the voluntary and private sectors and other public agencies; supporting community enterprise (for example, credit unions and cooperatives); and regenerating communities socially and economically by working with economic development initiatives to ensure sustainable development (Tree 1996: 27). Increasingly, the trend has been to make anti-poverty work more corporate, rather than being 'owned' by any single department, although resource constraints have imposed limits to the extent to which anti-poverty work can 'compete against the service priorities of the other strategic and statutory commitments within the policy process of local government' (Alcock *et al.* 1995: 2).

Social services, however, had very little to say, or do, about poverty, and many social services departments, even those within local authorities *with* anti-poverty strategies, still followed policies and practices which, in effect, continued to manage poor people. As discussed in the next section of this chapter, the anti-poverty philosophy adopted by many local authorities did not seem to permeate deeply into the culture of social services or social workers, nor did it seem to inform policy or practice, especially in regard to work with poor families with children.

Welfare rights advisers, many working within social services, continued to promote the take-up of benefits of existing social work clients and others, but as shall be discussed in the next chapter, with the introduction of community care, their role was also to change. Many became drawn into tasks which sometimes appeared to have more to do with maximising the income of their cash-starved departments, rather than assisting or empowering poor people to secure their 'rights' to independence and dignity in the community.

The denial of a poverty perspective

An anti-poverty perspective was missing from the analysis and response to many of the key issues that confronted social services and social work with poor families and children in the 1990s. This is despite the recognition that social services often had to deal with the 'casualties' of other social processes:

The system that the economic environment creates for low income people is vicious and not subtle. It not only creates poor people; it pauperises them, seeking out and stripping them of their last resources, forcing youths out of the home which might otherwise have helped, bringing together reluctant family members into one crowded dwelling. Whatever other problems this may create for society, it will create clients and claimants in large numbers for the social services. These departments will be rained upon.

(Schorr 1992: 18)

To a large extent social work with poor families in the 1980s, and particularly during the 1990s, has been dominated by child protection work, as a response to the increased awareness of, and concern with, child abuse and child neglect. However, much of the policy and practice in child protection has failed to engage with the implications of widespread poverty and benefit reliance among those families who, for one reason or another, become subjects of child protection procedures. This is despite the evidence to show the importance that poverty plays in these matters. For example, research has shown that debts, marital discord and unemployment are most commonly cited by parents as triggers which precede the abuse of children, even though in many instances it is problematic to talk about 'cause and effect' (National Children's Homes 1986, Becker and MacPherson 1986, Irvine 1988, Baldwin and Spencer 1993).

Many of the child death inquiries of the 1980s and 1990s have highlighted the impoverished circumstances of many of the families. The 1985 inquiry report into the death of Jasmine Beckford, for example, described the area where Jasmine and her family lived in Brent as one where the 'bare statistics of poverty' showed a high concentration of social problems and where families unquestionably suffered disproportionately from poor housing, unemployment, and lack of community facilities (Blom-Cooper 1985). The report into the death of Kimberly

Carlile in Greenwich (1987), and the Cleveland report (HMSO 1988) also referred to the multiple deprivations of the areas and the poverty of the local residents. A more recent example is that of a 15-month-old Southwark boy, Paul, whose family had been monitored by welfare professionals for many years. The report (Bridge Child Care Consultancy 1995) refers to the poverty of the family; there were no clean clothes for the unwashed children, no hot water, no proper toilet, few cooked meals, few toys. The local social services' main response was to provide occasional financial payments under its own limited financial powers, described above.

The lack of attention given to the poverty dynamic was also evident in other spheres of social work. In the early 1990s, for example, 'Satan seized the headlines', as alleged incidents of 'ritualistic' and 'satanic' abuse were added to the growing repertoire of evils committed against children (Webb 1991, Becker 1992). What was consistent in the reporting, but rarely commented upon or responded to by social services and social workers, was that many of the estates where these ritualistic or satanic abuses were alleged to have taken place were among the most deprived in the UK. The Nottingham case centred on the Broxtowe estate, described by the media as 'a deprived area ... a rundown estate of red-brick council houses' (*Mail on Sunday* 1990). Broxtowe ranked among the most deprived areas in the county, on the council's own deprivation indicators (Nottinghamshire County Council 1994). The Langley estate in Rochdale, with its '12,000 inhabitants, boarded-up shops, featureless houses, abandoned flats and disconsolate patches of dead greenery' (*Sunday Times* 1990) was described as a place 'where the poorest have to fight authority and sometimes each other to survive' (*Observer* 1990).

There are complex pathways to child abuse and neglect, but deprivation is now a well-established component (Baldwin and Spencer 1993). Abuse also occurs in all social classes but is more likely to be detected in poor households because of the social control nature of social services and child protection teams, and their location in or near to poorer·areas. Consequently, 'to pinpoint individual families who may be at risk is deeply stigmatising and methodologically suspect ... Community wide strategies to support families, promote children's health, development and well being must be the foundation of child care and child protection services' (Baldwin and Spencer 1993: 358). An emphasis on prevention and family support is likely to be a far more productive strategy than dealing with abuse, focusing on poorer families, once it has occurred.

The links between poverty and other areas of child care social work have also been well documented. For example, Holman (1980) and others (Hardiker and Barker 1988) have shown how, for some families, deprivation and financial poverty create barriers for the achievement of acceptable child care objectives, and precipitate children being taken away from parents or being received into the care of the local authority. Bebbington and Miles (1989) and many others (for example, Becker and MacPherson 1986, Beresford, Chemins and Tunstill 1987, Gibbons 1989, Gibbons, Thorpe and Wilkinson 1990) have shown a strong correlation between children entering the care system and socio-economic disadvantage, particularly in lone-parent families.

More recent research conducted by Strathclyde Social Work Department confirms these earlier findings (Freeman and Lockhart 1994). Seventy-eight per cent of children coming into care in Strathclyde are from families relying on benefit. Many came from one-parent families, the majority of whom are also on benefit. Of the children coming into care from households where a male carer was present, 60 per cent of the males were unemployed; 82 per cent of all children coming into care came from households where the 'head' was unemployed:

... you are over 4 times more likely to come into care if you come from a single parent family and more than 3 times more likely if you are in a family relying on income support or in a family with 3 or more children. 'Vulnerable' children in Strathclyde therefore are defined as those falling into 2 or more of 3 population groups i.e. single parent families, families with 3 or more children and families relying on income support.

(Freeman and Lockhart 1994: 12)

The overriding finding from these studies is stark: almost all the children brought into care, for whatever reason, are children of the poorest in society. Many of these poor children are not protected in care either, as the litany of residential child care scandals of the 1980s and 1990s clearly demonstrate (Becker 1992). Indeed, so serious and widespread were these scandals, affecting so many children, that Prime Minister John Major announced in 1996 a national inquiry into child abuse, particularly in local authority residential homes for children (DoH press release 1996a).

'Problem families' or poor families with problems?

Just a few years before the Broxtowe incident of alleged ritualistic abuse came to light, the social work area director and deputy director for Broxtowe wrote about the poverty that was so endemic on the estate and the effect that this was having for both local residents and social workers. They observed that:

Ironically, it is at this time of economic depression when areas such as the one identified in this article most need support to combat the undermining effects of poverty that departments are most ill-equipped to meet that challenge. Resources have become scarce in the face of mounting demand; attitudes and priorities shift, but to accommodate a more traditional, defensive role; the case-work model concerned with the traditional individual and family clientele re-emerges as the solitary approach of the statutory social work agency. Depressing, and in our view, doomed to be an inadequate solution.

(Dillon and Parker 1988: 339)

Social services and child care professionals have failed to engage with the issues of poverty and deprivation: 'Given the demoralisation, alienation and disintegration of relationships which may follow chronic stress arising from deprivation, as well as the major hindrances to health, education and practical functioning which accompany it, there are questions about why so few child care services are geared to tackling this problem systematically' (Baldwin and Spencer 1993: 364). Social workers appear to have become immune to the poverty dynamic in much of their work, despite the mass of research evidence that highlights its centrality to many of the problems encountered by poor families with children. A Department of Health review of child protection research findings (DoH 1995a), for example, suggests that:

> ... scrutiny falls almost exclusively upon those children who come to the notice of child protection agencies. They tend to be working class and poor; little is known about middle-class parents who mistreat their offspring or about children abused outside the home.

> (DoH 1995a: 21)

However, no effort has been made in the report, or within professional social work, to address the far-reaching implications of this statement. In launching the report the Health Minister made no direct reference to poverty, except to comment that 'A third [of children referred to child protection] came from lone parent families, two thirds were living in a household that lacked a wage earner' (DoH press release 1995c).

The implications of these figures, and the 'hidden' nature of abuse among better off or average income families, remains largely unexplored. The focus by policy makers and practitioners in child protection work, and by social workers working with families and children, is most often concerned with cases – so-called 'problem families' – rather than poor families with problems. There is an assumption that family structure, particularly lone parenthood, or being outside the labour market (unwaged and reliant on benefits), define and characterise the 'problem family' which then requires management, policing and regulation, rather than preventive family support. The poverty-related problems of many families who come into contact with social workers are redefined as 'symptoms' or 'presenting problems' of 'problem families'. The poverty dynamic is given little consideration; it is relegated to a position of minimal importance in determining the nature of the social work response to families with children living in poverty. This 'individualisation' of poverty (see also chapters 1 and 2) contributes to the management, and impoverishment, of the poor by social services and social workers.

A thorough consideration of the strategic importance of poverty would require an analysis of the aetiology of child abuse and neglect in its widest sense; the consideration of areas of broader socio-political significance, some of which are not directly child-related, such as inequality, unemployment, low income and substandard housing; as well as a focus on individual cases and the use of specific social work methods, approaches and purposes. This analysis is not on the agenda of most social services departments, nor is it a matter of concern, or interest, for many social workers. As with the relationship between poverty and ill health, or poverty and crime (discussed in chapter 2), there is considerable evidence to show the links between poverty and these and other social problems, including child abuse and neglect. But in all these spheres the poverty dynamic is regarded as either controversial and contested, or of minimal significance. This leads in most instances to its importance being overshadowed by more immediate professional concerns and interests, particularly a focus on the problematic nature of family structures and relationships within, and between, families, rather than on the expressed needs of poor people *as people living in poverty* and all that this engenders. Social services and social workers have largely managed poor families with children by defining them as dysfunctional families requiring individual or family treatment, rather than confronting and engaging with poverty as a structural and political issue. The social work 'mission' has 'centred on helping individuals to function more effectively in their social environment' (Clarke 1993: 19); it has encouraged poor clients to adapt, and manage, their poverty. As discussed in chapter 3, social services and social work have their origins in the Poor Law and the 'rescue' ethos of Christian charities. That influence is very much alive in the 1990s.

Social workers' attitudes to poverty and the poor

Policy, organisation and change in social services and social work cannot be divorced from the context of social, political, individual and professional attitudes and ideologies that help shape personal, professional and organisational identities, roles and responses (see chapter 1). It is now fairly well established within social services and professional social work that staff need to have a greater awareness and sensitivity to how their assumptions, beliefs and prejudices in the areas of race, gender, disability and sexuality affect their policies, organisation, practice and outcomes. But social workers have been reluctant to explore their beliefs and attitudes in relation to poverty and the poor, even though issues of race, gender, disability, poverty and exclusion overlap strongly (Becker 1988). There is a need to evaluate the extent to which certain social work values inhibit or distort social work services with poor people (Fuller and Stevenson 1983). Fundamentally: 'social workers' attitudes are a crucial factor in the way they will deliver services to the poor and how clients, in turn, will react to the services they receive' (Orten 1979: 94). Because many social work clients are poor and because, professionally at least, social workers are expected to have a positive attitude towards them, it is vital to study social workers' attitudes to poverty (Orten 1979: 3, Macarov 1981: 150, Becker and MacPherson 1986: 61).

Most studies of social workers' attitudes towards poverty and the poor originate from the United States and Australia. Orten (1979) suggests that if social workers have 'positive' attitudes towards the poor, this will be translated into positive behaviour. However, a study of Australian social workers found that while social workers were more likely to emphasise structural causes and structural solutions, social work practice at that time did not reflect a structural practice agenda (Considine 1978). This contradiction, between how social workers view the causes of poverty and how they respond to it, is a prominent feature of the research on social workers' attitudes to poverty (Blau 1974, Silberman 1977, Macarov 1981, Considine 1978, Becker 1988). Silberman has suggested that social workers with 'hostile' attitudes (equated as those who define poverty in individualistic terms) are more likely to implement such beliefs in their day-to-day practice, but that those with positive attitudes may be prevented from transforming their attitudes into 'positive' actions because of a number of institutional and other constraints (Silberman 1977: 81). It has been suggested that the more committed social workers are to the ideology of professionalism, and the higher they are in the agency hierarchy, the less likely they are to identify with the poor and support radical social action approaches (Epstein 1968, 1970a, 1970b). Epstein (1981) has shown how social work actions for, or on behalf of clients, can be analysed on a continuum from 'case' to 'cause' (see also Bull 1982). Case advocacy is concerned with individualised work for individuals or small groups. Class or cause advocacy is work on behalf of a group who share a similar status or set of problems. Epstein found that the majority of social workers practised both case and cause advocacy but that case advocacy was far more likely to be practised on poor clients than, say, on children and young people or those with physical impairments. Epstein concluded that social workers had little interest in anti-poverty action aimed at wider social change.

The study of social workers' attitudes towards poverty and the poor is relatively undeveloped in Britain and the rest of Europe (Becker 1987, 1988, Salonen 1993). However, what evidence there is indicates that social workers and others within social services have a lack of 'poverty awareness', and that this operates on a number of levels: social workers have little understanding of the complex processes that generate and maintain poverty; they have limited insight into how their political and welfare ideologies and attitudes to poverty affect their daily practice with poor people; they have failed to place poverty on the agenda for social work theorising, education, policy and practice.

Becker's (1987) study of 450 social workers shows that social workers, as a group, define the causes of poverty in structural, rather than individual terms. Eight out of ten social workers, for example, thought that people lived in poverty because of 'injustice and inequality'; this compared with only 16 per cent of the British public who had the same view at that time. Social workers were also more likely than the public to view benefit claimants with sympathy: 78 per cent of social workers (compared with only 25 per cent of the public) strongly agreed that most claimants on social assistance are in real need. Similarly, 53 per cent of social workers (23 per cent of the public) felt strongly that a lot of people entitled to claim social assistance failed to claim it. Social workers' beliefs about the adequacy of social assistance (supplementary benefit/income support) rested on their opinions about the purpose of these payments. The common view was that social assistance should provide for relative needs and allow for social participation and real choice. Consequently, many social workers thought that the existing rates of benefit were too low. However, social workers' opinions on this and other matters were deeply divided according to *which* claimant group was being considered. So, for example, social workers were more likely to view the scale rate as inadequate for families with young children than for school leavers or elderly people. Nearly one in ten social workers also agreed that *many* claimants 'are on the fiddle'.

Social workers' perceptions of the causes of poverty relate closely to their definitions of poverty: as a group social workers define poverty in relative terms, referring to the lack of resources and opportunities to live an 'adequate' or 'reasonable' life, relative to others. Social workers show concern that all citizens should have the opportunities and resources to make real choices and exert control over their lives; poor people lack access to opportunities, resources, an adequate lifestyle and social participation because, to a degree, they were seen as 'victims' and 'powerless' (Becker 1988: 245).

Social workers also believe that poor people who become users of social work services are 'different' from poor people who remain independent of social services. The dominant view was that poor social work clients were unable to cope by themselves, that they were inadequate in one way or another, hence their contact, voluntarily or reluctantly, with social services. This distinction between poor clients and other poor people is likely to influence the kind of service that users will receive: 'Personal social services that are directed at "non copers" may be quite different from those provided for people perceived to have other needs' (Becker 1988: 246). Social workers who were Conservative identifiers and who had the least education were most likely to individualise poverty. However, social workers as a group have a matrix of opinions, beliefs and values about poverty and the poor. Their attitude position (what they believe about the poor) and the intensity of their attitude (how strongly they believe it) range along a continuum from 'individualising' to 'social' for each issue under investigation (for example the causes of poverty, adequacy of social assistance, etc.). Attitudes are not always consistent nor are they consistently supportive: 'Individual social workers are often positive or negative or feel more strongly about one issue but may be more negative or feel less strongly about other issues. Their attitudes are characterised by inconsistency, paradox and contradiction – which is inherent in the operation and practice of social work itself' (Becker 1988: 247). The important point is not that there is a group of social workers with particularly hostile or positive views (although the evidence suggests that this is likely to be the case), but that *all* social workers have beliefs, opinions and views which are hostile towards some of the poor. Social workers, like the public more generally, make distinctions and judgements between different groups of the poor, between the 'deserving' and 'undeserving', between copers and non-copers, and so on. Most social workers also believe that they can have little strategic impact on poverty itself. They believe that it is necessary to respond at an individual or family level because it is here that change and adaptation are most likely to occur.

Social work methods and the ideology of casework

Traditionally, social work with families and children has drawn heavily on methods which focus on family members, either as individuals or as a group. This individualised or family focus, particularly as applied through casework methods and its derivatives (task-centred work, counselling, therapeutic work, etc.) has been at the core of professional social work since its origins (see, for example, Woodroofe 1962, Adams 1996). Jordan has suggested that 'the ideology which underlay social work with families of the poor was one of "rescuing" children from the influence of dissolute and feckless parents' (Jordan 1974: 27). He has gone on to develop his critique over many years, arguing that social work has become more 'coercive and restrictive', with staff checking behaviour and demanding compliance (Jordan 1990: 3). Similarly, Holman suggests that 'the casework method, so central to professional social work practice, when applied to people in poverty, only serves to maintain their depriving situation' (Holman 1973: 441). He too, over many years, has developed a sustained critique of social work and social services:

> With control rather than partnership to the fore, it is no surprise that social work support to families in order to prevent crises is no longer a priority … Sadly, the re-emergence of control in child care and rationing by condemnatory judgements in community care is a return to the practices of the Poor Law. Yet modern social work was supposed to replace that.
>
> (Holman 1993: 38–40)

These authors and others support a view that casework, by focusing on the workings and dynamics of poor individuals or families, fails to engage with the social and political construction of poverty: 'Traditionally, [the casework approach] has masked the social and political forces which shape individual lives. It has served to deny the collective problems faced by those who are oppressed and in poverty' (Davis 1991: 89). This critique is part of a body of social work theorising, developing from the 1970s, which has promoted a 'radical' or social perspective, arguing for analysis, approaches and methods within social work aimed at reducing inequalities and combating poverty and oppression (Curno 1978, Brake and Bailey 1980, Becker and MacPherson 1988). In the 1980s, many professional social work training courses highlighted the need to engage with the structural inequalities that generated and maintained oppression, discrimination and injustice for specific groups, particularly women, minority ethnic communities, and those with physical or mental impairments. There was an awareness that the 'Personal Social Services seem to be moving from a situation of being providers of barely adequate services for the poor towards becoming underfunded, overstretched and in some cases overwhelmed services for the oppressed' (Jowell 1985: vi). While social work did engage increasingly with oppressive structures and 'disabling barriers' around disability, race and gender, it failed to act with the same commitment and determination to combat oppression and exclusion generated by poverty. Indeed, most of the texts on social work theory or practice continue to neglect the poverty dynamic (see, for example, Coulshed 1988, Payne 1991, Adams 1996). Any lingering commitment to anti-poverty action within social work was swamped by the pace of change introduced by the Children Act and community care legislation at the end of the 1980s; by widespread departmental reorganisation in response to those legislative changes; by profound shifts in social services and social work culture and practices; by the rapid growth in managerialism; and by severe financial constraints. A concern for poverty, and what should, or could be done about it, was drowned in a sea of change.

While the rhetoric of social work training and practice in the 1990s has emphasised increasingly the shift to an 'empowering' rather than a 'treatment' paradigm for social work (Adams 1996: 20), the reality is that little appears to have changed for poor families. The *ideology* behind the casework method, with its focus on dysfunctional families, continues to dominate professional social work interventions in this field. Many social workers feel that they have neither the resources nor the power to make more than a marginal contribution to the situation of poor families (Becker 1988, Gibbons *et al.* 1990). Social workers define their professional objectives very much in individualising terms. Casework is not only the dominant *method*, but for many social workers has become the *purpose* of their intervention. Helping individuals and families in poverty through advice, guidance, counselling and networking, the provision of services and basic items, Section 17 (previously Section 1) assistance, are seen as the natural limits to effective and appropriate social work with poor families. Welfare rights work has been viewed as an activity outside the social work domain, until it was seen as a useful strategy for maximising the income of the local authority, in the context of community care assessments (chapter 6). Social services staff have largely failed to expose and protest about the poverty and deprivations of their vulnerable clients, concentrating instead on developing techniques for assessing clients and managing budgets

(Hughes 1993). The new managerialism, the language and ideology inherent within it, and the techniques that sustain it, obscure inequality and deprivation and contribute to the management of the poor.

This management function is perhaps inevitable given social workers position within the machinery of state regulation and social control (Derber 1983, Cousins 1987). Social workers have become ideologically 'incorporated' into their employing organisation; they owe their existence and power to the power of the state, and their function is largely to maintain institutional ends. For many tens of thousands of poor families with children, contact with social services, and with social workers in particular, continues to be fraught with danger (the greater risk that poor families will be investigated; that children will be received into care; that once in care they will experience further disadvantages and abuse, etc.). This contact is also stigmatising (poor families and children are labelled as failures or problems). Social workers have failed to recognise their own pivotal role in the continued management and impoverishment of poor people. There appears to be little commitment to shift resources, and power, away from professional agendas and onto poor families themselves (Becker 1988, ATD Fourth World 1996).

Towards an enabling and empowering social work

In his assessment of the way forward for social welfare, Bob Holman has proposed 'mutuality' as the basis for future social work with poor families. Mutuality is: 'the recognition of mutual obligations towards others, stemming from the acceptance of common kinship, expressed in joint action, towards a more equitable sharing of resources and responsibilities' (1993: 57). He goes on to suggest that:

the main purpose of the personal social services should be to support families (and individuals) vulnerable to these disadvantages. It should be to prevent them reaching the point where intervention and control is placed upon them. Within the blight of the enormous contemporary social deprivations, the aim should be to modify the devastating effects of social inequalities which now ruin the lives of so many.

(Holman 1993: 71)

Holman believes that community social work should be the 'core of the personal social services' and that neighbourhood-based family centres which meet widespread needs are more popular and valuable – and less stigmatising – than those services or approaches concerned with monitoring and correcting the behaviour of poor parents: 'The concept of mutuality thus leads to a picture of a new organisational structure for the personal social services, one in which a facility approach, community social work and family centres are the foundation' (p. 81).

A shift towards far greater locally responsive social services and social work is supported by others, including those who argue that the poor need to take more control over the issues and agenda for anti-poverty action (Beresford and Croft 1995). Smale and colleagues (1994), in their review of a range of research findings on community-based practice for the implementation of community care and the Children Act, suggest that: 'The research supports small locally based generalist area teams and services, with specialists within them, rather than centralised services provided through specialist divisions based on administrative categories of "clients"' (Smale *et al.* 1994, para. 1.27). They go on to acknowledge the critical importance of wider social policies: 'The right housing and income maintenance policies and adequate resources for social services are also crucial if people are to live independently' (Smale *et al.* 1994: para. 1.31).

Many of those concerned to break down the stigmatising barriers inherent within much social services organisation, provision and social work practice, now argue for a more localised model of service delivery, coupled with greater local control over resources and decision-making (see, for example, Burns, Hambleton and Hoggett 1994). However, it is important to remember the dangers inherent within 'local' frameworks: 'Social control can ... be enforced through myriad forms of neighbouring such as gossip, casual conversation and informal surveillance – all of which subject individuals to purportedly collective sets of norms and expectations' (Bulmer 1986: 32). Moreover, we should not forget that some of those on the right also argue for greater local control of resources – or self-government – whereby the views of local communities ought to determine welfare policy and priorities, and where local forms of stigma will supposedly deter people from poverty-producing anti-social behaviour (see chapter 1). There is a danger that the spotlight will again be directed at 'problem families' (and their so-called poverty-producing behaviour), rather than on the problems for families generated by poverty, low levels of benefits and other 'barriers' to independence and full citizenship. Social services and social workers need to forge new partnerships with poor people. There is much to learn from the anti-poverty strategies adopted by many local authorities, outlined above. Social workers will need truly to empower poor people and disadvantaged communities to have a greater say, and control, over the policy agenda, local priorities and allocation of resources.

The failure of social services and social workers to engage with, and respond to, the research evidence that has, for two decades and more, highlighted the strategic significance of poverty to the lifestyles and opportunities of many of the most vulnerable people in society – people who have traditionally made greatest use of personal social services – is of the utmost concern. It not only reflects a deep ambivalence towards the poor, but also to the importance of research evidence to inform professional interventions, competencies and effectiveness. Social work, as with other professions in and allied to medicine and health care, needs to promote research-based practice and policy (DoH 1994a). This, first and foremost, requires client-centred evidence: perspectives from the user's point of view, rather than professional judgements as to what is best for poor clients. By the mid-1990s, there was some indication that the government, through the Department of Health, was encouraging SSDs to seek out the views of users. This was particularly evident in the context of community care, where the views of users and family carers were, in theory at least, seen as central to the successful implementation of the policy. The reality, however, was that while consultation between SSDs and users/carers did increase, it was still not a truly consultative process, or empowering experience, for most clients (chapter 6). In the context of work with families and children, the Department of Health attempted to refocus child protection work with a greater emphasis on family support – prevention rather than reacting after the event (Chief Inspector of Social Services 1996). However, the power of SSDs and social workers to move towards a greater family support, consultative and enabling role may ultimately be determined by factors outside their professional control. Not least will be the treatment of poor citizens by politicians and policy makers in other spheres of social policy, particularly in social security. The Labour Party has argued that their policies will 'relieve the pressures on our hard-pressed public services, including social services. They will allow SSDs to reclaim some of their heritage of family support rather than their current role as pure family crisis agencies' (Milburn 1996: 12) [Document 12].

Whether this can be achieved is one of the greatest challenges facing social services and social work as we approach the new millennium. Prevailing social attitudes and the dominant political climate continue to define many poor people as responsible for their poverty and label them as 'dependent' on the state. In such a context, increasing the amount, and improving the quality and delivery, of state care provision, used mostly by poorer people, is unlikely to be a policy priority for any party in power. It is unclear how any government, or any SSD, can deliver on 'empowerment' when the policy direction is for containment, and contraction, in state welfare provision. These tensions are particularly evident in the field of community care, the subject of the next chapter.

CHAPTER 6

Excluding the poor: social services and community care

Introduction

The implementation in 1993 of the new community care arrangements was the outcome of more than four decades of politics, debate and reformulation of policy responses to the health and social care needs of elderly people and those with physical and mental impairments. The current structure of service provision, as was seen in chapter 3, is the most recent attempt by the state at creating a balance between the care and control of groups seen as 'vulnerable', 'different', 'dangerous' or 'poor'.

The belief that it is better to maintain these people in their own home, rather than in institutions, has been the guiding principle of community care policy since the 1950s (Allsop 1995: 95). A belief in the humanitarian value of community living has been coupled with a persuasive critique of the failings of institutions for people with physical impairments, those with mental health problems or learning difficulties, elderly people and the poor in general. Chapter 3 outlined the main values, beliefs and arguments of the anti-institution critique and showed how it has developed into both intellectual and pressure group movements promoting civil rights and equal opportunities for people with physical and mental impairments. The social model of disability, for example, has attempted to shift understanding of the nature of 'disability' away from an individualised medical pathology model of physical impairment, towards one concerned with the negative consequences of social reactions, labels and environments which effectively 'disable' people with impairments and exclude them from enjoying full civil rights. This critique has also challenged the language and ideology of 'care' itself, arguing that notions of 'dependency' and 'care giving' misrepresent and misunderstand both the needs of disabled people and their relationship with family carers and service providers (Morris 1991, 1993).

This chapter examines policy formulation and implementation in the field of community care during the 1980s and 1990s. It charts the politics, concerns, themes and objectives that have helped to shape the current structure and delivery of community care, and examines the impact on the very groups that, in theory at least, community care was intended to benefit, namely service users (for example, elderly people and those with physical or mental impairments), and family carers. Many of these people are also social security claimants, and are among the poorest in society. I am particularly concerned to examine the political agenda that has influenced community care policy and the development of the mixed economy of welfare, and the professional social services agenda that has shaped the delivery and management of care, and the management of an inadequate funding base. The evidence suggests that community care policy and implementation, rather than empowering and enabling vulnerable poor people to live secure, stable and independent lives in the community, has actually undermined their independence, security and autonomy, has forced them into greater dependence on social security and social services, and has exacerbated their poverty and social exclusion in the community.

Community care: politics and policy formulation from 1979

Up to 1979, when the Conservatives took power, the main thrust of the anti-institution critique had rested on a number of interrelated propositions, for example: that institutions had failed and were damaging the quality of life of vulnerable people; and that community care provided a 'better', more ordinary and independent life. This critique manifested itself in a number of forms, not least the emerging paradigms and pressure group movements calling for 'normalisation' or a social model of disability, both of which rejected the institutional segregation, isolation and exclusion that had characterised policy responses to the disabled and mentally impaired for over a century (see chapter 3).

Perhaps surprisingly, the Thatcher governments of the 1980s became new allies in this process of de-institutionalisation and change. To the anti-institution critique being promoted by many, especially disabled people themselves, was added some of the essential ingredients of New Right thinking, namely that the direct involvement of the state in welfare matters should be limited to support a vibrant pluralist economy of care, combining the best of private enterprise with voluntary and charitable giving, subject to the discipline and rigour of a free market, within the framework of the law. This was coupled with the policy imperative to reduce public expenditure on social programmes, particularly on cash and care.

In bringing about the transformation of health and social care, within hospitals and in the community, the government had to enlist the involvement of key players (commonly referred to as 'stakeholders'), and change the operation and practices of others. That the policy direction for care in the community was similar to that being argued for by the disability movement and other campaigning lobbies was more of a helpful coincidence than a reflection of government support for a social model of disability or for the civil rights of disabled people. Indeed, governments throughout the 1980s and first half of the 1990s managed to undermine, if not prevent, disabled people from securing their own legislation guaranteeing them full civil rights. The agenda of the Thatcher and Major governments was more concerned with the restructuring of the state's direct involvement in welfare by promoting a mixed economy of care, and curtailing social expenditure, rather than a commitment to embracing 'difference' and celebrating diversity.

The first Thatcher government's policies and priorities for health and social care were outlined in *Care in Action* (DHSS 1981). This prioritised certain groups (for example the elderly, those with mental health problems and those with special needs), and confirmed that the development of services in the community was to be the priority. The document also provided an early confirmation of the government's commitment to reducing public expenditure by careful targeting of resources and the better use of the informal, voluntary and private sectors in care – clearly identified as the cornerstone of any future community care provision. Here we see the ideological impetus for the new community care arrangements phased in during the 1990s. Direct state involvement in welfare in general, and in community care in particular, would be reduced and restructured by a number of means. First, by replacing some existing health service provision through the growth of private (for-profit) alternatives (residential or domiciliary), funded through social security benefits; second, by redefining some health care needs as social care, for example, continuing care; third, some direct personal social services provision would be replaced by provision from the private (for-profit) sector, by the voluntary (non-profit) sector, and by 'informal' family carers. The mechanism for this transfer of responsibility would later become the development of internal quasi-markets in health and social care, and the separation of the purchasing of services from their provision (Le Grand and Bartlett 1993, Wistow *et al.* 1994). As mentioned in chapter 4, the government intends to introduce the 'purchaser–provider split' into the field of social security from 1997, as part of its Change Programme, in an effort to improve the efficiency and delivery of benefits, and to reduce costs [see also Document 6].

Very soon after taking power, Mrs Thatcher's first government allowed supplementary benefit (now income support) payments to be made available to cover the full costs of private residential and nursing home care, but not the full costs of local authority residential care or domiciliary care services. Consequently, many vulnerable people, in particular the growing number of frail elderly, had little choice but to enter private residential or nursing care homes. Income support expenditure on private residential and nursing homes increased from £10 million in 1979, to £460 million in 1986, to more than £2 billion by 1992 (Bradshaw and Gibbs 1988, Knapp *et al.* 1992). The effect of this was also to provide a massive subsidy to the health service, by enabling it to discharge dependent patients to private residential care, so reducing its own continuing care commitments and costs. This was also true of local authorities, which were able to reduce their own provision in order to meet budget requirements, in the knowledge that the private residential sector would fill some of the gaps. The withdrawal of continuing care provision by the NHS, and its transfer to social services responsibility, denotes a changing boundary between health and social care, with the replacement of free health care with means-tested social care and charges (Wistow 1995).

Between 1982 and 1992, the number of residents in all homes for elderly people, and for the younger physically disabled, increased by 38 per cent, to a quarter of a million. This increase was attributable to a number of inter-related factors, not least the expansion in the private residential sector – a growth encouraged and facilitated through the new social security arrangements and by a government suspicious of, indeed hostile to, the public sector. The number of residents in private homes increased by almost 260 per cent over the period, while the numbers in local authority homes fell by 32 per cent (Chief Inspector of Social Services 1993). In 1978, 16 per cent of people in the residential sector were in private homes; by 1990 the proportion had risen to 43 per cent (Sinclair *et al.* 1990). By 1995, the private sector accounted for more than three-quarters of all places in residential care homes (Department of Health 1995d). Between 1979 and 1995 the private sector had grown from a relatively small-scale provider of residential and nursing home care, to become the market leader.

While the private residential sector in the 1980s and early 1990s was being stimulated by public money through the social security system, a perverse consequence was that residential, rather than domiciliary or home-based care, was being promoted. Moreover, the costs to the Exchequer were by no means insubstantial, with every sign that they would continue to rise. Clearly, not all the government's intentions for community care were going to be realised if the situation continued unchecked. By the mid-1980s many individuals and organisations, including the Social Services Committee of the House of Commons (1985) and the Audit Commission (1986), had expressed concerns about the operation of community care policy which, in effect, seemed to promote costly institutional care rather than care in, or care by, the community. While the vast majority of elderly people continued to live in their own homes, many frail elderly people were being forced into residential and nursing homes, either from the community or through the operation of hospital discharge arrangements. The Audit Commission concluded that something had to be done to challenge the perverse incentives of existing policies. To do nothing would be to witness the continued development of an uneven pattern of services; the continued switch from hospitals to residential care funded by social security; and the entrenchment of a pattern of care based on the private residential sector (Audit Commission 1986: 77). Making a reality of community care would require an attack on the competing and conflicting 'policy streams' and policy objectives that had corrupted existing care in the community. Policy formulation and implementation needed to be aligned more with policy intentions (Webb and Wistow 1987). Some have suggested, however, that there was no coherent community care policy during this period. Given the contradictory and conflicting policy objectives and practices in operation, Ham and Hill (1984) suggest that it is debatable whether any community care policy was actually being pursued.

Reforming community care: the Griffiths Report

At the centre of the major reforms in community care phased in during the early 1990s was a set of measures intended to limit the spiralling social security bill for residential and nursing home care; to promote an effective and coordinated community care policy; to reduce the inappropriate use of institutional care; and to continue the thrust of Conservative welfare policy in general – the withdrawal of direct state provision and the encouragement of choice through new and alternative structures, consistent with New Right ideology. The mixed economy of care, as it is commonly referred to, would also rely heavily on, even institutionalise, the contribution of unpaid family carers (see also chapter 3).

The government appointed Sir Roy Griffiths to head what was to become a high profile review of care in the community policy. His report, published in 1988, set the framework for the major changes that were phased in between 1991 and 1993, and which added community care to the growing list of social services statutory responsibilities (Griffiths 1988, Lister and Becker 1994). The Griffiths recommendations for reforming community care centred on the creation of internal quasi-markets and echoed earlier suggestions by Alain Enthoven (1985) for reforming the NHS. The Griffiths Report had a number of other principal recommendations. First, the main responsibility for planning community care at local level should lie with local authority SSDs. Second, responsibility for community care within central government should rest with a clearly designated minister. Third, local authorities should act as organisers and purchasers of services, but not primarily as providers. Fourth, earmarked resources should be transferred to local authorities to finance their new responsibilities [Document 11]. Griffiths suggested that local authorities had a very specific role to play. They should be responsible for identifying and assessing the community care needs of disabled and elderly people, people with mental health problems and people with learning difficulties (service 'users' as they are commonly called); arranging the support such people required, including all residential care; supporting the development of the voluntary sector; and maximising choice and competition through developing the role of the private sector and the mixed economy of care.

Having established where the prime responsibility for community care should rest and the role to be played by SSDs, Griffiths went on to highlight the centrality of family carers and the critical contribution that they made, and would continue to make, in the overall provision and structure of community care:

Publicly provided services constitute only a small part of the total care provided to people in need. Families, friends, neighbours and other local people provide the majority of care in response to needs which they are uniquely well placed to identify and respond to. This will be the primary means by which people are enabled to live normal lives in community settings.

(Griffiths 1988: 5)

Griffiths proposed that publicly funded services should operate in new ways, and that their first task should be to support, and where possible strengthen, these networks of carers (1988: 5).

The government's response to Griffiths

Not all of Griffiths' recommendations and suggestions were attractive to the then Prime Minister, Margaret Thatcher, or to some of the Cabinet who shared her deep-rooted suspicion of local authorities and local governance. Indeed, a Conservative critique of the 'waste' and 'lack of accountability' of local government had been a persistent theme of much of Mrs Thatcher's premiership. Nonetheless, the government's official response to Sir Roy's recommendations came four months after the report's publication, in a House of Commons statement delivered by the then Health Secretary, Kenneth Clarke. The statement indicated that the government now accepted Sir Roy's central recommendation that local authorities should be given the overall responsibility for community care, although other proposals were rejected (including a designated minister for community care and ring fencing of funding, with the exception of the mental illness specific grant). Kenneth Clarke also chose to pay tribute to the majority of carers who were 'dedicated and self-sacrificing' and who took on 'serious obligations to help care for disabled relatives and friends'. He went on to confirm that: 'the great bulk of community care will continue to be provided by family, friends and neighbours', and that 'Our proposals are aimed at strengthening support for those many unselfish people who care for people in need' (Clarke 1988). Family carers were to be, as they had always been, the cornerstone of care in the community (see also chapter 3).

It was some 15 months later, in November 1989, when the government finally published its community care White Paper, *Caring for People* (DoH 1989). This continued the approach of the Griffiths Report and outlined a number of key objectives for community care policy and practice. The objectives can be summarised as follows:

1   to promote the development of domiciliary, day and respite services to enable people to live in their own homes wherever feasible and sensible;
2   to ensure that service providers make practical support for carers a high priority;
3   to make proper assessment of need and good care management the cornerstone of high quality care;

4   to promote the development of a flourishing independent (private) sector
    alongside good quality public services;
5   to clarify the responsibilities of agencies and so make it easier to hold them
    to account for their performance;
6   to secure better value for taxpayers' money by introducing a new funding
    structure for social care.

(DoH 1989: 5)

As far as carers were concerned, the White Paper confirmed their central role as providers of community care:

... most care is provided by family, friends and neighbours. The majority of carers take on these responsibilities willingly, but the government recognises that many need help to be able to manage what can become a heavy burden. Their lives could be made much easier if the right support is there at the right time, and a key responsibility of the statutory service providers should be to do all they can to assist and support carers. Helping carers to maintain their valuable contribution to the spectrum of care is both right and a sound investment. Help may take the form of providing advice and support as well as practical services such as day, domiciliary and respite care.

(DoH 1989: 9)

In addition to supporting carers, personal social services would move away from the role of provider of services, to a role of 'enabler' – a role consistent with that suggested by Norman Fowler in his 1984 address to the annual social services conference in Buxton. Authorities were now instructed to make use of, and contract, services from the independent sector (private, voluntary, charities and trusts), where these were cost-efficient and of high quality. This partnership with different sectors, the mixed economy of care, was promoted as a move away from the traditional position of social services as monolithic provider – a position viewed by government as denying service users and their carers any real choice. Consequently, the provision of services was to be separated from their purchase (the 'purchaser–provider split'). Social services would take responsibility for assessing population and individual need, designing care arrangements, purchasing and ensuring that services were delivered to a specified quality. The traditional roles of 'financing' and 'regulation' were to be maintained by SSDs; the main change was that they would not necessarily deliver services themselves.

The NHS and Community Care Act 1990 established the legislative framework for the radical restructuring of *both* the NHS and community care system, bringing in the purchaser–provider split and internal markets in health and social care. It also established new patterns of mutual dependency among the main players in community care: local authorities would become dependent on independent, particularly private sector providers, to fulfil their responsibilities; independent providers became more dependent on local authorities for funding; in-house providers of local authority services increasingly had to operate in the same market conditions as the independent sector; health authorities became dependent on local authorities in order to discharge the most disabled patients from acute and long-stay wards; all sectors became dependent on family carers to continue to provide the main bulk of care, without whose efforts the system would face ultimate collapse (Trenery 1993: 115). These patterns of mutual dependency would, in theory at least, help to eradicate the perverse incentives and gridlock that had blighted effective community care for the past two decades. They would establish the conditions necessary for all the main players and agencies to become interdependent 'stakeholders' in the new arrangements. It had taken more than a decade for the Conservatives to establish the legislative framework, and it took another three years before the whole package of community care reforms was finally introduced. By this time Mrs Thatcher had been voted out of Downing Street, not by the public, but by her own party.

The politics of implementation

The NHS and Community Care Act also required local authorities to produce and publish an annual community care plan. The plans were originally expected to concentrate on the management and delivery of the key changes set out in the White Paper. In particular they were expected to include an assessment of the needs of the local population, along with strategic objectives for community care in the next three years, and how these related to national policy objectives. Other details to be included were those relating to the arrangements for the assessment of individuals applying to SSDs for care management, and finally the plans should show 'how services for people at home, including their carers are to be improved' (DoH 1989: 43).

However, by the time the ensuing *Policy Guidance* had been issued, both the timetable, and expectations, had changed (DoH 1990). The revised 'phased' implementation timetable for community care required SSDs to have in place new complaints procedures and inspection units by April 1991. By April 1992, departments were required to have published their first community care plan. The content of these plans was now to be less comprehensive, with the arrangements for individual assessments moved out of the first plans altogether. Original elements which did remain were the requirement for a needs assessment of the community which the plans intended to serve, as well as the need to inform service users and carers about services. In reality, the first community care plans were 'position statements' rather than strategic plans (Wistow, Leedham and Hardy 1993). By April 1993, SSDs would need to have established their own assessment and care management procedures for all vulnerable people who looked to the authority for support, and to have in place their charging and paying arrangements for contracting and purchasing.

As implementation drew nearer there was increasing anxiety about the policy and procedural implications of developing the mixed economy of care (Policy Studies Institute 1992). The King's Fund Institute suggested that the whole policy was flawed and that the belief in community care as a viable alternative to institutional provision was an 'act of faith' little tested in practice; uncertainty surrounded what would actually be achieved by implementation (Henwood 1992, Becker 1993). Notwithstanding the anxieties held by social services managers, practitioners and others about implementation, it became clear that SSDs had failed to consult with a number of the key stake-holders in the new mixed economy of care. Many service providers from the private sector complained that they had not been consulted by local authorities when the first plans had been drawn up (*Community Care* 1992b). While authorities had established fairly good lines of communication with the voluntary sector (particularly as voluntary organisations were often grant-aided by local authorities), few had such good relationships with the private sector. The private sector, however, was not particularly well organised to consult with local authorities: internal competition made finding 'representatives' prob-lematic (KPMG Management Consulting 1992). Nonetheless, the apparent snub to the private sector by local authorities prompted the then junior health minister, Tim Yeo, to proclaim: 'I am particularly dissatisfied with the failure of many authorities to co-operate effec-tively with the private sector. The government *expects* authorities to develop a more positive attitude towards the private sector' (*Social Work Today* 1992: 5, my emphasis). The following month, the joint DoH/SSI circular declared that authorities 'must also *ensure* that inde-pendent sector providers are properly consulted on 1993–94 Community Care Plans' (DoH 1992a). By the end of the year the Secretary of State, Mrs Bottomley, announced that she would be issuing binding directives *requiring* authorities to consult independent care providers and to guarantee a user's choice of private home (Bottomley 1992, Becker 1993).

Not only did SSDs have to improve their communication with the private and voluntary sectors, but they needed to work effectively with health authorities if community care was to be successful. Rivalries between health authorities and SSDs, in particular the failure of joint working and cooperation, had been recognised by many commentators as a cause of the gridlock in health and social care (Enthoven 1985, Audit Commission 1986, Griffiths 1988). These rivalries continued throughout the implementation period of the new reforms and raised such concern that joint Department of Health/Social Services Inspectorate circulars had to be issued on a number of occasions to improve the prospects of coordination, joint working and cooperation (DoH 1992a, 1992b). The Audit Commission suggested that commu-nity care plans may flounder if district health authorities failed to provide extra money for nursing support for people leaving residential care (Audit Commission 1992a, 1992b, 1992c, Neill and Williams 1992, Nocon 1994). The King's Fund Institute also expressed concern that the NHS was disengaging from its continuing care responsibilities. In some areas the NHS had reduced provision for continuing care beds to the point that many people were forced to pay for their own arrangements. In other areas, the report suggested, there was no NHS provision for non-acute nursing needs (Henwood 1992). The situation was considered so serious that a special 'support force' was established in 1992 to help collaboration. In October 1992, just six months away from the final implementation date, the then Secretary of State, Virginia Bottomley, announced that the finances to be transferred to SSDs would be *conditional* on there being agreement between local authorities and district health authorities on the key tasks to be performed jointly between them (Bottomley 1992).

Over the next few years there were some signs of improvement in joint working between SSDs and health authorities, as further guidance was published on joint commissioning of services and on the responsibilities of the NHS with regard to continuing care. By 1995, the Department of Health was able to acknowledge that: 'There is a common agenda between health and social services. Entrenched organisational apartheid is now a thing of the past and I am pleased at the increase in joint working across agencies since the introduction of the NHS and Community Care reforms' (DoH press release 1995b). As will be seen later, however, the boundary disputes continued over who should provide long-term continuing care for elderly and disabled people, and whether their needs were to be classified as health or social care. These policy and organisational tensions exacerbated the insecurities already experienced by many vulnerable and poor people.

The funding of community care: social services and the social security transfer

The final phase of implementation commenced on 1 April 1993. This was also the date on which local authorities took responsibility from the Department of Social Security for payments for vulnerable people being admitted into independent sector residential and nursing homes. Individuals who could afford to pay the fees privately could still make their own arrangements without contacting their local SSD. For those who could not afford to do this, social services were to become the modern day equivalent of Boards of Guardians, overseeing the use of public money on the care needs of those who required state financial support [Document 11].

The formula for funding community care and for transferring social security money to local authorities is complex, and only the most relevant features are referred to here (see Chartered Institute of Public Finance and Accountancy 1995 for a detailed guide). The Special Transitional Grant (STG) for community care began in 1993–4. This grant consists of a number of elements: one for infrastructure and implementation costs for the new system; one for taking over the responsibilities of the Independent Living Fund; one for the development of home care and respite care services; and one – the 'transfer element' – which is intended to replace the amount which would otherwise have been spent by the DSS on higher rates of income support for new residents in residential care and nursing homes. Over time, the DSS transfer and infrastructure elements of the STG will be incorporated into future years' Standard Spending Assessment (SSA) control totals. Between 1993–4 and 1997–8 local authorities will have received more than 2.5 billion pounds for community care, as well as access to additional specific grants for work in the fields of mental illness, training, AIDS/HIV work, among others.

The government had initially intended that the *whole* of the transfer element (equivalent, on average, to 75 per cent of the total funding package in the first year) should be spent by authorities on independent care providers. The rationale for this was partly that this money would otherwise have been spent by the DSS on residential and nursing home fees in the independent sector, particularly in private homes, so spending 100 per cent of the transfer element in this way maintained the status quo. In practice this would mean the bulk of the money being spent on private residential homes because the independent sector had not as yet extensively developed the domiciliary services market. The paradox, of course, is that the 'perverse incentive' of social security payments favouring the development of private residential provision at the expense of community care would effectively be maintained within the new funding structure, at least until the independent sector developed appropriate domiciliary alternatives. The local authority associations and the ADSS expressed concern that in some authorities the social security transfer would be less than 75 per cent of the total funding package in the first year, and for these authorities to meet the 75 per cent target, they would have to divert into the private sector money that was intended for community care infrastructure or for provision of their own services. Within weeks there was a government U-turn on the matter. Junior health minister Tim Yeo announced that authorities would now be required to spend 85 per cent or more (not 100 per cent as originally stated) of the transfer money on independent providers – equivalent to 63 per cent of total funds in the first year. This would allow SSDs some flexibility to spend some of the transfer on their own services or elsewhere (Becker 1993).

The '85 per cent rule' was successful in encouraging the rapid growth in domiciliary care provided by the independent, particularly the private, sector. Between 1993 and 1995 all the growth in home help and home care was in the independent sector, so that by 1995 independent providers accounted for 29 per cent of the total home care market, compared to 19 per cent in 1994 and just 4 per cent a year earlier. In most areas the private sector also increased its market share of meals on wheels provision, so that, in London for example, private providers accounted for one-fifth of all meals on wheels delivered to vulnerable people (Department of Health 1995b, 1996a). The funding formula was helping to develop rapidly the mixed economy of care, particularly private sector provision. Many of the costs of these developments were borne by poor people, as we shall see in the following sections.

Bearing the costs of community care: users and carers

To implement community care effectively, SSDs would need to engage in a major culture change, as they steered away from delivering services based upon their own professional interest or self-interest ('supply-led' services) to a position whereby provision became based on the expressed needs of users and their carers ('demand-led' or 'needs-led' services). The Audit Commission (1992a) expressed concern that valuing the perspectives of users and carers posed challenges to the traditional service-led culture of SSDs, and that many departments seemed to be resisting change.

Griffiths, the White Paper and the subsequent legislation and guidance all stressed the need for users and family carers to be involved in the process of community care, and to be properly consulted: 'All our guidance, and all our work with authorities, has from the beginning emphasised that people receiving care and their carers are entitled to express views about the support they would like, and that those views should be given proper weight' (DoH press release 1992). Despite the rhetoric of user/carer empowerment being promoted by government and social services, there was little evidence to suggest that departments had consulted these groups about community care priorities or policy. Fewer than one in twenty authorities had involved organisations of disabled people in formulating their first plans (Glendinning 1991), and people with multiple disabilities were particularly ignored. Over half the SSDs in England and Wales had ignored or failed to mention the needs of this group, and of the rest, 14 per cent identified their needs, but had no plans to provide specific services (Challenge 1992). The Carers National Association (1992) revealed that 69 per cent of carers in its sample had not been consulted at all, and a further 10 per cent were unsure as to whether or not they had been consulted.

Family carers and the privately borne costs of community care

There were about 6.8 million carers in Great Britain in 1990, equivalent to 15 per cent of people aged 16 and over (OPCS 1992). Women are more likely to be providing intensive forms of care, and caring for longer hours than men (OPCS 1992, Baldwin and Twigg 1991). Carers come from all social, ethnic and religious backgrounds. Their needs vary depending on the severity of the condition of the person cared for, their economic circumstances and the provision of services in their area (Social Services Committee 1990, Princess Royal Trust 1992, CNA 1992).

Many carers make major sacrifices in terms of careers, finances, time and personal freedoms, to look after family, friends or neighbours. As many as 1.5 million people nationally care for more than 20 hours per week. Often this work is extremely demanding, involving heavy lifting, washing, dressing, toileting, feeding, turning at night and so on. These tasks are particularly difficult for many carers who are themselves elderly or who have health problems. Two-thirds of elderly carers receive no help whatsoever from any statutory or voluntary agency – although they care for long hours each day. Many children also provide care for their parents and relatives in the community, at considerable cost to their childhood and development (Aldridge and Becker 1993, 1996, Dearden and Becker 1995).

Many carers do not recognise themselves as 'carers'; they view their actions as extensions of family or personal relations (Twigg, Atkin and Perring 1990). The term 'carer' has its origins in the language of social care agencies. Historically, carers have held an ambiguous and uncertain position within the social and health care system. Carers are rarely the focus of an intervention: they are not defined as 'clients', 'users' or 'patients' and carers have, in the past, seen their needs placed secondary (if ranked at all) to the needs of the specified client. However, the input of carers has been acknowledged as being critical in maintaining vulnerable people in the community, with or without professional support. As such, carers save the government tens of billions of pounds in alternative care costs which would otherwise need to be spent to maintain vulnerable people in the community, or elsewhere.

A number of reports provide information about the circumstances and experiences of carers and the strains that many of them endure. A 1992 survey by the Carers National Association, for example, found that nearly half had experienced financial problems as carers and 75 per cent wanted more professional support (CNA 1992). Glendinning (1992a) found that caring incurred economic, social and health costs. The extra costs of caring included one-off capital costs, special aids and adaptations and regular extra household expenditure (on heating, laundry etc.). Also, for many carers outside the full-time labour market, caring led to reduced or foregone earnings, lower future earning capacity because of interruptions to work, and financial insecurity in later life because they had not accrued sufficient entitlements to benefits, including pensions, in their own right (see also chapter 4). Warner (1994: para. 1.6) confirms that most carers rely on social security benefits and have few savings and below average disposable incomes. Many carers also experience isolation, loss of self-esteem and feelings of resignation; their health can suffer because of the weight of responsibility and care provision.

Up until the Griffiths Report there was little public discussion of how best to support carers, and even less discussion about the tensions between the needs of carers and the person(s) for whom they care (Glendinning 1992a, Twigg 1992). The Griffiths Report, and the subsequent White Paper and guidance, confirmed family carers as the cornerstone of care in the community, but failed to give them any entitlements to assessments or services in their own right, and failed to lead to any improvements in social security benefits for carers. Social security payments to carers, particularly the invalid care allowance, are inadequate to provide a secure and stable lifestyle (McLaughlin 1991). Monitoring the impact on carers of the community care changes shows that, as far as most carers are concerned, the new scheme made little difference to their lives. Warner (1994) suggests that, one year on from the 1993 implementation date, 80 per cent of carers said that the changes had made no difference to them and 8 per cent thought that services had actually got worse. A year later the picture had hardly improved at all: 69 per cent of carers thought community care had made no difference, even though it had been in place for two years (Warner 1995).

The Carers (Recognition and Services) Act 1995, implemented in April 1996, gives carers who are providing, or who intend to provide a substantial amount of care on a regular basis, the right to have their needs assessed when the person they care for is being assessed. Local authorities are legally obliged to assess the ability of a carer to provide and continue to provide care and take into account the results of this assessment when making decisions about any services to be provided for the user. To a large extent the Act enshrines principles of good practice that existed in some authorities for some time. However, the symbolic significance of the Act should not be under-estimated: it represents a real advance for carers in that it recognises, in law, their rights to be consulted and assessed (Arshey 1996). However, the Act does not carry with it any additional resources for SSDs in terms of implementation, or for meeting carers' needs or for providing services. For many carers the Act may give them the recognition that they require, but it fails to guarantee they will receive any extra support.

Organisations representing the interests of carers, and carers themselves, have increasingly voiced their own agenda, needs and rights. They say they require recognition, respect, access to information and services, practical help and support (which is flexible and responsive to individual need), time off and choice. Warner (1994) has suggested that primary carers should be given a core package of carers' support services, provided free to carers registered with their local SSDs. He has calculated (Warner 1995) that it would cost about £1.4 billion – less than 1p on income tax – to provide the million intensive carers with a four-hour break every week, a two-week holiday and three weekends a year. Moreover, many carers' and disability organisations are also lobbying for carers to have a right to an adequate independent income. They argue that there should be a considerable improvement in the current levels and coverage of benefits for family carers. This would include raising the level of invalid care allowance; improving the protection of carers' 'entitlements' to national insurance benefits in their own right; introducing new allowances to meet some of the extra costs of care-giving; and improving workplace conditions so that carers of working age can remain in the labour market for as long as possible (Caring Costs 1991).

Family carers bear many of the invisible costs of community care. As a group they have been excluded from consultation about community care plans and about the care programmes of those for whom they care; as individuals they experience exclusion by virtue of their low income and impoverished lifestyles, forced on them by having to bear the financial, social and health costs of caring. The social security system has not adequately compensated them for these additional costs, indeed it has largely ignored their situation, despite their pivotal contribution to care in the community. Glendinning comments that 'overlooking the privately-borne costs of community care may prove a short sighted and false economy. It may only increase the physical, emotional and social costs of informal care-givers, all of which may have substantial public policy implications in the longer term' (1992a: 7).

Cash limits, the funding crisis and the management of need

The level of funding for community care, by being predetermined, essentially capped the amount available to local authorities and established a cash limit on the amount that central government was willing to give authorities to spend on community *and* residential care for those who required public support. Additional sums could be spent by SSDs, but these would need to come from other local authority or social services budgets, for example from child care. The paradox for local authorities is that while service delivery and professional decision making was to become, in theory at least, demand-led rather than supply-led, the resources available to meet existing and new demands by users and carers were to be cash-limited. This change mirrors other policy initiatives, most notably the cash-limited social fund, where discretionary decision making became the means to regulate access to, and control expenditure on, the cash needs of the poorest (see chapter 4). The introduction of cash-limited budgets in cash *and* care represents the administrative mechanism for curtailing state expenditure on welfare and on the poorest in particular, and is an essential component of the strategy to restructure the welfare state.

The contradictions inherent between demand-led welfare and cash-limited budgets established and maintained a deceit in community care implementation: namely, that the needs and expectations of all users and carers, irrespective of the rhetoric of empowerment and needs-led services, could never hope to be met within a system that set a ceiling on the level of expenditure available to meet needs for social care (see also chapter 5). For those charged with implementing the deceit – SSDs and care managers in particular – the use of assessment, prioritising and eligibility criteria became key techniques to regulate and ration access to expensive forms of care, both residential, nursing and domiciliary, for users and carers. Under Section 47 of the NHS and Community Care Act, local authorities are required to assess the care needs of any person who appears to them to need community care and decide in the light of the assessment whether they should provide any services. The authority is also required to take special action in the case of disabled persons to decide the services required as mentioned in Section 4 of the Disabled Persons (Services, Consultation and Representation) Act 1986. The government estimated that, in the first year alone (1993–4), 120,000 frail elderly people would need to be assessed (Bottomley 1992). Under the Carers (Recognition and Services) Act 1995, carers also have a right to an assessment at the same time as the user is being assessed; local authorities must take into account the results of this assessment when making decisions about any services to be provided for the user. Those who can afford to purchase outright their care from the independent/private sector are able to buy provision without the need for a local authority assessment. Those who cannot afford to purchase outright their care from independent providers, and thus require public money, must have an individual assessment.

The management by social services and care managers of their cash-limited budget took a number of forms, including an attack on the formula and process governing the allocation of funds to local authorities. This attack started the year before implementation, when the Association of Directors of Social Services (ADSS) estimated that departments were only being given 42 per cent of the actual funds that were required to implement the new legislation (*Community Care* 1992a). The majority of SSDs faced immediate and substantial cuts in other services as they geared up for community care (Social Services Inspectorate 1992). Resources had already been diverted away from other client groups and statutory responsibilities, including issues around implementing the October 1991 Children Act. Between 1993 and 1997 the issue of funding was to dominate the discussion of community care, and was to haunt both SSDs and the government, as both sides attempted to blame the other for what was to become a crisis of funding and a crisis of credibility. At the 1994 social services conference in Harrogate, for example, the local authority associations declared that SSDs were facing a £226 million shortfall in community care funding for the coming year and called on the government to provide 'proper' funding to avert a crisis in care provision (ACC news release 1994b). The warning came too late. Just a week later the Isle of Wight was to become the first local authority to run out of money to implement community care. Four days later Gloucestershire County Council revealed that they were £1 million overspent in their community care budget and, with four months of the financial year still to go, would now only provide emergency care to people defined as 'at risk'. The council also withdrew home care services to thousands of people, many of whom were disabled (*Guardian* 1994h, *The Times* 1994b). A month later Surrey social services also made public its funding crisis. The Director of Social Services wrote to all private care homes in the county asking them to give free places to elderly and disabled people until the department could afford again to pay for this care, which would be in the new financial year – some 10 weeks away (*Sunday Times* 1995).

The funding problem for these and other authorities arose for a number of interrelated factors. A last minute change in the technical formula for distributing funds in 1994–5 meant that some departments lost out in the process. The demand for care in some parts of the country was also far greater than had been expected, with less money to meet greater demand. But by far the most important factor appears to be the general under-funding of community care by central government – funding which was never sufficient to deliver 'needs-led' services. The Association of County Councils warned that the consequences of this funding deficit would fall most heavily on the very people who needed community care services – users and carers (ACC news release 1994b).

Some users and carers fought back against the withdrawal of services by SSDs. Disabled pensioners from Gloucester, for example, went to the High Court to challenge the council's decision to withdraw home-based services. They secured a partial victory at best. The judges ruled that Gloucestershire had acted unlawfully in unilaterally withdrawing services without reassessing users' needs. However, the judges also ruled that local authorities were entitled to take into account the availability of resources when they decide what services they can afford to provide. In other words, when the department makes an assessment of needs, or a reassessment, it can take its available resources into account in prioritising needs. The judge commented that SSDs would have to compare the range of disabilities of those requiring services and then arrive at a decision as to whose needs could be met within the available resources (*The Times* 1995a). As far as SSDs were concerned, this ruling legitimised a strategy of prioritising one disabled person's need against another, within the budget. In Gloucestershire, after the High Court ruling, the local authority wrote to 1,200 clients telling them to reply if they wanted to be reassessed. Those who did not had their services withdrawn or cut. Radar (the Royal Association for Disability and Rehabilitation) sought advice as to the legality of this procedure. The ruling did allow those cash-starved councils, following a reassessment, to stop providing services to clients of lesser priority, but this was itself short-lived.

In a landmark decision, the Court of Appeal in July 1996 overturned the High Court ruling in what may well prove to be the most important case on the rights of disabled people to services in the community. The Court of Appeal ruled that hard-up councils are not legally entitled to take into account the size of their resources to order cutbacks. Disabled people in receipt of services under the 1970 Chronically Sick and

Disabled Persons Act cannot have their services removed or reduced whatever happens to a council's resources, unless the person's needs change. Disabled people's rights to services must be given priority over all the non-statutory services that SSDs currently provide.

The judgement applies to people who are 'permanently or substantially' disabled and who require services linked to the 1970 Act. It only applies to one section of community care activity. Authorities appear to be able to take resources into account when they are working with other client groups or when they are working under the NHS and Community Care Act 1990, in a way which they cannot under the 1970 Act. Consequently, other community care users, especially elderly people, may 'lose out' to disabled people. Moreover, social services will also have to tighten up their eligibility criteria for community care services and definitions of need, in order to manage their budget and to ration services. Ellis suggests that 'practitioners readily incorporate into their informal practice prioritisation criteria, assessment guidelines and proformas in a way which is designed to protect their interests as much as promote those of users and carers' (1993: 39). Now, with cash-limited budgets, practitioners are having to incorporate these considerations into their formal practice. In some instances this prioritising of care needs was done by introducing even stricter eligibility criteria. In others it was done with the assistance of checklists, giving a more objective appearance to assessment. In the London Borough of Hammersmith and Fulham, for example, the Barthel Scale was used to classify the degree of independence and to determine whether or not an elderly or disabled person was eligible for support, and whether it should be provided from health or SSDs (*Community Care* 1995a).

Prioritising needs, rationing services, and excluding some people from receiving support, have become key instruments in managing the cash-limited community care budget, before and after the full implementation. For example, the Royal College of Psychiatrists (1992) and the Mental Health Act Commission (1992) expressed concerns that cash limits imposed on, and by, local authorities had forced people with mental health problems down the list of social services priorities to the point that SSDs would not be able to identify or provide services to people with mental health difficulties living in the community and most at risk. A few years after implementation, in a survey of 600 care managers, half reported that some of their clients had unmet needs because of budget constraints; three-quarters of care managers reported that budget constraints were undermining community care implementation (*Community Care* 1995b). An Audit Commission report found that, on average, local authorities were spending 7 per cent more on community care than the Standard Spending Assessment set by the government. All authorities were ranking people in order of assessed need and then providing services only for high priority cases; some departments were also setting ceilings on costs and some were operating waiting lists (Audit Commission 1996). The process of assessment and prioritising care needs bore a striking resemblance to the process of 'considered decision making' adopted by social fund officers with regards to cash needs, requiring an initial ranking by predetermined groups and then by being sensitive to individual cases of need within these groups. This process, now adopted by care managers, had been heavily criticised by SSDs and the local authority associations just a few years earlier (see chapter 5).

The government, however, refused to accept that its funding was inadequate, arguing that it was the *management* of implementation that was the real problem. John Bowis, the minister then responsible for community care, commenting about the events in Surrey observed that: 'As the Audit Commission pointed out recently, weakness in financial management is an on-going problem in some local authorities' (*Sunday Times* 1995), while Stephen Dorrell, the Secretary of State for Health, was more direct: 'It is not the idea that is at fault. It is the delivery that is at fault' (*The Times* 1995c). Bowis went on to blame Labour and Liberal Democrat councils in particular:

Conservative councils have proved themselves worthy of the trust we had in them ... Where difficulties with community care have arisen, it is almost invariably the case that a Labour or Liberal Democrat council lies behind them. These authorities have a history of putting their own interests before those of the users of the services. Too many Labour and Liberal Democrat Councils have shown themselves unable to manage their community care responsibilities properly ...

(Conservative Central Office 1995)

With local authority SSDs and the government attempting to blame each other for the very visible problems of community care, SSDs adopted a number of strategies for overcoming, as best they could, the crisis in community care financing. As mentioned in chapter 5, directors of social services had rejected for many years any attempts by the Department of Social Security to blur the boundaries between cash and care, but in the initial community care bravado of 1989 and the belief that directors were to get more power and resources, many lost sight of the fact that finally and unequivocally, SSDs were to become income maintenance as well as social care agencies. As it became increasingly apparent that resources and the social security transfer were insufficient to provide a truly effective network of community care, SSDs increasingly looked to strategies for maximising their incomes and minimising their costs. Issues around means testing and charging policies, and welfare rights, took centre stage in the management of community care and the management of consumer demand. The costs of the funding crisis, and of the strategy to overcome it, were again borne most heavily by those who could least afford to do so – users and carers – the very people who, in principle at least, the community care reforms were intended to benefit.

Charges for residential care

A major strategy for managing the funding crisis has been to means test users and then charge them, where appropriate, for their care. Social services can make charges for many of their services, including some children's services (AMA/LGIU 1991, 1994). By law, local authorities have to make charges for 'residential accommodation' under the requirements of the 1948 National Assistance Act and the National Assistance (Assessment of Resources) Regulations. This legislation determines how charges are set and how much a resident is required to pay; there is little room for discretion (Bransbury 1995: 49, AMA/LGIU 1994: 13). In May 1990, about 40 per cent of elderly people in residential homes were paying the total cost of their care; 57 per cent were eligible for income support to help with fees while another 3 per cent resided in local authority funded homes (Laing and Buisson 1991). Thus, the large majority of residents in residential accommodation were on incomes too low to allow them to pay the total cost of their care. Some may have entered care as 'private' payers but will subsequently have become supported by social security as their savings diminished and they became eligible for income support. In authorities with a higher incidence of deprivation the proportion of people in this situation is more extreme. In Strathclyde, for example, 89 per cent of elderly people admitted to private, voluntary or local authority residential and nursing home care and who were assessed by social workers made no personal contribution to the cost of their residential care at all because of low income (Isobel Freeman 1995, personal communication).

Up until 1993 those elderly or disabled people who went into residential or nursing home care either paid the fees directly (if they were ineligible for income support because of their income or savings), or , if they had lower income/savings and were in private care, were eligible to have the fees met in part or full from the social security system (see also Document 11). From 1 April 1993, SSDs took responsibility for making arrangements for people who needed public financial support in order to enter residential and nursing homes. Social services will contract with independent providers to meet the home's charges in full, or if the resident, the home owner and social services agree, social services can assess the resident's contribution and the resident will pay this directly to the home with SSDs paying the balance. Residents eligible for income support and newly placed from April 1993 in independent sector homes will receive normal levels of income support including residential allowance, rather than the pre-1993 higher levels of income support. In May 1995 there were 281,000 income support claimants in residential care and nursing homes; the average weekly income support payment for residents with preserved rights under the pre-1993 system was £158 in residential care and £226 in nursing homes (DSS 1996a).

Departments attempted to recoup expenditure on private residential care costs, and some of the costs of placing people in their own local authority residential provision (which was not supported by social security), by using 'charging assessment rules' (jargon for 'means testing'), to see how much each resident should contribute towards his or her own care. These rules are based largely on the way resources are treated for income support purposes, and are governed by a Charging for Residential Accommodation Guide (CRAG) and amended by circulars issued by the Department of Health. From 1996, people have to pay *in full* for their residential or nursing home care if their assets, including their home, are worth more than £16,000. The state (via social services) pays the full costs of care only for those people with assets of £10,000 or less. Between £10,000 and £16,000 a sliding tariff applies, with costs shared between individuals and the state (Departments of Health and Social Security press release 1995).

Councils are allowed to put a legal charge on the property of people who go into residential care, to cover costs, although the property should be ignored if another partner still lives in it. Councils should not take the value of the property into account when determining charges for domiciliary care. However, Hereford and Worcester Social Services considered seeking a charge on people's homes when assessing them for domiciliary care. The department argued that high-dependency care in an individual's home can be as expensive, if not more so, than a nursing home place and it is inequitable if those in residential care have their house taken into account while those who stay at home are exempted from having such an asset counted. However, following political pressure, the council withdrew its proposals.

One outcome of taking the value of a person's home into consideration for residential care purposes, and not for domiciliary care, has been that during the early to mid-1990s around 40,000 elderly and disabled people each year transferred ownership of their homes to sons and daughters to avoid having to sell the property to meet residential care bills. The charging rules, in effect, seemed to 'asset-strip' the property-owning middle-class and their children, who saw their inheritance swallowed by the state, even though many of their parents had paid national insurance contributions for decades. This policy also created a further perverse incentive for local authorities to over-utilise residential care. They would get less income from providing a domiciliary care package than a residential/nursing home placement of the same gross cost, because the value of any property is not taken into account for domiciliary care purposes. Social services departments started to tighten up procedures on making a charge against property from 1994, to secure the revenue that they desperately needed. Many departments established procedures which paralleled the income support regulations for the treatment of income or savings disposed of deliberately to secure entitlement to benefit; social services treated those whom they suspected had transferred their home to a relative, so as to secure free residential or nursing home care, as still having those assets, and this was enforceable in law (*Independent on Sunday* 1995a). Many authorities also introduced a ceiling to the cost of domiciliary care packages supplied as an alternative to residential/nursing home care, so as to preserve funds.

In effect, many elderly and disabled people would be charged in full by social services, certainly up until the point where their income and assets withered to the degree that they were defined as 'low income' – when they became eligible for income support. Depending on the amount of income and savings left, they would then either be charged part of the residential fee or nothing at all. Either way, the consequence of this process was to impoverish many elderly and disabled people. It forced them, by requiring them to spend their savings (or have their assets taken into account), from a position of financial independence, to a position, ultimately, of dependence on income support and local authority funding for the payment of their care fees. Over time, as their frailty progressed and their savings declined, they were transformed from independent citizens in the community, to financially independent users of residential care services, to the dependent poor in institutions. They lost their personal and financial independence through a process of institutionalised impoverishment.

The spectre of many property-owning, middle-class, elderly people being forced to sell their homes to pay for residential and nursing home care led the government to propose a new 'partnership' between the state, private insurance and the individual. In May 1996, the government published its proposals on financing long-term care (DoH 1996b). These included a range of incentives for citizens to invest in private insurance policies or annuities, with the aim of stimulating the financial services industry to offer attractive, reliable products. It would be the responsibility of individuals to make provision for themselves, with the state retaining a safety net function for those who could not afford to do so. The Prime Minister, John Major, commented: 'If people take out insurance to help pay for their care, the state will reward their contribution by safeguarding more of their assets when that insurance runs out' (quoted in the *Sunday Times* 1996). The proposals were criticised by the Commons Health Select Committee on a number of grounds, not least that many poor people would find the proposals of no value. The Committee also advocated that the private insurance industry needed to be regulated closely (Health Committee 1996).

Charges for home-based care

In the context of non-residential services (in other words, domiciliary care provided in the home, or community care), local authorities have a power to make charges under the 1983 Health and Social Services and Social Security Adjudication Act (HASSASSA). The decision to charge for such services, including meals on wheels, home care and day care, is at the discretion of each authority, unlike charges for residential accommodation. Moreover, there are no national rules on the treatment of users' income or assets, although once an authority decides to charge then any charge it makes must comply with the test of 'reasonableness' set out in Section 17 of HASSASSA 1983 (Local Government Anti Poverty Unit 1995, AMA/LGIU 1994). Local authorities cannot, however, charge for services or care provided under the aftercare provision (Section 117) of the Mental Health Act 1983, although the Department of Health has confirmed that the government is considering changing the law to allow councils to charge severely mentally ill patients for accommodation and community care services (*The Independent* 1995b).

The Social Services Inspectorate has issued advice for its inspectors on how authorities might exercise these discretionary powers, and how 'reasonableness' can be determined. The SSI suggests that authorities might take account of the full cost of providing the service, the income profile of the 'generality of users' and so on (SSI 1994, AMA/LGIU 1994). Once an authority sets a reasonable charge it must then also establish that the charge is reasonable for the individual to pay. Clearly, this raises considerable issues for disabled, elderly and other groups, may of whom are also on low incomes:

As charges have become more widespread, so has their importance as a policy issue. The pressures to charge, particularly in the context of severe budget restrictions, are immense. But the duty to safeguard the most vulnerable and poorest, often those using these services, is also paramount. This is the essential dilemma facing authorities: to raise revenue from charges to ensure that service levels are maintained whilst not impoverishing individual users. These two objectives are incompatible. All that local authorities can do is trade one off against the other. The extent to which people on low incomes will be protected will depend upon the extent to which the authority forgoes potential income.

(Local Government Anti Poverty Unit 1995: 1)

Forgoing potential income is increasingly difficult as the government actually reduces the amount of money available to local authorities on the assumption that authorities *will* charge for social care, regardless of the fact that to do so or not is discretionary. Since 1990 the government has actively encouraged the use of charges wherever possible for community care services. The government now assumes that 9 per cent of the costs of non-residential adult services will be recovered through charges nationally. Based on this assumption, the amount of Revenue Support Grant given by government to all local authorities was reduced by £260 million in 1995–6, regardless of the actual level of any income received nationally or locally by authorities (Local Government Anti Poverty Unit 1995). In 1993–4, £609 million was raised by English and Welsh authorities through charges for community care (*Community Care* 1996b).

It is not surprising, therefore, that most local authorities have introduced charges for social care since the introduction of the HASSASSA legislation in 1983, and particularly since the community care reforms of the early 1990s. The AMA has monitored these developments, producing a number of reports examining charges in 1983, 1988 and 1993–5. Between 1983 and 1988, for example, the AMA reports that metropolitan authorities attempted to keep charges down as far as possible, reflecting their growing awareness of the low income status of many of their traditional service users, and a commitment to anti-poverty approaches. Indeed, there were slightly more authorities in 1988 making no charges for social care than in 1983. However, the data indicate no coherent strategy on this: some authorities would charge for one service but not another and there was wide variation across Britain (AMA 1992, AMA/LGIU 1991, 1994). This latter point should come as no surprise. One of the main characteristics of discretionary schemes – be they in 'cash' (for example the social fund) or 'care' (local authority charging policies) is geographical variation and inequities.

By 1995, however, the picture for local authority charges for social care had changed considerably: 'The number of local authorities charging for non-residential social services, and for children's services, has grown immensely over the last four to five years' (Local Government Anti Poverty Unit 1995: 1). Only 13 per cent of authorities did not charge for home care, for example. The phased introduction of the community care reforms from the early 1990s, and the government's assumptions about the extent to which charges would be levied by authorities, had made a speedy impact on authorities, many of which found it increasingly difficult or impossible to refrain from making charges for a range of social care services. The government's funding system, making the assumption that authorities would receive 9 per cent of non-residential costs through charges, exacerbated this situation.

In the early 1990s there was a move away from flat charges towards charges that took account of users' ability to pay. In 1995, only 12 per cent of authorities had flat rate systems, about half the number of 1992–3. Increasingly, local authorities had to grapple with complex and often technical considerations about the least damaging charging policy, which, as far as possible, was fair, equitable and just: 'there are choices that authorities have to make about the structures of any charges levied, since this can have a dramatic impact upon the living standards of users' (Local Government Anti Poverty Unit 1995: 1, see also Thompson 1995). To an extent the cost of this 'anti-poverty' approach was that most authorities failed to achieve a net income from charges of 9 per cent of costs, the figure assumed by government for funding purposes. Only a third of authorities reported that they had achieved this rate of recovery; indeed two-thirds of authorities reported that increases in charges had failed to achieve proportionate increases in revenue because of the cost of collection and user resistance to paying. Those authorities with high levels of deprivation – Strathclyde and many of the London boroughs, for example – are least likely to be able to generate the levels of income from charges that might be possible from more affluent parts of the country. In Strathclyde, for example, 53 per cent of home help clients are in receipt of social security benefits and 63 per cent are exempt from charges because they are on low income (Isobel Freeman 1995, personal communication). In the London Borough of Waltham Forest, the SSD raised just 1.4 per cent of its social services spending in charges, compared with 18.4 per cent in Buckinghamshire (*Community Care* 1996b).

Some authorities systematically took the incomes of other family members into account when assessing available income, despite the fact that the legislation does not empower them to do so, and others would not waive or reduce charges to individual users in any circumstances, despite the need to consider what is reasonable for each individual to pay. Moreover, most departments failed to communicate adequately what would happen if users failed to pay charges (Local Government Anti Poverty Unit 1995: 3, Bransbury 1995: 50; Chetwynd *et al.* 1996). How local authorities structure and administer these charging policies will have a very real impact on the users of social care and family carers, many of whom will be on low incomes or will become income support claimants as they are forced to spend their income and savings on fees and charges. The imposition of charges is likely to distort demand, deterring poor people who need home care from applying for it and deflecting services to more wealthy elderly people who need them less (Sinclair *et al.* 1990). Monitoring of the impact of charges in the mid-1990s provides some indication of the consequences for various vulnerable and poor groups. Studies of local authorities (National Consumer Council 1995, Baldwin and Lunt 1996) found that each authority had different charging structures and that these were confused and confusing. A study by Scope (formerly the Spastics Society) found that almost one in five disabled people had to turn down some care from social services because they could not afford the services (*Guardian* 1995g). Chetwynd and colleagues' (1996) qualitative study of the impact of charges on 36 disabled people discovered that users found the whole charging process very confusing. Because disabled people had a high level of dependency on the care provided they had little scope to reduce or withdraw from services, even when charges were introduced or went up. Moreover, they had few, if any, alternatives – they could not exit or transfer to the private sector because the costs of services in this sector were perceived as more expensive, nor could they expect more care from their family carers. The impact of charges on users' financial circumstances was significant. Many had to make economies in their other expenses to pay social care charges, and many found that they could not save for larger items or household goods. People also had a deep sense of anxiety about the future – particularly those who knew that they would need higher levels of care over time. People were also unclear about why they were having to pay for services previously provided free.

This wide variation in the structure and rate of local charges has led to some, particularly disability organisations, but also the Labour Party, to call for greater national uniformity in charges for non-residential care (see for example Chetwynd *et al*. 1996, Milburn 1996, and Document 12). Moreover, it raises questions about what benefits should be taken into account in assessing income – for example Chetwynd and colleagues question whether attendance allowance and disability living allowance should be counted as income at all. For many disabled people, charges for social care count as a charge on disability – they have to pay charges to allow them to do everyday activities which non-disabled people can do free of charge. In other words, charges suppress their equal opportunities and reinforce their exclusion; it is the additional price they pay for their difference. It is only when their savings have been drained and when they become eligible for income support that they can receive free or subsidised social care. But in this process they also bear further costs; in the pursuit of independence, equal opportunities and full civil rights, they are forced to give up their financial independence to become dependent on income support and local authority assistance.

On another level, charges have implications for the boundaries between social and health care, and for the wider discussion of individualism versus collective responsibility (see also chapter 3). Wistow has suggested that social care, as opposed to health care, is increasingly being characterised and defined by charges: 'the central distinction between the NHS and social care is that the former is available free at the point of delivery (with the exception of charges for prescriptions, eye and dental examinations). The latter must charge for residential services and have discretionary powers to charge for non-residential care' (Wistow 1995: 13). Oldman has made a similar point: 'where a need is met determines in part whether it is health or social care ... Increasingly social care is seen as long-term or chronic care; care for when one will not get better. Health care, by contrast, is often equated with acute care for which one does not pay' (Oldman 1991: 3). The debate around who has, or should have, responsibility for 'continuing care' has fundamental implications for all citizens, including the poor. Define continuing care as health care and it is received as a non-stigmatising, universal, free service by better-off and poor alike; define it as social care and all potential beneficiaries are subject to means tests and charging policies, which redistribute costs away from the NHS and transfer them to local authorities and onto individuals themselves.

For more than a decade the NHS has been shifting the responsibility for continuing care to SSDs and the private residential and nursing home sector – in which means tests and charges apply. The government only intervened in this process when, in the 1990s, a Leeds hospital discharged a doubly incontinent, brain-damaged patient, who could not feed himself, to a private nursing home on the grounds that it could not improve his condition. Following the outcry, the government maintained that health authorities must provide long-term continuing care even for high-dependency 'incurable' cases. However, the 'boundary war' continues, and there is great regional variation across Britain in the type and source of continuing care available to elderly and disabled people. So, for example, some people, all with the same needs, will receive free long-term care from the NHS; others will be in private nursing homes but paid for by the NHS; others will be in private homes, means-tested but receiving a free place because of low income; others will be means-tested and having to pay for their care because they are 'better-off' (Health Committee 1996).

Wistow suggest that, as SSDs charge for many services that were previously provided free by the NHS, this will have a number of outcomes, not least a diminishing of the social contract on which the post-war welfare state was founded, namely that 'payments made at one point in time generate entitlements to cash and/or care as needs subsequently arise' (1995: 15–16). He argues that: 'Elderly people and people with disabilities are being required to pay for continuing care services they not only expected to be provided through the NHS but for which they might reasonably feel they have already paid ... As such [this] represents a significant shift in the balance between collective and individual responsibilities' (Wistow 1995: 15–16, see also *The Independent* 1995c). The changing boundary between health and social care is not simply a matter for technical definition and resolution, including how best to devise, apply and deliver charges, but is more fundamentally about the boundary between free and means-tested services on the one hand, and about collective and individual responsibility on the other, between state provision and privatisation (Wistow 1995).

It also raises complex issues about how elderly people and others will pay for their social and residential care, be this provided from the statutory, private or voluntary sectors. Oldman, examining a number of ways in which elderly people might in future pay for their own care, asks whether better-off people will prefer to buy their care from the private sector while SSDs will focus their services solely on the poor (1991: 15). This two-tiered outcome is highly probable, but it is far more complex than this. The process of care management and charging for social care actually forces some people to become dependent on social security if they are to receive financial support for their social care costs; the *process* itself impoverishes them. In effect, charging for social care disempowers people by forcing them to pay for the additional costs of their difference. If they are to receive services free of charge – services which meet some of their civil rights and provide them with equality of opportunity – they must become reliant on income support and all that this entails. At the same time, the changing boundaries between health and social care are undermining the long-standing contract between the individual and the state. As more people find themselves denied universal and free services during times of frailty, disability and old age – and as they have increasingly to pay for their care – the emphasis will increasingly be on individuals and families to secure their own future through their own efforts, maximising the opportunities offered by private insurance and the markets. The shift from collective responsibility back to individualism will have far-reaching implications for the poorest. The state will retain a residual welfare function, reserved for those who cannot afford to make independent provision for themselves.

Welfare rights

Many users of social services, and family carers, fail to receive all their entitlements to social security. Welfare rights, considered a maverick part of the social work task for most of the 1980s, became vaguely respectable in the 1990s, as departments saw the potential, for their clients and themselves, of the pursuit of welfare rights and income maximisation.

It has been known for some years that there is a problem of low take-up of benefits among social services clients (Silburn, MacPherson and Becker 1984, Becker and MacPherson 1986). Alcock and Vaux's research among home-care clients confirms that many still fail to claim all their entitlements to a wide range of means-tested and other social security benefits despite being in contact with a social worker/care manager (Vaux and Alcock 1995, Alcock and Vaux in press, see also Hayball 1993, Rainbow 1993, Fimister 1995). Welfare rights take-up work with users of community care services will not only increase their income (which will help them to live within the community), but will also bring much-needed money into the local economy and into SSDs, in the form of additional income from charging. Maximising the income of vulnerable people may, for some, lead to them being exempted from charges (because they receive income support, for example), but on the whole such initiatives are likely to bring more people into the net of charges than remove them (Alcock and Vaux in press). All authorities need to maximise the incomes of community care service users and their carers if independent living and security are to be a reality (Becker 1990).

The National Welfare Rights Officers Group (NWROG, now the National Association of Welfare Rights Advisers – NAWRA) suggests that decisions about the appropriate care package that a user receives should not be taken until a benefit check has been carried out. Benefit checks should also be offered to carers: 'If carers are to play the major role that is envisaged for them in the community care system, then their ability to cope will be profoundly influenced by their ability to get by financially' (NWROG 1991: 2). The NAWRA argues that welfare rights advisers have a number of distinct roles in the planning and implementation of community care, which also generate a number of ethical issues concerned with maximising incomes for clients which may later lead to their becoming eligible for charges for social care. Nonetheless, NAWRA argues that welfare rights advisers are best deployed in planning and evaluating the system of benefit checks and in training and supporting the staff who will carry them out. There will be a continued role for advocacy in relation to Benefit Agencies and SSDs, as well as the need to use technical expertise in designing service charges and means tests. Clearly, SSDs need to develop their expertise in welfare rights advice and advocacy; unless they do so many users and carers will fail to receive all their entitlements, and they and SSDs will be denied much-needed income (Becker and MacPherson 1986).

Direct payments: cash for care

One means of reducing the propensity of the community care process to impoverish users may be to give them cash directly so that they choose how to spend it on their own care needs. While the money will still be from public funds, the arrangement will provide users with power and control over their own situations, rather than having their care determined by others, no matter how well-intentioned.

Social services departments, as has been described, provide, or arrange for others to provide, community care or residential care *services* to people in need, following an assessment. While departments do have some limited powers to make small financial payments to poor families with children (see chapter 5), it has been illegal for departments to give out *cash* to other poor or vulnerable clients for them to buy their own care services. Section 29(6) of the National Assistance Act 1948 prohibits local authorities from making direct payments to clients, although Section 65 of the Health Services and Public Health Act 1968 allows local authorities to make grants and loans to voluntary organisations whose activities consist of, or include, relevant services or services similar to the local authority. Consequently, many authorities make payments to voluntary organisations to act as brokers, which then use these payments to provide cash directly to clients to facilitate independent living. There has been a significant increase in these brokerage arrangements since 1993 (Nadash and Zarb 1994, AMA 1995); over 60 per cent of responding authorities were already operating payment schemes to third parties or directly to clients in some instances, and 90 per cent said that they would make direct payments to individuals rather than through third parties if the legislation permitted (AMA 1995). Sheffield is one authority which has, for some years, provided direct payments to a small number of elderly people, and people with physical or mental impairments (*Direct Payment to Users Scheme Newsletter* 1995).

Since the 1980s there have been those, particularly organisations of disabled people, who have called for the law to be changed so that disabled people can receive cash to buy and manage their own choice of care services, rather than receiving services organised and arranged by others. The case for these direct payments is one of enabling and empowering disabled people to have choice and take financial control over their own lives, to promote their independence, rather than letting others make decisions on their behalf or in their best interests. The creation of the Independent Living Fund (ILF) in 1988 was an example of this type of direct payment scheme. The intention of the ILF was that a small number of severely disabled people (those who faced the largest losses with the changeover from supplementary benefit to income support and the abolition of additional requirements – see chapter 4) should be able to access a special cash pool to pay for their additional needs for personal support and care assistance. The ILF proved very popular among disabled people, indeed so much so that expenditure on these payments was far greater than planned; by 1993 the fund was making cash payments to 21,500 people, with expenditure exceeding £100 million. Disabled people valued the control and independence that ILF payments gave them, even though the new opportunities also generated new problems, not least those associated with becoming employers of care assistants, and the ensuing national insurance and tax implications (Kestenbaum 1996, Bond 1996). Evidence from the ILF and elsewhere indicates that direct payments are not only valued by recipients but also offer potential savings on direct service provision (Kestenbaum 1992, AMA 1995). In some cases this might be because private agency care workers are themselves low paid. The AMA found that:

Disabled people using the direct payments option almost invariably expressed greater satisfaction with the choice and control over their support arrangements and the reliability of provision than those using managed services ... 80% of service users reported a need for additional personal assistance hours compared to 40% of those receiving direct payments ... Support arrangements, financed through direct payments schemes were on average 30–40% cheaper than equivalent service based support. The average hourly unit cost of support for people receiving payments is £5.18 compared to £8.52 for service users.

(AMA 1995: paras. 4–8)

The success of the ILF in meeting some of the aspirations of disabled people for independent living and control over their own affairs helped to fuel the movement calling for the principle of such payments to be extended and be made more widely available to other groups, including those with learning difficulties, those with mental health problems and elderly people. In November 1994, the then Secretary of State, Virginia Bottomley, announced plans for the government to legislate to permit direct payments to be made from SSDs to disabled people to enable them to buy their own care services, in lieu of community care provision (AMA 1995: 1). A technical advisory group was established with representatives from the local authority associations, to help advance the initiative. One year after Bottomley's announcement the government published the Community Care (Direct Payments) Bill, which would, when it became law, prove to be a watershed in the cash and care divide: once and for all SSDs were to become income maintenance agencies as well as service providers/ arrangers. Their limited financial powers in respect of making Section 17 payments to poor families (chapter 5) would appear to be small change when compared to the scale of spending and the value of individual payments involved in making direct payments to disabled people.

The Bill gave local authorities the power to make direct payments to someone they had assessed as needing community care services. It also allowed authorities to means test clients to see how much they should receive as a payment and how much they should pay towards their care (DoH press release 1995d). The Bill was followed shortly afterwards, in January 1996, by a consultation paper which set out how the scheme might operate and a number of alternatives regarding which groups of people would be eligible in the first instance to receive payments. Payments would not be available to buy local authority services, private or voluntary residential care, except for brief respite periods, nor could they be used to pay a close relative. The parliamentary debates (see *Lords Hansard* 12 February 1996, cols. 397–458, *Commons Hansard* 9 March 1996, cols. 372–434) show the level of concern over some of the proposals, including the anxiety that some groups, particularly those over 65 and those with learning difficulties, were to be excluded from receiving direct payments. The government continually emphasised that there was a need to tread cautiously in this new area, and that local authorities would need to monitor developments carefully; the scheme would work best from the outset if it was tightly defined and limited to a small number of people 'willing and able' to manage their own care. After much discussion, it was agreed that the policy would be implemented in stages, with the first groups to benefit being adults (over 18 and under 65) with physical impairments or learning difficulties: 'Once direct payments have been available for a year, the Government will look at the scope for extending payments to other groups' (DoH press release 1996b, Document 13). The Bill received Royal Assent in July 1996.

It will be up to SSDs to decide who is 'willing and able' to take advantage of direct payments, although people with mental health problems and elderly people are outside the scope of the scheme in the first instance. There will be no automatic entitlement to payments, indeed, local authorities can choose whether or not they wish to introduce such a scheme in their area – there is no compulsion – which, in effect will mean that there will be wide geographical variation, as with charging policies. Moreover, while the user is to decide what to purchase, SSDs must agree on how the money will be spent and users must show that their choice is as cost-effective as the package that could be provided or arranged by social services. Social services will have powers to seek repayment of any money not properly spent on meeting the assessed needs.

One danger of the scheme as outlined is that the assessment, monitoring and gatekeeping function of SSDs could disempower, rather than empower, some disabled people, and undermine *their* choice and freedom to manage their own care. Because direct payment schemes involve allocating a level of funding to people related to their degree of disability, this will involve SSDs setting eligibility criteria for different levels of funding relating to different levels of disability. It will force the assessment process to look for 'objective measures' of disability (for example dependency scales), and create a whole new dimension of conflict between assessors and potential beneficiaries. The process of setting levels of funding related to different levels of disability is well under way in many authorities prior to the introduction of the scheme.

While it is wholly acceptable that public bodies should develop systems to ensure as far as possible the correct use of public money, direct payments, when implemented at the local level, may exacerbate the inequities that disabled people already face at the hands of welfare professionals. The evidence on SSDs' usage of Section 1 (now 17) cash assistance (chapter 5), and their strategies for managing the cash-limited community care budget, suggest that SSDs may be stretched to manage direct payments with fairness, impartiality and equity. The view that the 'professional knows best' who is 'willing and able' to manage their own care may well introduce more paternalism and judgemental-ism into the social care system, in addition to the problems faced by SSDs in dealing with fraud and misused money. Moreover, the introduction of direct payments may encourage the further development of a 'grey market' of low paid care workers, who have little job security and work long hours for little renumeration. But, of most significance, is that finally, SSDs will have become mainstream income maintenance agencies – providers of cash – to people with physical impairments or learning difficulties initially, but to include other vulnerable groups in the future. As this transformation takes place, the traditional divide between cash and care will be swept away once and for all. Social services in Britain, as with similar social care agencies across Europe, will be responsible for care *and* cash.

Direct payments: social services as an agency of income maintenance

Social services are already dealing with direct income maintenance issues, including complex rules and procedures for means testing and charging vulnerable clients for residential and community care. Departments have had some direct income maintenance responsibilities for a considerable time. Chapter 5 described how they are empowered to provide payments to poor families with children. In 1982–3, local authorities also took from the DSS the responsibility for housing benefit administration. Fimister (1995) suggests that the transfer of housing benefit and of social security (for community care) in the 1990s were designed to preserve central government's control over the key elements, while difficult operational matters were 'exported' to local authorities, along with the blame when things went wrong, particularly problems arising from under-financing. While this partly explains the movement towards greater integration of cash and care (with a transfer of cash responsibilities to SSDs and local government, rather than the transfer of care responsibilities going to central government or the social security system), there is also a powerful argument that cash and care *need* to be better integrated to respond to the *whole* requirements of vulnerable people, many of whom are on low income and need services in addition to money (see chapter 3). In some cases the separation of cash and care into two different agencies of the welfare state has not been beneficial to poor people, who have been left without money, care or even both. When SSDs become responsible for direct payments it will be a further step in the direction of them becoming agencies of social security. This shift, and the lack of attention given to it in the social services' and social work media, is perhaps the more ironic given social services' and social workers' long-standing hostility to taking on income maintenance responsibilities, and their vehement opposition to any suggestion that they should help social fund officers in their decision-making concerning poor people's cash needs (chapter 5).

Direct payments offer real opportunities for disabled people to gain greater choice and control over their own lives. However, this opportunity also carries with it considerable risks, for users and for SSDs. There is a real danger that SSDs, by becoming mainstream income maintenance agencies, will incur many more problems of the type already associated with their responsibilities for managing community care, particularly if each authority's direct payments budget is itself cash-limited. Fimister (1995) questions 'the uncritical assumption' that a system of direct payments has necessarily to be run by SSDs. He suggests that while the movement to direct payments is welcome, a more desirable approach would be for such payments to come from the national social security system, preferably as part of a comprehensive disability income scheme, rather than from SSDs. His arguments reflect wider anxieties about social services and social work moving even further into direct cash provision, with all the associated problems and dangers. These dangers include social workers taking on a more coercive role, requiring conformity from poor clients before cash and care are given (Handler 1968). Rather than SSDs (with their local variations and discretionary arrangements) taking on more income maintenance responsibilities, Fimister argues that these responsibilities are better located within a national, uniform social security system. However, Fimister's proposals have been overtaken by events. Direct payments *will* be delivered by SSDs.

Towards the integration of cash and care

The 1993 community care changes have unleashed a cascade of change which has blurred even more the boundaries between cash and care, between social security and social services. The Benefits Agency and the Department of Health issued advice to SSDs and benefit offices on

how best to improve liaison between the two departments over community care issues, including the need for SSDs to supply benefit agency
offices with information about changes affecting the social security benefit entitlements of community care users (DoH 1993). Considering the
hostility to previous suggestions by the DSS to improve liaison with
SSDs, particularly over the social fund (chapter 5), it is perhaps surprising that the new advice has not generated more attention or concern.

As direct payments are extended to other groups, perhaps even to
family carers in due course, and as liaison arrangements between SSDs
and social security are improved, there will be more pressure to move
towards some system of joint assessments of cash *and* care needs. Fitch
(1995) observes that there is already a 'striking similarity' in the assessment procedures used by the DSS to see whether people should receive
the disability benefits attendance allowance and disability living
allowance, and by local authority SSDs to see whether people should
receive care services under the NHS and Community Care Act.
Moreover, the charging assessment rules used by SSDs to determine the
amount residents will pay in residential or nursing home care are based
on income support regulations.

It will also become increasingly difficult to make a case for distin-
guishing direct payments from the other disability benefits provided by
social security. The case for transferring to SSDs the delivery of benefits which include a 'care' element (see chapter 4), such as disability
living allowance, severe disablement allowance and invalid care
allowance, will become more compelling. In this context it will also be
hard, if not impossible, to maintain the case for keeping the budget and
responsibility for social fund community care grants within social
security; there is little reason to deny SSDs the community care grant
budget if they are responsible for direct payments and community care.
The additional resources from the community care grant budget would
also give SSDs greater scope in tailoring packages of care to meet the
cash *and* care needs of poorer, vulnerable, clients. The community care
grant budget could be transferred as part of a revised social security
transfer, and over time built into the Standard Spending Assessment.
This would increase SSDs' responsibilities for making discretionary
cash payments and remove the ring fence around the community care
grant budget created by its location within the Department of Social
Security, making it possible for the money to be used also for funding
general care services.

There is evidence that the government is considering the further
transfer of 'care' responsibilities/costs from the social security system
and onto social services. Many vulnerable people, including those in
supported accommodation schemes and social housing, receive housing
benefit to cover rent ('bricks and mortar'), but also to cover some element for charges relating to personal needs (for example for counselling
and support services). The government intended to abolish this 'care'
element to housing benefit from October 1996, paying housing benefit

for bricks and mortar only. Many vulnerable people would, as a consequence, have little choice but to go into residential care because of their
need for personal support, or social services would have had to pay for
the care element from its own community care budget (if it wished to
maintain that person in social housing or supported accommodation in
the community). In July 1996, the government unexpectedly withdrew
the draft regulations pending the findings of an urgent interdepartmental
review of the arrangements for funding supported accommodation
through housing benefit. The outcome of this review will have major
implications for community care and social services in particular. If the
costs of the 'care' element in supported accommodation are taken out of
housing benefit and shifted onto social services, then there will be even
more pressure on hard-pressed departments. It will also be a further
example of the contraction in the responsibilities of the national social
security system to meet 'care-related' costs, and the transfer of these
responsibilities to SSDs. Given this transfer, again it would be hard to
maintain a case for not transferring other 'care' costs out of existing
social security benefits, particularly disability benefits.

Page, Bochel and Arnold (1995) comment that far greater integration
and coordination of cash and care, including housing services and housing benefit, is required. Assessments could also benefit from a more
explicit holistic intention in which accommodation, care and finance are
looked at together. Although at present the assessment process is
intended to 'trigger' the involvement of housing and professionals from
other agencies, effective liaison arrangements are still rare (Page *et al.*
1995, see also DoH 1994b, Clapham, Monro and Kay 1994). The
'poisoned chalice' facing SSDs is that while better assessment and
integration of cash and care, including housing benefit and housing services, are undoubtedly an advance, the politics of such developments
suggest that the responsibility, and costs, will be transferred from central government (and the national social security system), to local
authority SSDs, and that the outcome of this process will be characterised by regional variations, discretion, selectivity and charges.

As pressure grows for integration, and for treating vulnerable people
as 'whole persons', new models of delivering cash, care and housing
will need to be explored, perhaps on an experimental basis, as with new
social security initiatives (chapter 4). Alcock and Vaux's work on the
non-take-up of benefits among vulnerable home care clients led them to
conclude that a client-centred approach to take-up issues is necessary
among social services and social security staff, and that one-stop shops,
in which all benefit needs are dealt with through one contact, would be
beneficial to clients (Alcock and Vaux in press). The concept of the one-
stop shop can be extended to include not only meeting the diverse
benefit needs of vulnerable claimants, but also to include the meeting of
their social care and housing needs, through one point of contact. This
will require even greater integration of cash and care.

The evidence reported in this and the preceding chapters suggests that, for many poor elderly people, those with physical or mental impairments, and family carers, the reality of community care is a life on inadequate social security benefits, subjected to harsh treatment from both social security and social services. Social services departments have little option but to charge many users for social care, and to exclude others entirely from receiving support because of the requirement to manage cash-limited community care budgets. As they take on further income maintenance responsibilities, not least direct payments, there is every likelihood that this will unleash a cascade of further change, in particular the transfer of more responsibilities from the social security system to SSDs. The pressure for improving the delivery of cash and care, and for treating vulnerable people as whole persons, is likely to challenge even further the traditional boundary between social services and social security. Whether this challenge is a threat, or whether it offers new hope and opportunities for poor people, is just one of the issues explored in the final chapter.

CHAPTER 7

Towards a social reaction model of poverty and exclusion

This final chapter argues that to understand the relationships between cash, care and poverty we need to define poverty and exclusion as the consequences of social reactions, social and individual attitudes, policies, structures and practices which act as 'barriers' to independence and security for millions of people on low income. To refocus the poverty agenda we need to develop a social reaction model of poverty and exclusion.

Refocusing the poverty agenda

Some academics and others have attempted to refocus the research and policy agenda away from the concept of 'poverty' and the individualising consequences of existing academic and policy concerns, to the dynamics of social exclusion, social polarisation and marginalisation. The European debate about poverty is now far more concerned with social exclusion: 'Society is seen by intellectual and policy elites as a status hierarchy or a number of collectives, bound together by sets of mutual rights and obligations which are rooted in some broader moral order. Social exclusion is the process of becoming detached from this moral order' (Room 1995: 105–6). Williams and Pillinger argue that:

the concept of *social exclusion* has moved the focus from poverty as a *relative* condition, resolved through distributional mechanisms, to an understanding of poverty as a *relational* dynamic. In other words, poverty is about more than access to material resources, it is about the social relations of power and control, the processes of marginalisation and exclusion, and the complex and multifaceted ways in which these operate.

(1996: 9–10, emphasis in original)

A greater concentration on social exclusion would also take the focus off 'poor people' and encourage us to 'ask questions such as why they are poor and what the mechanisms are that are creating and sustaining that poverty' (Lister, quoted in Friedrich Ebert Foundation 1993: 51). Moreover, Lister poses some important questions concerning the agency and contribution of poor people in any refocusing of the poverty agenda:

many people in poverty themselves don't want that label poverty attached to them because there is still a stigma attached to it. And so we have a dilemma; how to stop Governments from getting away with denying the reality of poverty, but at the same time listen to what people in poverty themselves are saying about not wanting to think of themselves as poor. We need a strategy which gives due place to their perceptions of the situation and what they themselves are doing to change it.

(Lister, in Friedrich Ebert Foundation 1993: 51–2)

A focus on the processes and mechanisms that create and sustain poverty and exclusion requires poverty to be conceptualised as a structural rather than an individual problem, and in social reaction rather than individualising terms. As Alcock asserts:

who becomes or remains poor is a consequence of structural social forces. What causes poverty therefore is not individuals finding themselves or placing themselves in particular circumstances, but the reasons why those circumstances result in their receiving resources that are inadequate for their needs. It is this relationship which we need to understand if we are to understand the causes of poverty ...

(Alcock 1993: 27–8)

Lessons from the disability movement

In conceptualising poverty in social reaction terms, and in refocusing the poverty agenda, there is much to be learnt from the disability movement and the social model of disability (see chapter 3 for a full exposition of the model). The importance of the social model of disability, for our purpose here, is the way in which it provides an alternative paradigm or way of thinking to the individualised pathology model of 'difference' and 'disability'. Consequently, it is not physical impairment which causes 'disability', rather society's reaction to impairment, through its disabling environments and socially constructed barriers.

The social model of disability also offers insights into how a so-called 'disadvantaged' group can take control over the definition of the key issues, and how it constructs itself as a new social movement with considerable influence and power. The social model is being promoted by a strong and influential coalition of disabled people and their supporters. Drawing on the success of the American disability movement and its achievements in bringing about the Americans with Disabilities Act, the lobby is expressing and asserting itself increasingly in terms of human and civil rights, rather than specific rights for disabled people (Bynoe 1991, V. Scott 1994, Gooding 1994, Milne 1995, Scott-Parker and Holmstrom 1995). The disability movement is also arguing that, far from being a cost on the Treasury to introduce anti-discriminatory and civil rights legislation, net savings would be achieved as disabled people require fewer benefits, pay more in taxes and consume more goods and services (Barnes 1995).

Many policies in cash and care during the 1980s and 1990s have helped to politicise the concept and experience of disability, 'prompting disabled people, academics and professionals alike to address the limitations and contradictions of official policies and articulate instead an entirely different set of assumptions and premises governing the relationship between individual disabled people and the state' (Glendinning 1992b: 106). The social model, to a large extent, has become 'the new orthodoxy' (Oliver and Barnes 1993: 274). The way in which it is being promoted has turned 'disability' into a pressing political concern and raises important issues for those concerned to understand poverty as social exclusion, and to promote a dynamic social reaction model of poverty.

Developing a social reaction model of poverty

For many millions of people poverty and social exclusion are the consequences of 'social barriers' – reactions, attitudes and language, policy and service arrangements, institutions and agents, which label the poor as 'different', and marginalise and punish them by denying them full civil rights. These barriers are institutionalised in much contemporary social policy and social administration, and are built upon a foundation of hostile social attitudes, individual prejudice and discrimination, which exist towards groups defined as 'different' – for example people with physical or mental impairments, Black people, lone parents, foreigners and poor people themselves.

To conceptualise poverty in social terms we need to reject the dominant paradigm that constructs 'the poor' as a group, or groups, which are 'different' to the 'non-poor', separated and distanced from the rest of society by virtue of their own behaviour and difference. We need to conceptualise and understand the poverty of individuals within these groups as the consequence of social reactions, social attitudes, institutional structures and barriers, and professional practices which label people with little money and little power as 'different'; which then devalue them, deny them equal opportunities and full citizenship, and punish them for being 'poor'.

Cash, care and social reactions

The poverty agenda, in both research and policy, has focused sharply on material and economic considerations. Economic and material aspects of poverty are critical in understanding its cause and nature. Jordan has argued that 'a theory of poverty and social exclusion is necessarily *an economic theory of exclusive groups* (how people interact in relation to their economic risks, capacities and resources)' (Jordan 1996: 7, emphasis in original). Enabling people to find and to retain employment which pays a decent wage is perhaps the most important single factor which will promote the reality of 'social security', stability and independence for millions of citizens, and it is a necessary precondition for the achievement of wider social programmes (Silburn 1992: 146).

However, focusing almost exclusively on material and economic aspects has been at the expense of a consideration of social attitudes, welfare ideologies and political reactions to poor people. The cultural, ideological and political environments in which social policy is formulated by politicians and others, and implemented by welfare professionals, determines strongly the kind of response that poor people receive from social security and personal social services. Understanding welfare ideologies and social attitudes helps us interpret and explain the nature, functions and limits of cash and care as they relate to, and affect, poor citizens. Social services and social security, as agencies of 'welfare', and social workers, care managers and social security personnel, as agents of the state, have developed, operate within and contribute to the dominant, and often contradictory welfare belief systems and welfare ideologies that construct the poor as feckless and 'failures'. Poverty and exclusion are experienced not just in material and economic terms, but also as *reflections* of welfare ideologies, attitudes, beliefs and reactions.

Attempts to measure and respond to poverty and social exclusion must therefore recognise that they are a cultural as well as a material process: 'To develop sensitive and sophisticated measures of people's incomes while only partially to investigate the state of the public mind is to impoverish poverty research' (Golding 1995: 231–2). There is a need for greater attention to be given to the collection, analysis and interpretation of data on public perceptions of poverty and exclusion, rather than maintaining the traditional focus on defining and measuring poverty: 'How people construe poverty, their attitudes, prejudices, and beliefs, are significant ... they set the limits to what is politically feasible. What people know and believe about benefit levels or the circumstance of claimants and low-paid people, not to mention their broader visions of social inequality, will form the framework within which they can be persuaded of the virtue or otherwise of redistributive policies in aid of poorer groups' (Golding 1991: 39). There also needs to be far greater study of the attitudes, reactions and responses of other key players in the policy process, particularly politicians and welfare professionals, and how these and organisational structures and environments impact upon the condition and experience of poverty and exclusion.

As has been shown in preceding chapters, social security and personal social services in the UK are increasingly becoming programmes for the poor. Social security has a mass role to play in society – as a scheme open and available to all citizens at various stages in their lives. However, it is the poorest who account for the significant part of social security expenditure – increasingly so as the better off seek alternative income maintenance arrangements outside the state scheme – particularly through private means. Similarly, personal social services, including social work, community care and social care, are also services used most heavily by poor people and those on low income, especially those on means-tested benefits. The majority of social services' users, particularly families with children, come to social services specifically with financial and benefit-related problems. Others come because low income or poverty has exacerbated or precipitated further problems, strains or tensions, at the individual, family or community level. Many users of community care, especially people with physical or mental impairments, elderly people and family carers, are also claimants and many are widely acknowledged to be among the poorest. It is these people – those who cannot afford to buy their care outright from the independent sector – who must rely most heavily on public funds to pay for their care needs, and who must access these funds via a social services assessment and means test.

Those who receive cash and care find that they are often regarded as failures, 'scroungers' or cheats; they are controlled, degraded and stigmatised by the very systems which, insidiously, present themselves as caring and aiding:

in the very process of being helped and assisted, the poor are assigned to a special career that impairs their previous identity and becomes a stigma which marks their intercourse with others. Social workers, welfare investigators, welfare administrators and local volunteer workers seek out the poor in order to help them, and yet, paradoxically, they are the very agents of their degradation.

(Coser 1965: 145)

For many poor users of social security and social services, including social work and community care, contact with state provision is a public symbol of 'failure' and 'dependency'. There is differential treatment of the various groups who use state provision in cash and care – between those defined and prioritised as 'most vulnerable' – and those who are excluded from receiving cash, care or both. This is increasingly common in the context of cash-limited resources for meeting needs for money and services. Policy formulation and implementation in cash and care, designed to exclude some and regulate or manage the behaviour of others, rests upon a foundation of hostile attitudes towards the so-called 'undeserving' poor.

This ideological climate, and the treatment of poor people by welfare organisations and professionals, also exert a strong influence on the way in which poor people define themselves: 'Some of the poor have come to conclude that poverty does not exist. Many of those who recognise that it exists have come to conclude that it is individually caused, attributed to a mixture of ill-luck, indolence and mismanagement, and is not a collective condition determined principally by institutionalised forces, particular governments and industry' (Townsend 1979: 429). For some, 'self-blaming' can develop as a 'spoiled identity' and give an overriding sense of stigma and shame, characterised by apathy and feelings of dependency, which can threaten the very 'fabric of identity' (Goffman 1961, Matza 1969, Kerbo 1976, Breakwell et al. 1984).

In a period where the policy agenda in cash and care is largely determined by the political imperative to curtail social expenditure, particularly on the poor, targeting 'undeserving' groups for cuts in cash benefits or social services, or for other 'punitive' treatments, is likely to generate public support. Moreover, it helps fuel the very belief that crime, abuse, failure and dependency are part and parcel of the 'welfare culture', thus fostering an uneasiness among claimants about receiving benefits, among poor clients about using social services, and among taxpayers about the value of contributing towards these and other state welfare programmes. As cash benefits and care services become targeted even more at the most vulnerable and poorest, these state programmes will be viewed increasingly as 'reserved for the poor' and will be characterised and transformed into 'poor services'. Moreover, as the better off seek alternative sources of support – independent of the state – the sense of failure experienced by poor people, their polarisation from mainstream economic and social life, and their exclusion, will become more acute. This can only frustrate even further the intentions of politicians and policy makers to reduce 'dependency' on state welfare and to promote the values of independence and personal responsibility. Existing reactions, structures and policies in cash and care have become part of the problem of poverty – social barriers to independence and security – rather than solutions.

A social reaction model of poverty and exclusion provides an alternative analysis and way forward. It is not the receipt of welfare, cash and care, which create and sustain 'dependency', rather it is society's reactions to claimants and clients, which label them as failures, 'problem families', 'workshy' and so on, and which then punish them accordingly. These reactions, particularly as evidenced through the organisation, operation and practice of cash and care, coupled with a lack of paid employment opportunities providing decent wages, are the main social barriers to independence and security for poor people.

How do we explain the exclusionary consequences of contemporary social services and social security? At one level this can be explained by the profound lack of awareness of poverty issues among politicians, policy makers and many professionals charged with implementing cash and care policy. For example, social services, social workers and care managers, despite their day-to-day contact with people on low income and in poverty, are ambivalent and confused about their roles and tasks in relation to poverty and money matters. In many spheres of contemporary social services policy and implementation the poverty dynamic is rarely recognised as an issue of strategic importance. This may partly reflect social work's lack of a theoretical base, in particular its inability to generate, apply and sustain a social as opposed to an individualised pathology model of impairment and poverty. It may also reflect social services and social work's traditional focus on individuals and families, and their emphasis on assisting people to manage or adapt to their circumstances, financial or otherwise.

The dominant assumptions underlying cash and care policy and implementation are that the poor are a group apart, somehow 'different' to the non-poor, and somehow responsible for their poverty. The condition and experience of poverty is constructed in terms of the personal characteristics and behaviour of the poor themselves, rather than in terms of the social processes and barriers that define, maintain and reinforce poverty, polarisation and exclusion. The emphasis has been on regulating the behaviour, lifestyles and choices of the 'undeserving' poor, to reduce 'dependency' on welfare, encourage them off benefits and back into work, wherever possible. This individualistic model has also manifested itself in a debate about whether 'poverty' in the UK exists at all. The claim that 'real' poverty has been abolished shifts attention away from the structural determinants and social characteristics of poverty, and places the focus on the 'undeserving' poor. Again, the social reaction to poverty is individualising; it denies the structural significance of poverty while emphasising the problem for society of 'undeserving' low income groups.

Partnership and inclusion

As we have already seen, people with physical impairments have been instrumental in developing a social model of disability and in promoting and applying that model in the policy arena. Poor people are also well aware of the social barriers that maintain their poverty, polarisation and exclusion. These barriers include the very organisation and operation of social security and social services, including the attitudes, reactions and practices of many welfare professionals. Given the opportunity, resources and power poor people will be able to identify a multitude of other social barriers, at the macro and micro levels, which serve to exclude them from full citizenship and social and economic participation. Many of these barriers have already been identified and articulated by poor people. They include the low level of income support; the lack of affordable and adequate child care provision; the low earnings disregards for some social security benefits; the lack of employment opportunities and adequately paid jobs which provide decent living wages.

Poor people need to play a strategic role in developing a social reaction model of poverty and exclusion and in formulating anti-poverty responses. Beresford points to the links between disabled people's fight to secure citizenship rights and a parallel cause for the poor:

There are constructive links to build upon between the rights approach to poverty and disabled people's concern with civil rights. There are two key sources of insight for understanding the relation between disability and poverty, both of which have been marginalised in dominant discussions. These insights come from the overlapping perspectives of people with experience of poverty and disabled people.

(Beresford 1994: 2–3)

Traditionally, the perspectives of poor people have seldom been sought by politicians, policy makers and welfare professionals in cash and care. The push for the eradication of poverty has been led by the poverty lobby, academics, professionals and others, rather than the poor themselves. A social reaction model of poverty and exclusion, and policies and strategies to prevent poverty, need to draw heavily on the views, expertise and agency of the poor – poor people must not be excluded from the debates and policy-making arena. The barriers to their voices being heard in anti-poverty debates must be dismantled:

The argument that people with experience of poverty should be more fully involved in anti-poverty action is now well rehearsed. A strong case is made for it on philosophical, practical and political grounds. Including poor people challenges the exclusion which anti-poverty campaigners rightly highlight as a central effect of impoverishment. It makes possible more relevant, effective and participatory analysis and research. It is likely to lead to more successful and appropriate campaign methods and results. The effectiveness of the disabled people's movement pressing for anti-discrimination legislation offers a powerful and overlapping example of the strength of such broad-based involvement. Campaigns against the poll tax and Child Support Agency offer other important lessons.

(Beresford and Croft 1995: 14)

There is no denying the complexity and difficulty in breaking down the barriers that exclude poor people from being heard and from taking a full part in social and economic life. The publications of ATD Fourth World offer valuable insights into how partnership between poor people and welfare professionals might be developed in the UK – partnerships which 'empower' all sides (see for example ATD Fourth World 1996). It is not the place here to rehearse these debates in any more detail; rather the point must be to emphasise the centrality of concepts such as 'partnership' and 'inclusion', and how they must form the value-base on which to move forward.

Promoting a social reaction model of poverty and exclusion, accompanied by a more positive political rhetoric and sensitive treatment by social administrators in cash and care – with an emphasis on respect, consultation, partnership and inclusion – would do much to break down the sense of stigma, failure and social exclusion that characterise the current process and outcomes of cash and care policy for poor people. This will require reformed administrative arrangements for the delivery of cash and care which minimise the judgemental and intrusive application of techniques and tests, including means tests, designed to differentiate between, and categorise, different poor groups. It will require different ways of working and talking between poor people and welfare professionals. It will require far greater poverty awareness among welfare professionals, policy makers and politicians, who need to understand how their own views, attitudes and reactions to poverty have become part of the social barriers that exclude, regulate and manage poor people.

Moreover, it will require closer coordination, and possibly greater integration, of cash and care, so that poor people are treated as 'whole' persons with coexisting needs for money and services. Different organisational structures for delivering cash and care in as 'seamless' a manner as possible need to be tried, utilising the expertise of poor people themselves in determining how best this might be achieved. It may be that the needs of poor people are better served by the integration of cash and care functions into one organisational structure; or it may be that they are better served by these functions remaining separate, but with improved channels of communication and coordination between cash and care. This may lead to the introduction, perhaps on an experimental basis, of 'one stop shops' in which cash, care, housing and other services are provided to all citizens, including the poor. The point to highlight here is the need to examine these issues and options in far more detail, to find better ways of delivering cash and care. Throughout, there is the need to include poor people in these discussions as partners with expertise in their own right.

The partnership approach will pay dividends in personal, economic and social terms. A positive attitude towards poor service users and benefit claimants will help to establish and reinforce their own positive self-image (Rosenthal and Jacobson 1968, Wills 1978), which, at the individual level at least, is important to promote a sense of self-worth and empowerment and, at the social level, is important in promoting a sense of communal purpose, cohesion and solidarity. Within the context of cash and care, non-judgemental and positive regard, offered universally to clients and claimants without recourse to notions of 'deservingness' or otherwise, would help to reduce the pauperising and 'disabling' nature of existing social reactions and much social welfare. It would require the poor to be seen, and to act, as 'agents' in their own right, taking responsibility, resources and power from the established agencies and agents of the welfare state, so that they can exert stronger control over the policy agenda. Where partnership has been attempted along these lines there is evidence that it has been of great benefit to poor people and to welfare professionals alike (ATD Fourth World 1996).

Rather than punishing the poor in an effort to get them off benefits and reduce 'dependency' – a policy which has been destructive to individuals and families, socially divisive and ultimately self-defeating – the poor need to be respected as agents and experts in their own right, 'partners' rather than 'villains'. Welfare provision must be seen as a badge of citizenship rather than a mark of failure.

A minimum income standard

In our development of a social reaction model of poverty and exclusion we also need to have some benchmark from which to better understand the levels of income required to enable people to live an ordinary life, free from poverty. Veit-Wilson (1994) points out that the UK is one of the few developed countries in which 'the government does not set a minimum income standard to define its view of minimal adequacy – the lowest level required for people to be able to take part in ordinary social life and stay out of poverty' (1994: ii). Moreover, in 1992 the European Commission recommended that member governments set such a minimum income standard at a level considered 'sufficient to cover essential needs with regards to respect for human dignity'. Veit-Wilson confirms that 'basic needs are not just physical needs; they include the need to participate in the life of society. In other words, basic needs can only be defined in relation to the standards of living of the whole of society' (1994: ii).

Veit-Wilson goes on to outline how such a minimum income standard might be set. He suggests that the population (not just experts) should be asked what they consider to be the minimum necessities which no one should be without, and then researchers should discover the income levels at which different household types acquire these minimum necessities. Whether the government then sets benefit levels below, above or at the level of the standard would be a political and economic decision. Clearly, if benefit levels are set below the minimum income standard, we should not be surprised to find many, if not all, people on benefits experiencing deprivation and poverty. If the benefit level is set at a higher rate than the minimum income standard then the condition of poverty should be abolished for many millions of people. These are political decisions, but it is possible to alleviate poverty, and prevent poverty, by first calculating a minimum income standard and then establishing a benefit level which is non-pauperising. This would also end the long-standing debate about the 'adequacy' of benefits, the culpability of the poor, and so on, because the whole process would be transparent, and the politics of poverty open to public scrutiny. Establishing a minimum income standard is a necessary step in the development of a social reaction model of poverty and exclusion. If we know the level of minimum income required to enable people to live a minimum standard with regards to human dignity, we can then see more clearly, and understand them for what they are, the social reactions and social barriers which deny people on low income the opportunity for dignity and freedom from poverty.

The fundamental challenge facing politicians, policy makers, welfare professionals, academics and poor people themselves, is whether there can be a genuine shift from an individualised, pathology model of poverty to one which is dynamic and social. This will require far-reaching changes in the ways in which poor people are viewed and treated – away from regulation, management and exclusion – to a position of respect, partnership and full citizenship. It will require a conceptual and policy shift, away from reactions and responses which define the poor as the problem, to one of *responding to poverty*. Is this a challenge that we are ready to face, and ready to pay for?

List of Documents

1   Frank Field on poverty and welfare reform   168
2   New Labour on social security reform   169
3   Peter Lilley on poverty   170
4   Michael Portillo on the public sector   172
5   Peter Lilley's 'little list'   173
6   Improving delivery of benefits – the Change Programme   175
7   Privatising the delivery of benefits   177
8   The Social Security Advisory Committee on private provision   178
9   CPAG's agenda for social security   179
10   Social services and social work   181
11   Griffiths Report on public finance for residential and nursing home care   183
12   New Labour's policy for social services   185
13   Direct payments   187

Document 1
FRANK FIELD ON POVERTY AND WELFARE REFORM

Rowntree set the parameters of the poverty debate in Britain this century. Yet, as we have seen, it is one thing to attempt to define an outcome sufficient to guarantee 'merely physical efficiency'; it is quite another to translate this into benefit rates or minimum wage proposals. **Seeking an exact definition of poverty in money terms and translating the findings into a workable benefit system is a political eldorado. We need to sidestep this futile exercise.**
   The aim should be twofold. We have seen that the welfare state in this country has been skewed almost exclusively to the question of combating poverty. Such an emphasis stems directly from the impact of the early social surveys conducted by Booth and Rowntree. In most other European countries the debate has been cast much more widely to address the question of how best to underpin working families' living standards. A reconstruction of Britain's welfare must bring our debate into line with that which has dominated the European agenda for most of this century.
   Moving away from an exclusive debate about poverty is therefore a first priority. The long-term interests of the poor can best be served by setting their needs in the context of a much wider political agenda. The second move is to begin offering individuals a welfare income which harnesses their self-interest and wish for self-improvement so that they are motivated to leave the welfare roll, rather than, as at present, merely to maximise their income while remaining on welfare. Neither of these objectives will be achieved if income support levels are regarded as the official poverty line income.
   Income support rates should simply be regarded as offering a minimum income level. To use the rates to measure the numbers of poor is perverse, given that both Booth and Rowntree used appearances rather than income to 'measure' the numbers of poor in their surveys. Moreover, as we have seen, the way the minimum benefit rates have been calculated has been, at best, arbitrary. Nobody who has any experience of living on the income support rates, or observed others doing so, has any illusion about the modest standard of living afforded by them, even for those with the most able budgetary skills. **The aim is not to define or redefine these levels with greater accuracy, but to free people from income support altogether. How can this be achieved?**
   A political party must first recognise how dire the problem is, acknowledge its scale, and set out a strategy which aims to replace means-tested dependency, even though such a programme will take twenty or more years to achieve. This goal then becomes a yardstick by which to judge all welfare reforms; do they help or hinder the achievement of this objective?
   Hard choices follow from this decision. The aim is to free people from means-tested dependence. Any redirected or new expenditure must go towards extending the coverage of national insurance benefits, not in raising what has been called the poverty line income itself.

From: Field, F. *Making Welfare Work: Reconstructing Welfare for the Millennium*, Institute of Community Studies, London (1995) pp. 75–7.

Document 2
NEW LABOUR ON SOCIAL SECURITY REFORM

Shadow Social Security Secretary CHRIS SMITH MP today published Labour's plans for getting unemployed people off benefits and into work, arguing that this was the best way to reduce the social security bill.

Mr Smith said that Beveridge had never meant the welfare system to keep unemployed people trapped in dependency, but had intended it to act as a springboard back into work. He pointed out that the number of people dependent on benefits had doubled from one in 12 to one in six of the population since the Tories came to power in 1979.

The MP said:

'Labour's benefit-to-working strategy is at the heart of our approach to welfare reform. It is better to have a nation at work than a nation on benefit, and the policies we are publishing today set out our plans for changing the welfare system to achieve this aim.

'Today we are unveiling both Labour's vision for a system which meets the needs of the claimant and not the other way around; and also some practical ways of removing Tory benefit traps. Our proposals include:

- Personalising the benefits and employment services, by giving tailor-made help with job-seeking and skills, as the JET scheme in Australia and GAIN programme in California do;
- A network of 'One-Stop Shops' for benefits and employment advice, with the aim of a single, user-friendly form for claiming all the major benefits;
- Actively encouraging, rather than penalising, volunteering, which helps unemployed people gain work experience, skills and contacts;
- Recognising and helping unemployed people's own efforts to rebuild their skills, for example by encouraging, rather than penalising by the '16 hour' rule, part-time studies;
- Adding together the weekly amounts people on Income Support are allowed to earn before their benefit is affected so that they can do occasional work while unemployed, to allow a gradual re-entry to the world of work;
- Running a pilot scheme to enable people to keep their Income Support for a month after finding work, to help with the initial costs of taking up a job; and
- Giving people taking temporary or uncertain work an automatic re-entitlement to Income Support at their previous rate, so they are encouraged to take the chance of a job.

'Our proposals for assisting people to move out of benefit dependency will, over time, save substantial amounts for the tax payer, and we will set clear targets for savings.

'Our plans mean a revolution in the way the DSS operates, and an entirely new relationship between the Benefits Agency and those who come into contact with it. Under Labour the social security system will treat people as individual citizens, rather than as passive recipients of giros'.

From: Labour Party news release 'Labour: DSS should help with jobs, not just giros', 24 June 1996.

Document 3
PETER LILLEY ON POVERTY

I am not one of those who deny the right, indeed the duty, of the Church to speak out on political issues. Christianity affects every aspect of life and therefore must encompass politics. On the issue of poverty the Church has always played a supremely important role. For centuries it was the principal channel of sustenance to those unable to help themselves. And by its teaching the Church has continually reinforced our senses of duty towards 'all them who in this transitory life are in trouble, sorrow, need, sickness or any other adversity'.[1]

The message is clear. We have a duty to help those unable to help themselves. The rich must help the poor; the healthy care for the sick; the strong support the weak. That is an obligation Conservatives accept just as do other parties. As that great Christian and Tory Samuel Johnson said, 'A decent provision for the poor is the true test of civilisation'.[2] It is part of our common Christian heritage in this country. And it would be wrong for any party to claim to monopolise it.

NO CONSENSUS ON MEANS

Nonetheless, although we all want to help those in need, there remains a sharp divide between the parties in our approaches to these issues, our analyses and our policies for tackling need.

OPPOSITION APPROACH

The opposition approach is still based on a hostility towards, and misunderstanding of, the free market. They see the market as based on selfishness and greed, generating poverty and inequality. They assume it is a zero sum game so that the wellbeing of some must have been attained at the expense of poverty for others. And they believe unequal incomes reflect the arbitrary selfishness of employers rather than the relative scarcity of different skills, efforts and abilities. So they believe the state should intervene, not just to tackle need, but to impose a just and equal pattern of incomes. Indeed an obsession with equality often displaces concern for poverty by the politics of envy. They fondly hope that the state can raise earnings ahead of people's productivity without destroying jobs, impose burdens on employers without reducing employment, and penalise risk, effort and skills without affecting the amount of investment, enterprise, and new skills.

CONSERVATIVE APPROACH

By contrast Conservatives see the free market as essentially positive. It releases and rewards human creativity. And it allows people to prosper only insofar as they satisfy the wants of others. Over time it has enabled the vast majority of people in Britain to achieve a decent income. Of course the market cannot directly help those who, through sickness, incapacity, caring responsibilities or temporary misfortune, are unable to participate in it. But it generates the wealth which enables us, as taxpayers or charitable givers, to meet the needs of those who cannot themselves participate in the market. The obligation of a government like this one, which believes in the free market, is twofold: to help those who cannot help themselves, and to provide a framework within which all those able to work can support themselves and generate the resources to help others. In short: to help the helpless and to enable the able. [...]

WE ARE HELPING PEOPLE IN NEED

Paradoxically, our success in raising general living standards intensifies accusations that 'Conservatives do not care about the less well off', that we have 'let the poor get poorer' or even that this has been the direct result of 'cuts in benefits'. These accusations misrepresent our motives, our policies and our achievements. We do care – our policies aim to help the least well off. And the results prove that they do. In fact, even the least well off have seen improvements over the last 15 years.

I have always avoided sterile debates about how best to define poverty. But the people most of us normally think of as least well off are those who depend on benefits. No-one thinks that benefits permit a life of luxury. But in most cases benefits are higher in real terms that in 1979. [...]

It is significant that claims that the 'poor have got poorer' do not generally focus on benefit levels. Instead they largely relate to statistics for households with the lowest tenth of reported incomes. A growing proportion of them are self-employed, many of whom report low or even negative incomes, particularly in the early years of setting up business. The other group which has grown rapidly – doubling its share of those on low incomes – is the unemployed, most of whom return to work after a while. Whatever their reported incomes show, those in the lowest tenth of incomes enjoy higher real living standards as measured by their spending – which is 30 per cent up on that of their counterparts in 1979.

Over the same period the proportion of people in the bottom tenth of income who own consumer durables has risen enormously. For example fewer than a third had a fridge-freezer in 1979. Now the overwhelming majority (84 per cent) do. Almost no low income household in 1979 had a video. Now nearly three quarters have one. Some 40 per cent had a car in 1979. Now 57 per cent have one. To most people the idea that well over half the group alleged to demonstrate ever-deepening poverty nonetheless have a car – at least gives pause for thought! [...]

1 *Book of Common Prayer*, 1662, Communion service.
2 Samuel Johnson, Boswell: *Life* ii, 130.

From: Lilley, P. 'Equality, generosity and opportunity: welfare reform and Christian values', Speech, Southwark Cathedral, 13 June 1996.

Document 4
MICHAEL PORTILLO ON THE PUBLIC SECTOR

A revolution is taking place in public sector management. Hardly noticed today but when historians look back on this period of history they will see clearly that huge changes were made.

In the early 1980s the State consumed over 47 per cent of British national income. It employed over 700,000 civil servants. That number has been cut by 25 per cent. It managed around 50 more nationalised industries than today. They ran at a total loss to the Exchequer of £3 billion a year.

So the scope and size of the public sector have changed dramatically in the last 10 years. We now get much more for a lot less. Better services for less cost. In the next 10 years it will change just as dramatically.

Consider all the initiatives: privatisation, contracting out, market testing, the creation of agencies, the Citizen's Charter, delegated budgets, local pay and grading arrangements, greater competition for senior Civil Service posts, performance pay, private finance and the introduction of resource accounting.

And we are improving roles and responsibilities within the public sector, for example through the introduction of grant-maintained schools and NHS trust hospitals. The delegation of key tasks to a local level represents a huge change.

On top of that we are squeezing the budgets of central government departments and others in the public sector. That process emulates the pressures of competition in the private sector. It is a discipline that sharpens performance, bringing out the best in management and encouraging the emergence of the can-doers.

Those changes mean that the State now seeks to do only the things that it alone can do, or that it does best at least for the time being. Competition and value for money are watchwords. Managers increasingly account for what they do, know the cost of the resources they use, and feel under strong pressure to improve their cost effectiveness.

Today I want to describe how and why such a huge transformation is taking place. I will highlight some of the Government's achievements and indicate where further progress is underway.

Principles

There are four main principles that guide our approach to public sector reform.

- First, we believe that the State should not do that which others can do better.
- Second, we believe that financial arrangements in the State sector should make costs clear to managers and the public, should relate pay to performance and, above all, should ensure that managers feel the consequences of their decisions, good or bad.
- Third, we believe in sweeping away monolithic and centralised rules and procedures which stifle individual enterprise and prevent managers from managing.
- Fourth, we believe in competition, including competition from the private sector in offering public services.

From: Portillo, M. 'A revolution in the public sector', Speech at the Hertford College, Oxford Deregulation Seminar, 7 January 1994.

Document 5
PETER LILLEY'S 'LITTLE LIST'

When the Prime Minister asked me to take on this Department, I was delighted. Not because it is bigger than Defence, Education, Health and the DTI put together. Not just because both Margaret Thatcher and John Major cut their ministerial teeth here, but because this is the fiftieth anniversary of the Beveridge Report. And John has given me the challenge of shaping a humane, Tory social policy, for the next century. That great Tory Dr Johnson said 'The true test of a civilised society is generous provision for the poor'. That's a test which we amply fulfil. [...]

But to escape recession we must curb public spending, including social security. But improving benefits is not just a question of spending more money. It's how we spend it that counts. So when I took office, I set out six principles to guide our future policy:

● to focus benefits on the most needy,
● to restore incentives to work,
● to encourage personal responsibility,
● to simplify the system,
● to adapt it to the needs of beneficiaries not bureaucrats,
● and to crack down on fraud.

Because every pound lost to fraud means less for those in real need.

Be in no doubt. This Government and this Secretary of State will not tolerate fraud. It's an insult to the law-abiding majority. I have set a target of tracking down five hundred million pounds. And I mean to get it back. I'm closing down the something-for-nothing society.

This summer I announced tougher rules affecting so-called 'New Age Travellers'. Most people were as sickened as I was by the sight of these spongers descending like locusts, demanding benefits with menaces. We are not in the business of subsidising scroungers.

And we've tightened up on bogus asylum seekers. It's right to help genuine victims of persecution. But not those whose persecution is fraudulent. It's outrageous when people claim using a dozen invented names. So we've clamped down on forged claims. And already nearly 20,000 have evaporated into thin air.

There are scores of other frauds to tackle. So, Mr Chairman, just like in the Mikado,

'I've got a little list'.
Of benefit offenders who I'll soon be rooting out.
And who never would be missed.
They never would be missed.
There's those who make up bogus claims.
In half a dozen names.
And councillors who draw the dole.
To run left wing campaigns.
They never would be missed.
They never would be missed.
Young Ladies who get pregnant just to jump the housing list.

And Dads who won't support the kids of Ladies they have. … kissed.
And I haven't even mentioned.
All those sponging Socialists.
They'd none of them be missed.
They'd none of them be missed.
And I've got 'em on my list.

From: Lilley, P. Speech to the 109th Conservative Party Conference, 7 October 1992.

Document 6
IMPROVING DELIVERY OF BENEFITS – THE CHANGE PROGRAMME

Today I can announce that we are on track with the 'Change Programme' I launched in February to make a 25% improvement in operational efficiency. It is an ambitious plan to make the same sort of dramatic improvements in efficiency in this Department as many private companies have made in recent years. The Change Programme will save the taxpayer £$\frac{3}{4}$ billion a year, without reducing benefits and while enhancing service to our customers.

STREAMLINING INCOME SUPPORT

We currently spend around £3 billion a year on just administering services to our customers. That is a huge cost to taxpayers. So one of the most fruitful areas for change is to streamline the administration of benefits. Income Support is one of the biggest and most complex benefits, with 4 million claims a year, and costing £1.7 billion a year to administer. Its procedures have built up layer upon layer as new changes were tacked on to old processes. That happens in any organisation. In the DSS we have the added problem that aspects of our procedures are often specified in statute, regulation or as the result of judicial rulings. So they come to seem particularly hallowed and unchangeable.

We could not hope to achieve a substantial improvement in efficiency by more pruning and working harder. We had to find ways of working more efficiently, and more streamlined processes to achieve our basic objectives. That is why I asked the Benefits Agency to review the whole process of claiming benefit, from initial contact to payment. The procedures had never before been set out in a systematic, centrally co-ordinated way. So the only people who know all the complexities of how it is done are front line staff delivering the benefit. Their role in analysing, describing and suggesting improvements to the system has been absolutely crucial. A review team has now finished making a 'process map' showing each step of the way in the process of handling a claim for Income Support. They examined which steps are essential and which add to costs, delays and errors.

The process map analysed for the first time how complex the process has become. And the map paves the way for dramatic increases in efficiency [...]

BUILDING SYSTEMS FOR THE FUTURE

The process review indicates that there is scope for a step change in efficiency as we redesign and streamline our processes to deliver our objectives. But it is a mistake to assume we will then achieve a new plateau of maximum efficiency. Evidence of all organisations suggests that processes can continuously be improved. Just as important as achieving a step change is setting in place the structures and incentives to achieve continuous improvement thereafter.

The reason such complex processes as those in handling Income Support had developed was inherent in the way Whitehall has funded operations. Money and resources have been allocated in proportion to work done not results achieved. So more complex processes and making good past mistakes attract increased funding. No business units of a department are rewarded for achieving their given result more efficiently or more accurately.

In future we must pay for results. The DSS already does that in certain circumstances. Funds are matched to what we want delivered by competition, for example, in the contracts set with in-house or external providers in areas like audit or facilities management. In Information Technology we first charged internally for services, then outsourced delivery, and have recently contracted for a new system through the Private Finance Initiative.

The ultimate objective is to pay the right benefit, to the right person on time, every time. A precondition is to separate the two roles of purchaser and provider. The people who specify contracts and monitor performance need to be distinct from the people who deliver the result. That should be the norm throughout the department, not just when a service is outsourced, but also where it is delivered in-house.

Separating purchaser from provider will bring three benefits:

First, and most important, it will enable us to motivate, reward and develop the full potential of our staff. They know the business. They are keen to do it better. They can improve it, if they have proper opportunities and incentives.

Second, it will enable us to draw on outside expertise if and when appropriate. And to experiment with different ways of involving the private sector.

Third, it will make it possible to draw on outside capital, as we do through PFI, for example in the development of the benefit payment card.

From April 1997, all Agencies will re-organise to separate purchasers from providers and will manage both front-line and support services through Service Level Agreements.

EFFECT ON STAFF

Greater productivity will mean fewer staff posts. But, as I stressed when I launched the Change Programme, a 25% increase in efficiency does not translate into a 25% decrease in the numbers of staff. And we must do all we can to accommodate change by natural staff turnover and redeployment. The Change Programme is ambitious. Nothing will happen overnight, but we are on track to be able to make continuing efficiencies in years to come. The Department of Social Security will remain a very large employer.

CONCLUSION

Within the more flexible framework I have described changes will be judged by two criteria.

- First, it is essential to maintain the ethos of public service and to maintain standards.
- Second, it is essential to achieve value for money.

I do believe they are mutually compatible.

From: Lilley, P. 'Efficiency improvements on target', Speech to DSS Managers, 17 July 1996.

Document 7
PRIVATISING THE DELIVERY OF BENEFITS

Peter Lilley, Secretary of State for Social Security, today announced further private sector involvement in the Department's drive to improve the delivery of benefits.

In answer to a parliamentary question from Mrs Marion Roe (Broxbourne), Mr Lilley said:

'In February, I launched the Change Programme to achieve a step change in the effectiveness of the Department of Social Security and all its Agencies. It will involve streamlining benefit processes, introducing new information technology and greater involvement of the private sector.

'I have today approved three initiatives involving greater collaboration with the private sector as the next stage of the Department's drive to review and improve the delivery of social security.

'The first initiative will involve an invitation to the private sector to submit proposals for taking over the operation of the Child Benefit Centre in Washington, Tyne and Wear. This will involve the administration of Child Benefit, One Parent Benefit and Guardian's Allowance. The intention is that staff working in these areas will be taken on by the appointed contractor.

'The second initiative will involve three private companies – or consortia – appointed following open competition to work in conjunction with the Benefits Agency in running benefit delivery in three of its thirteen areas (Yorkshire, West Country and East London & Anglia Area Directorates) for twelve months.

'All three companies will assist the Benefits Agency with the development of new business processes and information technology. They will be invited during the twelve month period to submit proposals for any elements of the Agency's business which could be run differently, including the possibility of further parts of the operation being run by the private sector.

'The third initiative is to launch the procurement process for an Information Systems/Information Technology strategy to enable greater sharing of data between benefit systems, working closely with the private sector to provide the most up to date technologies, expertise and funding.

'These initiatives are designed to improve the administration of the benefit system. They will not change any individual's benefit entitlement.'

From: DSS press release 'Peter Lilley announces new initiative under the Change Programme', 19 July 1996.

Document 8
THE SOCIAL SECURITY ADVISORY COMMITTEE ON
PRIVATE PROVISION

6.1   In the fields of incapacity, disability and unemployment, we see little scope for developing private provision to an extent which would impact on state benefits. There clearly is a market for private insurance in these fields and it will doubtless continue to develop, as it has done in recent years, to meet new needs. However, we believe that the state should remain the major provider of benefits for long-term sickness, disability and unemployment. The universal coverage of the state scheme is its great virtue and is essential for the protection of the most vulnerable who might find private cover difficult to afford or even to obtain, if they represented a high risk.

6.2   In the future, mortgage interest insurance may assume greater importance. Already, homeowners with mortgages exceeding £125,000 need to con- sider insuring any excess because housing costs payable with income support are in most cases limited to the interest on £125,000 mortgages. At present, the coverage of such insurance is limited and existing borrow- ers may find difficulty taking out such insurance. But, given the development of suitable packages – perhaps with mortgagors themselves taking out insurance to spread the risk rather wider – this is an area where greater reliance on the private sector might be possible in years to come.

6.3   With regard to pensions, we are at a turning-point in the development of retirement income. Private provision is continuing to grow but the intrica- cies of the pensions industry are such that the individual needs to consider very carefully how best to invest to provide for an income in retirement.

6.4   Our principal concern is for those who are most vulnerable – the low paid (especially women), the long-term unemployed, those with interrupted work patterns and sick and disabled people – who cannot benefit from the expansion in private and occupational pensions. But this is not our only concern. The contributory state pension is an inter-generational contract, under which current earners pay for the pensions of those who have retired, in return for the contributions they had previously paid for the pensions of earlier generations. We regard this as a fundamental commit- ment on the part of the whole community. This does not preclude the possibility of future changes in a number of possible directions. Options have been suggested from many different sources across the political spectrum. We would need to consider these very carefully before making any recommendations and we reserve the right to return to this matter in due course. For the present however, we advise that there will be a contin- uing need for state provision for an adequate income during retirement for a significant minority of vulnerable people and that the contributory prin- ciple of the state pension scheme should be retained.

From: SSAC *State Benefits and Private Provision*, Benefits Agency Publishing Services Ltd., Leeds (1994) pp. 21–2.

Document 9
CPAG's AGENDA FOR SOCIAL SECURITY

This discussion document has highlighted the need to reform the social security system in order to meet modern challenges facing our society in the late 20th century. We have examined various models which could be adopted and have assessed each model against a range of criteria which CPAG believes to be fundamental to the aims of any modern social security system. In so doing, we have highlighted the difficulties of meeting competing and sometimes contradictory goals. The value of fundamental reform of social security lies in its ability to meet as many of the criteria set out as possible. This will not be achievable in a short space of time – the changes that have occurred in the 50 years since the Beveridge Report cannot be addressed in one parliament. However, policy reform could begin immediately, led by an overarching vision of what we want the social security system to provide.

For over 30 years CPAG has called for action to reverse trends in poverty and inequality. Our proposals for action are based on a framework of principles which underpin the criteria which have been set out. We recognise the importance of preventing poverty. To alleviate poverty is only second best. What society needs are policies which prevent poverty, rather than stop-gap measures which merely compensate and redistribute resources once it has struck. We view poverty not only as material deprivation but also as the denial of opportunities and the chance to participate fully in society. Changes in our families and our working lives are likely to continue. At times of such insecurity the value of a social security system in which everyone has a stake is ever more significant.

CPAG has always recognised that social security policies need to be part of a package of complementary measures including economic, labour market, welfare and fiscal policies. The interaction of social security with other policies should be addressed; a modern welfare state must strike the right balance between work and welfare strategies.

Turning broad overarching policy into practice is not the job of organisations such as CPAG, but our proposals for change offer some suggested ways forward. They are broadly in line with the 'family and work' model outlined above. Among other options, CPAG supports:

- Moves away from means-tested benefits towards a modern social insurance system which is more inclusive in offering cover to low-paid workers and those who are in unstable employment.
- A national minimum wage.
- A fairer tax structure, more closely related to ability to pay.
- Greater individualisation in the payment of non-means-tested benefits.
- Increases in benefits to an adequate level and their annual uprating in line with earnings or the retail price index, whatever is greater.
- The development of a national childcare strategy, involving investment in the supply of services.
- Equal maternity rights for all women, regardless of length of employment.

The social security system is clearly in need of reform. Failure to address the changes which have taken place in society and to redress the growing inequality in the distribution of resources is already impinging on the lives of many families – however, we choose to define them. In a world of change, striving to provide a secure future for all is perhaps society's most important goal.

From: Harker, L. *A Secure Future? Social Security and the Family in a Changing World*, Child Poverty Action Group Ltd., London (1996) pp. 41–2.

Document 10
SOCIAL SERVICES AND SOCIAL WORK

Local authorities are agents of law. More than thirty Acts of Parliament confer powers and duties on them to provide personal social services administered by SSDs. This is an untidy legal legacy which takes complexity to the point of strangulation. For social workers to act outside their powers is illegal, while to fail in their duties is liable to put them in peril of a public inquiry, an Ombudsman investigation for maladministration or a prosecution. Yet within the context of SSDs and the probation service, discretionary social work is also practised, notably the probation officers' role in counselling and conciliation in divorce proceedings, and SSDs' involvement in preventive and rehabilitation work. The exercise of legal duties and discretionary powers leaves social work in an equivocal position.

The main categories or client groups who are deemed in law to require service or protection are an historical legacy derived from the Poor Law (abolished in 1948) and from medical and penal services. They are vulnerable or dependent people because of age or condition, or deviants from the accepted norms of society, but assessed as likely to benefit from support, counselling and core or benign social control. One view is that those whose welfare needs were long term and peripheral to a medical and largely hospital model were of low priority, and the obligation to care and protect ranked below that of caring and curing.[1] A social model was gradually evolving which recognized that humans have a social entity, and throughout their lives live in social relationships. Social work and the personal social services required their own identity if they were to be effective in promoting social functioning at times when people were beset with difficulties and impediments. For effective intervention, as social work increasingly moves from an institutional to a community base, the inherited categorical and distinctive client group approach becomes stigmatizing, restrictive and outmoded. Social work is needed by newly emerging groups in response to social change. Yet it is on the horns of a dilemma. Its intervention through offering care, support and practical assistance commands public approval and sympathy for handicapped people of all ages. These are the deserving. This is an unsophisticated view, for given adequate support and technical aids, increasing numbers of handicapped people demonstrate their independent social functioning and rightfully resent being labelled. With elderly people intervention is designed to protect, to promote capacity and maintain independence for as long as practicable and this intervention wins social approval. Intervention is more ambiguous and is viewed more controversially when protection requires a measure of control under the legal powers and duties vested in local authorities but exercised by social workers. The law may be invoked to protect children from mental, physical or sexual abuse by adults. Social workers, including probation officers who are themselves qualified social workers, intervene in and out of court to protect adolescents from unnecessary custody. Recent legislation requires specially approved social workers who have had additional training to intervene in mental illness crises to prevent self-damage or avoid danger to others, and to ensure that community resources are explored before compulsory hospital admission is imposed. Very occasionally, social workers intervene to seek the removal of an elderly person living in unsafe or neglectful circumstances. This continuum of care and control, necessary because any society needs a social defence system, makes social work a very public activity and vulnerable to public scrutiny.

1 Pinker, R.A. *Research Priorities in the Personal Social Services.* Social Science Research Council, London (1978) p. 21.

From: Cooper, J. 'The future of social work: a pragmatic view' in M. Loney *et al.* (eds) *The State or the Market*, Sage Publications, London (1991) pp. 59–60.

Document 11
GRIFFITHS REPORT ON PUBLIC FINANCE FOR RESIDENTIAL
AND NURSING HOME CARE

6.39 I recommend that public finance for people who require either residential home care or non-acute nursing home care, whether that care is provided by the public sector or by private or voluntary organisations, should be provided in the same way. Public finance should only be provided following separate assessments of the financial means of the applicant (using a means test consistent with that for income support) and of the need for care. These assessments should be managed through social services authorities as follows.

6.40 The social services authority should establish a system, including arrangements for consultation when necessary with others, for enabling it to decide whether residential care (including what is now the care provided in non-acute nursing homes) is the most appropriate way of meeting care needs, in the light of the other options available. Depending on the individual's circumstances, consultation might include private or voluntary carers including informal carers, and health carers, as well, of course, as the person directly affected. The social services authority would take the final decision. In doing so, it would take into account all the information available from its own sources, and assessments of the individual's health care needs provided through the health authority and the relevant GP.

6.41 In some urgent cases decisions to provide residential care may have to be taken and implemented without full consultation. In those circumstances consultation should be arranged as soon as possible thereafter.

6.42 As part of the assessment process, the social security system should contribute an assessment of the financial means of the applicant, leading to a decision about whether there is an entitlement to an income related social security benefit (described hereafter as 'residential allowance'). The rate of residential allowance should be set in the light of the average total of income support and housing benefit to which someone living other than in residential care would be entitled. It would be for the social services authority to pay the balance of costs, if it concluded that residential care was the most appropriate way of meeting the individual's care needs.

6.43 When the financial assessment showed that there was no entitlement to the income related residential allowance, the information collected should enable the social services authority to decide how much of the total cost of the residential care should be charged to the individual.

6.44 Some people may seek residential care even though the social services authority cannot agree that their care needs justify such care. In those circumstances there should continue to be entitlement to the residential allowance, but no financial support should be given by social services authorities.

6.45 A decision is required about which social services authority should be responsible for financing care for an individual who moves between one authority's area and another's. I recommend that financial responsibility should be based on the individual's "ordinary residence". This is consistent with current social services legislation.

6.46   If the recommendations are accepted, transfer of resources between social security and specific grant for social services authorities will be needed to take account of the changed responsibilities. Equally a transfer in the opposite direction will be necessary to take account of the fact that residents of local authority provided residential care (commonly known as Part III) will be supported on the same basis as those in private and voluntary homes. The net effect will depend on the rate at which the social security residential allowance is set and will call for detailed assessment. 'Public Support for Residential Care' (the report of a Joint Central and Local Government Working Party) provided useful illustrative calculations.

6.47   The pace of this transfer will depend on decisions about continuing support for existing residents both of private and voluntary homes and of Part III accommodation. It is important that the implementation of the changes proposed and the transfer of resources between agencies does not adversely affect the delivery of care to such individuals. Two approaches are possible: preservation of existing financial entitlements from the current funding agencies or preservation of the right to the existing form of care, but with responsibility for its management located clearly with the social services authority. If the latter is chosen, then a targeted specific grant, of the kind I recommended in paragraph 6.31, would be necessary to smooth the transition of responsibilities between the social security system and social services authorities, because of the wide variation between areas in the number of such recipients.

From: Griffiths, R. (Sir) *Community Care: Agenda for Action*, HMSO, London (1988) pp. 19–20.

Document 12
NEW LABOUR'S POLICY FOR SOCIAL SERVICES

Labour's social services policy offers such a new approach. It is based on four key points.

Firstly, Labour's social services policy will operate in a new environment where a nationally-led anti-poverty strategy will seek to tackle the unemployment, deprivation and sheer lack of hope that have come to dominate too many local communities in our country. Social services have been on the frontline of the social and economic changes that have confronted Britain during the last two decades. People using social services tend to have become ever more dependent so making the job of social workers ever more difficult. Perhaps that is not surprising. Since 1979 unemployment and crime have doubled. Child poverty has trebled. The poorest people in our society have seen their real incomes fall. Our country is now more divided than at any point this century.

SSDs have all too often picked up the tab for social division and economic failure. This situation cannot go on. Here I do share something with the inevitability merchants. Our country will cease to be able to afford its key public services if our economy is not modernised and our society is not re-united. Without the realisation of Tony Blair's vision of a stakeholder society in which young people feel hope again, our country's caring services will simply be overwhelmed.

Central government has to give a lead to make stakeholding a reality. We need a government that shares the public sector values of SSDs. One that will take responsibility and not shelve it. So that SSDs do not operate alone but in a context where there is a new national effort to improve opportunity, spread prosperity and strengthen community.

Labour's plans to tackle youth and long term unemployment, to end poverty pay through a national minimum wage, to provide people with incentives to work rather than living on welfare and to start building homes again will offer a fresh start for Britain. We will tackle dependency and offer routes to independence by making people stakeholders in the economy and society of our country. In the process our plans will relieve the pressures on our hard-pressed public services, including social services. They will allow SSDs to reclaim some of their heritage of family support rather than their current role as pure family crisis agencies.

Labour's stakeholding approach will also allow care service users to help shape services and offer better support to Britain's seven million strong army of carers. We should never forget that without their participation the whole edifice of care in this country would simply crumble.

Secondly, Labour will be seeking a new partnership with SSDs as planners and deliverers of care, not based on major new additional legislative burdens, but instead built on agreed and enforced national standards.

One of the very real tragedies in community care is the enormous geographical variation in service policies, service standards and service availability. After all if central government simply passes the buck to health authorities to determine eligibility criteria for continuing care it should be no surprise to find that services in Durham end up quite different from those in Dorset. Ministers of course say that local flexibility has to have priority because local needs differ so markedly from place to place. But an elderly person needing rehabilitation services in Durham has needs no different to an elderly resident in Dorset.

Unfortunately, the care you get and indeed the price you pay now depends on where you live. Such a lottery should have no part to play in a civilised system of community care. That is why Labour supports the Health Select Committee's call for a nationally set framework which specifies the eligibility criteria for long term care to define what the NHS as a national service will always provide. We will also seek in agreement with patients, providers and statutory bodies to give national clarity to local charging policies for special services [...]

Labour's approach to social services springs from our belief that care policies should encourage and support independence, be flexible enough to meet changing needs, optimise the use of scarce resources, give people more control over their own lives and provide access on an equitable basis regardless of which part of the country a person lives. For our caring services to succeed they need to be delivered as part of an overall community strategy designed to provide a continuum of housing, health and social services.

That will require new national standards. It will require new forms of co-operation both nationally and locally. It will require the realisation of our stakeholding vision. It will require in short a new approach to new challenges in a new era. Above all else it will require a new government. I look forward to working with you in the months and years ahead.

From: Milburn, A. 'Labour's policy for Social Services', Speech to the Silver Jubilee Seminar, Association of Directors of Social Services, 6 February 1996, pp. 8–11, 15–16.

Document 13
DIRECT PAYMENTS

'Direct payments will bring more choice and control for disabled people', says Minister.

New legislation allowing local authorities to give people cash payments to enable them to make their own arrangements for their community care services today received Royal Assent.

John Bowis, Health Minister responsible for community care, said:

'This legislation opens up fresh opportunities for disabled people. Direct payments will bring them more choice and control. It is a major development in community care and one which has been long sought by disabled people. I am grateful for the support the Government received from a wide range of groups during the passage of the bill.

'In preparing this legislation, we have placed great importance on the views of people who will benefit from direct payments. Community care is designed to increase the choice available to service recipients and to ensure that services are more closely tailored to individuals' needs. This scheme will develop these principles further'.

Payments will be an alternative to services arranged by local authorities. As direct payments are a new concept in community care, it is intended to introduce the policy in phases with the first groups to be physically and learning disabled adults under 65. Once direct payments have been available for a year, the Government will look at the scope for extending payments to other groups.

NOTES TO EDITORS

1. The Community Care (Direct Payments) Bill will allow local authorities to give people cash payments as an alternative to community care services directly arranged by local authorities. The Bill was introduced in the House of Lords on 17 November 1995.

2. All disabled people under 65 will be eligible to receive direct payments (and people who begin to receive direct payments before the age of 65 will be able to continue to do so afterwards) although it is the local authority's decision whether or not direct payments are appropriate in each individual case. After the first year of implementation the Government aims to consider whether there is a case for extending the scheme to include the elderly, a much larger group. Around half the authorities who responded to consultation on the bill said they wanted eligibility to be restricted.

3. The powers contained in the Act will be permissive – authorities themselves will need to decide whether to take advantage of it. Direct payments will be an alternative to community care service, where authorities assess a need for them. There will be no overlap with social security benefits.

4. No implementation date has yet been set for the Act; regulations need to be laid out and guidance issued before the Act is brought into force.

From: Department of Health press release 'Community Care (Direct Payments) Bill receives Royal Assent', 4 July 1996.

BIBLIOGRAPHY

Abel-Smith, B. and Townsend, P. (1965) *The Poor and the Poorest*, Occasional Papers in Social Administration, No. 17, London: G. Bell and Sons Ltd.

Adams, R. (1996) *The Personal Social Services: clients, consumers or citizens*, London: Longman.

Addison, P. (1975) *The Road to 1945*, London: Jonathan Cape.

Alaszewski, A. (1988) 'From villains to victims' in A. Leighton (ed.), *Mental Handicap in the Community*, London: Woodhead-Faulkener.

Alcock, P. (1993) *Understanding Poverty*, London: Macmillan.

Alcock, P., Craig, G., Dalgleish, K. and Pearson, S. (1995) *Combating Local Poverty: summary*, London: Local Government Management Board.

Alcock, P. and Vaux, G. (in press) 'Reconciling cash and care: home care charges and benefit checks in social services', *British Journal of Social Work*.

Aldgate, J. and Tunstill, J. (1994) *Implementing Section 17 of the Children Act – The First 18 Months: a study for the Department of Health*, Leicester: Leicester University.

Aldridge, J. and Becker, S. (1993) *Children Who Care: inside the world of young carers*, Loughborough: Loughborough University.

Aldridge, J. and Becker, S. (1996) 'Disability rights and the denial of young carers: the dangers of zero-sum arguments', *Critical Social Policy*, 16, 3, pp. 55–76.

Allsop, J. (1995) *Health Policy and the NHS: towards 2000*, London: Longman.

Alston, J. and Dean, K. (1972) 'Socioeconomic factors associated with attitudes towards welfare recipients and the causes of poverty', *Social Service Review*, 46, pp. 13–23.

Andrews, K. and Jacobs, J. (1990) *Punishing the Poor: poverty under Thatcher*, London: Macmillan.

Arshey, H. (1996) 'Missed target', *Community Care*, 28 March, pp. 24–6.

Ashley, P. (1983) *The Money Problems of the Poor*, London: Heinemann.

Association of County Councils news release (1994a) 'Funding fears for social services', 2 November.

Association of County Councils news release (1994b) 'ACC presses for action over community care underfunding', 21 November.

Association of Metropolitan Authorities (AMA) (1985) *Caring for Unemployed People: a study of the impact of unemployment on demands for personal social services*, London: Bedford Square Press/National Council of Voluntary Organisations.

Association of Metropolitan Authorities (1992) *Social Services Charging Policies: results of the Association of Metropolitan Authorities/Association of County Councils/Association of Directors of Social Services survey of charging practices in social services departments between 1990 and 1992*, London: AMA.

Association of Metropolitan Authorities (1995) 'Direct payments to people with disabilities', Social Services Committee Item, 10 February.

Association of Metropolitan Authorities/Association of County Councils/ Confederation of Scottish Local Authorities (1988) *Social Fund – Practice Guide and Position Statement*, London: AMA.

Association of Metropolitan Authorities/Local Government Information Unit (LGIU) (1991) *Too High a Price? examining the costs of charging policies in local government*, London: LGIU/AMA.

Association of Metropolitan Authorities/Local Government Information Unit (1994) *Commentary on Social Services Inspectorate Advice Note on Discretionary Charges for Non-Residential Adult Social Services*, London: AMA.

ATD Fourth World (1996) *Talk with Us, Not At Us: how to develop partnerships between families in poverty and professionals*, London: ATD Fourth World.

Audit Commission (1986) *Making a Reality of Community Care*, London: HMSO.

Audit Commission (1992a) *Community Care: managing the cascade of change*, London: HMSO.

Audit Commission (1992b) *Homeward Bound: a new course for community health*, London: HMSO.

Audit Commission (1992c) *The Community Revolution*, London: HMSO.

Audit Commission (1996) *Balancing the Care Equation*, London: HMSO.

Bailey, R. and Brake, M. (eds) (1975) *Radical Social Work*, London: Edward Arnold.

Baldock, J. (1994) 'The personal social services: the politics of care', in V. George and S. Miller (eds) *Social Policy Towards 2000: squaring the welfare circle*, London: Routledge, pp. 161–89.

Baldwin, N. and Spencer, N. (1993) 'Deprivation and child abuse: implications for strategic planning in children's services', *Children and Society*, 7, 4, pp. 357–75.

Baldwin, N. and Twigg, J. (1991) 'Women and community care – reflections on a debate', in M. Maclean and D. Groves (eds), *Women's Issues in Social Policy*, London: Routledge, pp. 117–35.

Baldwin, S. and Lunt, N. (1996) *Charging Ahead: the development of local authority charging policies for community care*, Bristol: Policy Press.

Balloch, S. and Jones, B. (1990) *Poverty and Anti-Poverty Strategy: the local government response*, London: Association of Metropolitan Authorities.

Bamford, T. (1990) *The Future of Social Work*, London: Macmillan.

Bank-Mikklesen, N. (1980) 'Denmark', in R. J. Flynn and K. E. Nitsch (eds), *Normalization, Social Integration and Community Services*, New York: University Park Press.

Barclay, P. (1982) *Social Workers: their roles and tasks*, London: NISW/Bedford Square Press.

Barclay, P. (1995) *Income and Wealth*, vol. 1 (Joseph Rowntree Inquiry), York: Joseph Rowntree Foundation.

Barnes, C. (1992) 'Discrimination, disability benefits and the 1980s', *Benefits*, 3, pp. 3–7.

Barnes, H. (1995) 'Harry Barnes explains why MPs should back his bill', *New Statesman and Society*, 10 February, p. 26.

Barr, N. and Coulter, F. (1990) 'Social security: solution or problem?', in

J. Hills (ed.), *The State of Welfare: the welfare state in Britain since 1974*, Oxford: Clarendon Press.

Bartley, M., Blane, D. and Davey Smith, G. (1996) 'Poverty, inequality and health', *Benefits*, 17, pp. 2–4.

Bean, P. (1980) *Mental Illness: changes and trends*, Chichester: J. Wiley and Sons.

Bebbington, A. and Miles, J. (1989) 'The background of children who enter local authority care', *British Journal of Social Work*, 19, 5, pp. 349–68.

Becker, S. (1987) 'Social workers' attitudes towards poverty and the poor', unpublished PhD thesis, Nottingham University.

Becker, S. (1988) 'Poverty awareness' in S. Becker and S. MacPherson (eds), *Public Issues Private Pain: poverty, social work and social policy*, London: Insight/Carematters Books, pp. 242–50.

Becker, S. (1989a) 'Poor women', *Community Care*, 12 January, pp. 14–16.

Becker, S. (1989b) 'Keeping a poor woman down', *Community Care*, 19 January, pp. 23–5.

Becker, S. (1990) 'The sting in the tail', *Community Care*, 12 April, pp. 22–4.

Becker, S. (ed.) (1991) *Windows of Opportunity: public policy and the poor*, London: Child Poverty Action Group Ltd.

Becker, S. (1992) 'Personal social services', in P. Catterall (ed.), *Contemporary Britain: an annual review 1992*, Oxford: Blackwell/Institute of Contemporary British History, pp. 313–22.

Becker, S. (1993) 'Personal social services', in P. Catterall (ed.), *Contemporary Britain: an annual review 1993*, Oxford: Blackwell/Institute of Contemporary British History, pp. 341–56.

Becker, S. and Bennett, F. (1991) 'Conclusions: a new agenda', in S. Becker (ed.), *Windows of Opportunity: public policy and the poor*, London: Child Poverty Action Group Ltd, pp. 103–16.

Becker, S. and MacPherson, S. (1985a) 'Scroungerphobia – where do we stand?', *Social Work Today*, 18 February, pp. 15–17.

Becker, S and MacPherson, S. (1985b) 'Cash counsel: the art of the possible', *Social Work Today*, 25 February, pp. 16–18.

Becker, S. and MacPherson, S. (1986) *Poor Clients: the extent and nature of financial poverty amongst consumers of social work services*, Nottingham University: Benefits Research Unit.

Becker, S. and MacPherson, S. (eds) (1988) *Public Issues Private Pain: poverty, social work and social policy*, London: Insight/Carematters Books.

Becker, S. and Silburn, R. (1989) 'Back to the future: the process of considered decision-making', in G. Craig (ed.), *Your Flexible Friend: voluntary organisations, claimants and the social fund*, London: Social Security Consortium/Association of Metropolitan Authorities, pp. 24–40.

Becker, S. and Silburn, R. (1990) *The New Poor Clients: social work, poverty and the social fund*, Sutton: Community Care/Reed Business Publishing.

Bell, M., Butler, E., Marsland, D. and Pirie, M. (1994) *The End of the Welfare State*, London: Adam Smith Institute.

Benefits Agency (1994) *The Benefits Agency's Fight against Fraud 1993/94*, Leeds: Benefits Agency.

Benefits Agency (1995) 'Crackdown on benefit fraud achieves record savings', *Fraud Bulletin*, 10 July .

Benefits Agency/Employment Service (1995) *Benefits Review (Income Support and Unemployment Benefit) Report on Methodology and Findings*, Leeds: Benefits Agency.

Bennett, F. (1995) *Security at Risk*, London: NACAB.

Bennett, F. (1996) 'Private insurance – who pays the price?', *Poverty*, 93, pp. 10–12.

Benyon, J. (1994) *Law and Order Review 1993: an audit of crime, policing and criminal justice issues*, Centre for the Study of Public Order, Leicester: University of Leicester.

Benzeval, M., Judge, K. and Whitehead, M. (eds) (1995) *Tackling Inequalities in Health: an agenda for action*, London: King's Fund.

Beresford, P. (1994) 'Poverty alleviation and reduction: DPI elaborate paper for the World Summit on Social Development', mimeo.

Beresford, P., Chemins, J. and Tunstill, J. (1987) *In Care in North Battersea*, Surrey: University of Surrey, Guildford.

Beresford, P. and Croft, S. (1986) *Whose Welfare – private care or public services?*, Brighton: Lewis Cohen Urban Studies.

Beresford, P. and Croft, S. (1995) 'Time for a new approach to anti-poverty campaigning', *Poverty*, 90, pp. 12–15.

Beresford, P. and Green, D. (1996) 'Income and wealth – an opportunity to reassess the UK poverty debate', *Critical Social Policy*, 16, 1, pp. 95–109.

Berthoud, R., Benson, S. and Williams, S. (1986) *Standing Up for Claimants*, London: Policy Studies Institute.

Beveridge, W. (1942) *Social Insurance and Allied Services*, Cmnd. 6404, London: HMSO.

Beveridge, W. (1948) *Voluntary Action: a report on methods of social advance*, London: Allen and Unwin.

Black, Sir D. (1980) *Inequalities in Health: report of a research working group*, London: DHSS.

Blair, T. (1995) *Speech to the Annual Trades Union Congress*, Brighton, 12 September.

Blau, P. (1974) *On the Nature of Organisation*, New York: John Wiley and Sons.

Blom-Cooper, L. (chair) (1985) *A Child in Trust: the report of the panel of inquiry into the circumstances surrounding the death of Jasmine Beckford*, London Borough of Brent: Kingswood Press.

Blunn, C. and Small, M. (1984) 'Mental handicap', *Community Care*, 16 February, pp. 18–20.

Bolger, S., Corrigan, P., Docking, J. and Frost, N. (1981) *Towards Socialist Welfare Work*, London: Macmillan.

Bond, H. (1996) 'State of independence', *Community Care*, 4–10 April, pp. 20–21.

Bottomley, V. (1992) Speech to the social services conference, Isle of Wight, 2 October.

Bradshaw, J. (1990) *Child Poverty and Deprivation in the UK*, London: National Children's Bureau.

Bradshaw, J. (1993) *Household Budgets and Living Standards*, York: Joseph Rowntree Foundation.

Bradshaw, J. and Gibbs, I. (1988) *Public Support for Private Residential Care*, Aldershot: Avebury.

Bradshaw, J. and Lynes, T. (1995) *Benefit Uprating Policy and Living Standards*, York University: Social Policy Research Unit.

Bradshaw, J. and Millar, J. (1991) *Lone Parent Families in the UK*, London: HMSO.

Brake, M. and Bailey, R. (eds) (1980) *Radical Social Work and Practice*, London: Edward Arnold.

Bransbury, L. (1995) 'The legal framework', in NISW/LGAPU *Charging for Social Care*, London: NISW/LGAPU, pp. 49- 52.

Breakwell, G. M., Collie, A., Harrison, B. and Propper, C. (1984) 'Attitudes towards the unemployed: the effects of threatened identity', *British Journal of Social Policy*, 23, 1, pp. 87–8.

Brewer, C. and Lait, J. (1980) *Can Social Work Survive?*, London: Temple Smith.

Bridge Child Care Consultancy (1995) *Paul: death through neglect*, London: The Bridge Child Care Consultancy.

Brisdenen, S. (1986) 'Independent living and the medical model of disability', *Disability, Handicap and Society*, 1, 2, pp. 173–8.

Brown, H. and Smith, H. (eds) (1992) *Normalisation: a reader for the nineties*, London: Routledge.

Brown, M. and Madge, N. (1982) *Despite the Welfare State*, London: Heinemann.

Brown, M. and Payne, S. (1990) *Introduction to Social Administration in Britain*, London: Unwin Hyman.

Brown, P., Hadley, R. and White, K. J. (1982) 'A case for neighbourhood-based social work and social services', in P. Barclay (ed.) *Social Workers: their roles and tasks*, London: Bedford Square Press, pp. 219–35.

Bryson, A. and Marsh, A. (1996) *Leaving Family Credit*, London: HMSO.

Bull, D. (1982) *Welfare Advocacy: whose means to what ends?*, Sheila Kay Memorial Lecture, Birmingham: BASW.

Bull, D. and Wilding, P. (eds) (1983) *Thatcherism and the Poor*, London: Child Poverty Action Group.

Bulmer, M. (1986), *Neighbours: the work of Philip Abrams*, Cambridge: Cambridge University Press.

Bulmer, M., Lewis, J. and Piachaud, D. (eds) (1989) *The Goals of Social Policy*, London: Unwin Hyman.

Burns, D., Hambleton, R. and Hoggett, P. (1994) *The Politics of Decentralisation – revitalising local democracy*, London: Macmillan.

Butcher, T. (1995) *Delivering Welfare: the governance of the social services in the 1990s*, Milton Keynes: Open University Press.

Butterworth, E. and Holman, R. (eds) (1975) *Social Welfare in Modern Britain*, London: Fontana.

Bynoe, I. (1991) 'The case for anti-discriminatory legislation', in I. Bynoe, M. Oliver and C. Barnes (eds), *Equal Rights for Disabled People*, London: IPPR.

Camden, London Borough of, (1985) *Camden's Submission to the DHSS on Reform of Social Security*, London: Camden Borough Council.

Carers National Association (CNA) (1992) *Speak Up, Speak Out*, London: CNA.

Caring Costs (1991) *Taking Care, Making Do*, London: Caring Costs/CNA.

Challenge (1992) *A Challenge to Community Care*, London: Challenge.

Chartered Institute of Public Finance and Accountancy (1995) *Community Care Funding Two Years On*, London: CIPFA.

Chetwynd, M., Ritchie, J., Leith, L. and Howard, M. (1996) *The Cost of Care*, Bristol: Policy Press.

Chief Inspector of Social Services (1993) *Raising the Standard: the second annual report of the Chief Inspector, Social Services Inspectorate 1992/93*, London: HMSO.

Chief Inspector of Social Services (1995) *Partners in Caring: the fourth annual report of the Chief Inspector, Social Services Inspectorate 1994/95*, London: HMSO.

Chief Inspector of Social Services (1996) *Progress Through Change: the fifth annual report of the Chief Inspector, Social Services Inspectorate 1995/96*, London: HMSO.

Child Poverty Action Group (CPAG) (1982) Evidence to the Barclay Committee, unpublished.

Church House (1985) *Faith in the City: a call for action by Church and Nation* (Report of the Archbishop of Canterbury's Commission on Urban Priority Areas), London: Church House.

Clapham, D., Monro, M. and Kay, H. (1994) *A Wider Choice: revenue funding mechanisms for housing and community care*, York: Joseph Rowntree Foundation.

Clarke, J. (ed.) (1993) *A Crisis in Care? challenges to social work*, London: Sage.

Clarke, K. (1988) Statement to Parliament on the Future Arrangements for Community Care, Department of Health press release, 12 July.

Clasen, J. (1994a) *Paying the Jobless: a comparison of unemployment benefit policies in Great Britain and Germany*, Aldershot: Avebury.

Clasen, J. (1994b) 'Soziale Sicherung and social security – convergence or divergence?', in B. Dietz, J. Bardelmann, and Schafer, T. (eds), *Soziales Europa? Bedingungen und Perspektiven einer 'Sozialen Integration' Europas*, Giessen: Focus Verlag, pp. 63–76.

Clode, D. (1996) 'The way it is', *Community Care*, 4–10 April, pp. 22–3.

Cloward, R. A. and Piven, F. F. (1979) *Regulating the Poor: the function of public welfare*, London: Tavistock.

Coates, K. and Silburn, R. (1970) *Poverty: The Forgotten Englishmen*, Harmondsworth: Penguin.

Coffield, F., Robinson, P., and Sarsby, J. (1980) *A Cycle of Deprivation? a study of four families*, London: Heinemann.

Cole-Hamilton, I. (1991) 'Poverty makes you sick', *Poverty*, 80, pp. 12–15.

Commission on the Future of the Voluntary Sector (1996) *Meeting the Challenge: voluntary action into the 21st Century*, London: CFVS.

Commission on Social Justice (1994) *Social Justice: strategies for national renewal*, London: Vintage.

Community Care (1992a) 'Charting the swing of the axe', 21 May, pp. 18–19.

Community Care (1992b) 'SSDs did not consult private sector', 18 June, p. 1.

Community Care (1995a) 'Hard times', 26 January, pp. 16–19.

Community Care (1995b) 'Care managers speak out', 30 March, pp. 16–17.

Community Care (1996a) 'Bitter option', 25 April, pp. 18–19.

Community Care (1996b) 'Community care charges up by a quarter says Labour', 16–22 May, p. 1.

Conservative Central Office (1995) *Conservative Party News* (press release), 20 April.

Conservative Way Forward (CWF) (1994) *Social Security: time for a revolution*, London: CWF.

Considine, M. (1978) 'The death and resurrection of conservative ideology: Australian social work in the seventies', *Social Alternatives*, 1, 2, pp. 50–5.

Cooke, F. (1979) *Who Should be Helped?*, New York: Sage.

Cooper, A. and Nye, R. (1995) *The Rowntree Inquiry and 'Trickle Down'*, London: Social Market Foundation.

Cooper, J. (1993) 'The future of social work: a pragmatic view', in M. Loney *et al.* (eds), *The State or the Market*, Milton Keynes: Open University Press, pp. 58–69.

Corden, A. (1983) 'Come and get it', *Community Care*, 20 February.

Corrigan, P. and Leonard, P. (1978) *Social Work Practice Under Capitalism: a Marxist approach*, London: Macmillan.

Coser, L. A. (1965) 'The sociology of poverty', *Social Problems*, 13, pp. 140–8.

Coulshed, V. (1988) *Social Work in Practice*, London: Macmillan.

Cousins, C. (1987) *Controlling Social Welfare*, London: Wheatsheaf.

Craig, G. (1995) 'The Privatisation of Human Misery: reclaiming the facts about poverty', inaugural lecture, University of Humberside, 5 December.

Curno, P. (1978) *Political Issues and Community Work*, London: Routledge and Kegan Paul.

Dahrendorf, R. (1995) *Report on Wealth Creation and Social Cohesion in a Free Society*, London: The Commission on Health Creation and Social Cohesion.

Davis, A. (1991) 'Hazardous lives – social work in the 1980s: a view from the Left', in M. Loney *et al.* (eds), *The State or the Market: politics and welfare in contemporary Britain*, London: Sage. pp. 83–93.

Daily Telegraph (1993) 'Major spells out his vision for Britain', 4 February.

Daily Telegraph (1994a) 'Lilley seeks foreign ideas on benefit cuts', 23 August, p.1.

Daily Telegraph (1994b) 'Blair gives a guarded welcome', 25 October, p. 4.

Daily Telegraph (1995a) 'Lilley defends record over poverty claims', 15 February, p. 23.

Daily Telegraph (1995b) 'The origins of crime', 30 May, p. 18.

Deacon, A. (1978) 'The scrounging controversy: public attitudes towards the unemployed in contemporary Britain', *Social and Economic Administration*, 12, 2, pp. 120–35.

Deacon, A. (1991) 'The retreat from state welfare', in S. Becker (ed.), *Windows of Opportunity: public policy and the poor*, London: Child Poverty Action Group Ltd.

Deacon, A. (1995) 'Spending more to achieve less? Social security since 1945', in D. Gladstone (ed.), *British Social Welfare: past present and future*, London: UCL Press.

Deakin, N. (1993) 'A future for collectivism', in R. Page and J. Baldock (eds) *Social Policy Review 5*, Canterbury: Social Policy Association.

Dean, H. and Taylor-Gooby, P. (1992) *Dependency Culture: the explosion of a myth*, Hemel Hempstead: Harvester Wheatsheaf.

Dearden, C. and Becker, S. (1995) *Young Carers – the facts*, Sutton: Reed Business Publishing.

Dennis, N. (1993) *Rising Crime and the Dismembered Family: how conformist intellectuals have campaigned against common sense*, London: Institute of Economic Affairs.

Dennis, N. and Erdos, G. (1992) *Families Without Fatherhood*, London: Institute of Economic Affairs.

Department of the Environment (1992) *The Functions of Local Authorities in England*, London: HMSO.

Department of Health (1989) *Caring for People: community care in the next decade and beyond*, Cmnd 849, London: HMSO.

Department of Health (1990) *Community Care in the Next Decade and Beyond: policy guidance*, London: HMSO.

Department of Health (1992a) *Implementing Caring for People*, Circular, 11 March.
Department of Health (1992b) *Implementing Caring for People*, Circular, 25 September.
Department of Health (1993) *Community Care: liaison between the Benefits Agency and social services departments*, Local Authority Social Services Letter [LASSL (93) 8], March.
Department of Health (1994a) *A Wider Strategy for Research and Development Relating to the Personal Social Services*, London: HMSO.
Department of Health (1994b) *Implementing Community Care: housing and homelessness*, London: HMSO.
Department of Health (1995a) *Child Protection: messages from research*, London: HMSO.
Department of Health (1995b) *Community Care: detailed statistics on personal social services for adults, England 1994*, London: DoH.
Department of Health (1995c) *Local Authority Social Services Statistics: staff of local authority social services departments at 30 September 1994, England*, London: DoH.
Department of Health (1995d) *Personal Social Services: residential accommodation in England 1995, statistical bulletin 1995/21*, London: DoH.
Department of Health (1995e) *Social Services: maintaining standards in a changing world: an introduction for elected members and chief officers of local authorities*, London: HMSO.
Department of Health (1996a) *Community Care Statistics, 1995, Personal Social Services: day and domiciliary services for adults*, London: DoH.
Department of Health (1996b) *A New Partnership for Care in Old Age*, London: HMSO.
Department of Health press release (1992) 'Virginia Bottomley announces government support for community care', 2 October.
Department of Health press release (1995a) 'Minister responds to ADSS survey of social services budgets', 16 March.
Department of Health press release (1995b) 'Stronger partnership between NHS and social services offers benefits to patients, says Gerald Malone', 27 April.
Department of Health press release (1995c) 'John Bowis launches child abuse research. Closer working with families needed', 21 June.
Department of Health press release (1995d) 'Stephen Dorrell welcomes Direct Payments Bill', 17 November.
Department of Health press release (1996a) 'Prime Minister announces review of children's homes', 13 June.
Department of Health press release (1996b) 'Community Care (Direct Payments) Bill receives Royal Assent', 4 July.
Department of Health and Social Security (DHSS) (1971) *Government Report to Establish a Framework for Developing Better Services for Vulnerable Groups*, London: HMSO.
Department of Health and Social Security (1975) *Better Services for the Mentally Ill*, Cmnd. 6233, London: HMSO.
Department of Health and Social Security (1979) *Report of the Committee of Inquiry into Mental Handicap Nursing and Care (The Jay Report)*, Cmnd 7468, London: HMSO.
Department of Health and Social Security (1981) *Care in Action*, London: DHSS.

Department of Health and Social Security (1985a) *Reform of Social Security*, vol. 1, London: HMSO.

Department of Health and Social Security (1985b) *Reform of Supplementary Benefit – Background Papers vol. 3*, Cmnd 9519, London: HMSO.

Department Of Health and Social Security (1985c) *Reform of Social Security* (White Paper), Cmnd 9691, London: HMSO.

Departments of Health and Social Security press release (1995) 'Long-term care – capital allowance doubled', 28 November.

Department of Social Security (1989) *Annual Report by the Secretary of State for Social Security on the Social Fund 1988–1989*, London: HMSO.

Department of Social Security (1992) *Social Security: the government's expenditure plans 1992–93 to 1994–95*, London: HMSO.

Department of Social Security (1993a) *The Growth of Social Security*, London: HMSO.

Department of Social Security (1993b) *Containing the Costs of Social Security: the international context*, London: HMSO.

Department of Social Security (1994) *The Government's Expenditure Plans 1994–95 to 1996–97*, London: HMSO.

Department of Social Security (1995a) *Income-Related Benefits: estimates of take up in 1992*, London: HMSO.

Department of Social Security (1995b) *Households Below Average Income – a statistical analysis 1979–1992/93*, London: HMSO.

Department of Social Security (1995c) *Social Security Departmental Report: The Government's Expenditure Plans 1995–96 to 1997–98*, London: HMSO.

Department of Social Security (1995d) *Personal Pensions Statistics 1993/94*, London: HMSO.

Department of Social Security (1995e) *Income-Related Benefits: estimates of take up in 1993/94*, London: HMSO.

Department of Social Security (1996a) *Income Support Statistics: May Quarterly Enquiry 1995; residential care and nursing home report*, London: DSS.

Department of Social Security (1996b) *Reply by the Government to the Third Report of the Select Committee on Housing Benefit Fraud*, London: HMSO.

Department of Social Security (1996c) *Male Earning Mobility in the Lifetime Labour Market Database, Working Paper*, London: DSS.

Department of Social Security press release (1993) 'Social security and economic policy cannot be separated says Peter Lilley', 23 June.

Department of Social Security press release (1994a) 'Peter Lilley announces plans to halt "Benefit Tourism"', 4 February.

Department of Social Security press release (1994b) 'Housing benefit review focuses on rising expenditure', 15 June.

Department of Social Security press release (1994c) 'Peter Lilley clamps down on benefit tourism', 11 July.

Department of Social Security press release (1994d) 'Peter Lilley invites ideas to improve benefit delivery', 20 July.

Department of Social Security press release (1994e) 'Peter Lilley stops prisoners' housing loophole', 12 October.

Department of Social Security press release (1994f) 'Peter Lilley announces £600m package of new work incentives', 29 November.

Department of Social Security press release (1994g) 'Peter Lilley announces £300 million boost to fight against fraud', 30 November.

Department of Social Security press release (1994h) 'Peter Lilley curbs soaring housing costs', 30 November.

Department of Social Security press release (1994i) 'James Arbuthnot announces firms shortlisted to automate benefit payment system', 9 December.

Department of Social Security press release (1995a) 'William Hague publishes regulations for new incapacity for work test', 21 February.

Department of Social Security press release (1995b) 'Regulations to curb housing benefit laid', 29 June.

Department of Social Security press release (1995c) 'Pension Bill receives Royal Assent', 20 July.

Department of Social Security press release (1995d) 'Peter Lilley publishes response to social security expenditure reviews', 8 August.

Department of Social Security press release (1995e) 'UK defuses pensions time-bomb', 23 November.

Department of Social Security press release (1996a) 'Billion pound housing benefit fraud revealed', 19 January.

Department of Social Security press release (1996b) 'Value of British pension funds rises to £600 billion', 23 January.

Department of Social Security press release (1996c) 'What are you doing after work?', 30 January.

Department of Social Security press release (1996d) 'Peter Lilley outlines radical reform of social security administration', 28 February.

Department of Social Security press release (1996e) 'Peter Lilley launches new initiatives against fraud', 5 March.

Department of Social Security press release (1996f) 'Alistair Burt announces extra help for job starters', 2 April.

Department of Social Security press release (1996g) 'Peter Lilley challenges legal authority of European Commission spending plans', 3 April.

Department of Social Security press release (1996h) 'Alistair Burt announces earnings top-up rates', 20 May.

Department of Social Security press release (1996i) 'Lord Mackay announces winner of Newcastle estate PFI', 20 June.

Department of Social Security press release (1996j) 'Lord Mackay announces major PFI initiative for DSS estate', 28 June.

Department of Social Security press release (1996k) 'Peter Lilley announces new initiatives under the Change Programme', 19 July.

Derber, C. (1983) 'Managing professionals: ideological proletarianization and post industrial labour', *Theory and Society*, 12, pp. 309–41.

Dhooge, Y. (1985) *Responding to Unemployment: the project description*, London: South Bank Polytechnic.

Dhooge, Y. with Becker, S. (1989) *Responding to Unemployment and Poverty: a training manual for social services*, London: Southbank Polytechnic.

Dickens, R., Fry. V. and Pashardes, P. (1995) 'The Cost of Children and the Welfare State', *Findings*, 89, York: Joseph Rowntree Foundation.

Digby, A. (1989) *British Welfare Policy*, London: Faber and Faber.

Dillon, M. and Parker, J. (1988) 'Faith, hope and charity', in S. Becker and S. MacPherson (eds), *Public Issues Private Pain: poverty, social work and social policy*, London: Insight/ Carematters Books, pp. 331–9.

Direct Payment to Users Scheme Newsletter, Spring 1995, No. 2, Sheffield: Family and Community Services Department.

Donnison, D. (1982) *The Politics of Poverty*, London: Martin Robertson.

Dorrell, S. (1996) Speech to the Annual Conference of the Association of Directors of Social Services, June.

Doyal, L. and Gough, I. (1991) *A Theory of Human Need*, Basingstoke: Macmillan Education.

EEC (1977) *The Perception of Poverty in Europe*, Document V/17/77-E, Brussels: Commission of the European Community.

Ellis, K. (1993) *Squaring the Circle: user and carer participation in needs assessment*, York: Joseph Rowntree Foundation/Community Care.

Enthoven, A. (1985) *Reflections on the Management of the NHS*, London: Nuffield Provincial Hospital Trust.

Epstein, I. (1968) 'Social workers and social action: attitudes toward social action strategies', *Social Work*, 13, 2, April, pp. 101–8.

Epstein, I. (1970a) 'Organisational careers, professionalization and social worker radicalism', *Social Service Review*, 44, June, pp. 123–31.

Epstein, I. (1970b) 'Professionalization, professionalism, and social worker radicalism', *Journal of Health and Social Behaviour*, 11, March, pp. 67–77.

Epstein, I. (1981) 'Advocates on advocacy: an exploratory study', *Social Work Research and Abstracts*, 17, 2, pp. 5–12.

Esping-Anderson, G. (1990) *The Three Worlds of Welfare Capitalism*, Oxford: Polity Press.

Evans, M., Piachaud, D. and Hunter, H. (1994) *Designed for the Poor – Poorer by Design? the effects of the 1986 Social Security Act on family incomes*, London: STICERD.

Feagin, J. R. (1972a) 'America's welfare stereotypes', *Social Service Quarterly*, 52, 4, pp. 921–33.

Feagin, J. R. (1972b) 'God helps those who help themselves', *Psychology Today*, November, pp. 101–10, 129.

Feather, N.T. (1974) 'Explanations of poverty in Australian and American samples: the person, society, or fate?', *Australian Journal of Psychology*, 26, pp. 199–216.

Fiegehen, G., Lansley, P. and Smith, A. (1977) *Poverty and Progress in Britain 1953–73*, Cambridge: Cambridge University Press.

Field, F. (1989) *Losing Out: the emergence of Britain's underclass*, Oxford: Blackwell.

Field, F. (1995) *Making Welfare Work: reconstructing welfare for the millennium*, London: Institute of Community Studies.

Fimister, G. (1984) 'Digging deeper into their pockets', *Social Work Today*, 22 October, pp. 16–18.

Fimister, G. (1995) *Social Security and Community Care in the 1990s*, Sunderland: Business Education Publishers.

Financial Times (1993) 'Benefit fraud costs £5bn a year, say officials', 26 October, p. 1.

Financial Times (1994a) 'Housing benefit cuts drawn up', 29 April, p. 13.

Financial Times (1994b) 'Prospects of housing benefit cut recedes', 13 October, p. 12.

Financial Times (1994c) 'TUC denounces jobseeker's bill', 3 December, p. 5.

Financial Times (1995a) 'Blair pledges extensive review of welfare state', 13 July, p. 6.

Financial Times (1995b) 'Tougher benefit regime fails to deliver savings', 9 October, p. 1.

Financial Times (1996) 'Invalidity benefit changes fail to make big savings', 15 April, p. 6.

Fitch, M. (1995) 'Cash and care in the community', *Benefits*, 14, pp. 23–5.

Freeman, I. and Lockhart, F. (1994) 'The reception of children into public care.

What do we really know?', Paper at the Association of Directors of Social Work Conference, 29 March.

Friedrich Ebert Foundation (1993) *Old and New Poverty in the Welfare States: a challenge to reform our social security systems?*, Euroseminar, London: Friedrich Ebert Foundation.

Fuller, R. and Stevenson, O. (1983) *Policies, Programmes and Disadvantage: a review of the literature*, London: Heinemann.

Furnham, A. (1982) 'Why are the poor always with us? Explanations for poverty in Britain', *British Journal of Social Psychology*, 21, pp. 311–22.

Furnham, A. and Gunter, B. (1984) 'Just world beliefs and attitudes towards the poor', *British Journal of Social Psychology*, 23, 3, pp. 265–9.

Gallup, G. (ed.) (1976) *Gallup International Public Opinion Polls: Great Britain 1937–75*, New York: Random House.

George, V. and Page, R. (eds) (1995) *Modern Thinkers on Welfare*, Hemel Hempstead: Prentice Hall/Harvester Wheatsheaf.

George, V. and Wilding, P. (1994) *Welfare and Ideology*, Hemel Hempstead: Harvester Wheatsheaf.

Gibbons, J. (1989) 'Helping poor families with pre-school services', *Social Work Today*, 1 June.

Gibbons, J. (ed.) (1992) *The Children Act 1989 and Family Support – principles into practice*, London: HMSO.

Gibbons, J., Thorpe, S. and Wilkinson, P. (1990) *Family Support and Prevention: studies in local areas*, London: HMSO.

Gladstone, D. (1995) 'Universal welfare: locating care in the mixed economy', in D. Gladstone (ed.), *British Social Welfare: past, present and future*, London: UCL Press, pp. 161–70.

Glazer, N. (1988) *The Limits of Social Policy*, London: Harvard University Press.

Glendinning, C. (1991) 'Losing ground: social policy and disabled people in Great Britain 1980–1990', *Disability, Handicap and Society*, 6, 1, pp. 3–17.

Glendinning, C. (1992a) *The Costs of Informal Care: looking inside the household*, London: HMSO.

Glendinning, C. (1992b) 'Residualism vs rights: social policy and disabled people', in N. Manning and R. Page (eds) *Social Policy Review 4*, Canterbury: Social Policy Association, pp. 89–110.

Glendinning, C. and Millar, J. (eds) (1992) *Women and Poverty in Britain: the 1990s*, Hemel Hempstead: Harvester Wheatsheaf.

Goffman, E. (1961) *Asylums*, New York: Doubleday.

Goldberg, E. M. and Warburton, R. W. (1979) *Ends and Means in Social Work*, London: NISW.

Golding, P. (ed.) (1986) *Excluding the Poor*, London: Child Poverty Action Group.

Golding, P. (1991) 'Poor attitudes', in S. Becker (ed.) *Windows of Opportunity: public policy and the poor*, London: Child Poverty Action Group Ltd, pp. 39–54.

Golding, P. (1994) 'Indicators of social exclusion: their practical feasibility; public attitudes to social exclusion', Seminar Paper, Centre for Research in European Social Policy and Employment Policy, 17–18 June.

Golding, P. (1995) 'Public attitudes to social exclusion: some problems of measurement and analysis', in G. Room (ed.), *Beyond the Threshold: the measurement and analysis of social exclusion*, Bristol: Policy Press, pp. 212–32.

Golding, P. and Middleton, S. (1982) *Images of Welfare: press and public attitudes to poverty*, London: Martin Robertson.

Gooding, C. (1994) *Disabling Laws, Enabling Acts: disability rights in Britain and America*, London: Pluto Press.

Goodman, A. and Webb, S. (1994) *For Richer, For Poorer: the changing distribution of income in the United Kingdom, 1961–91*, London: Institute of Fiscal Studies.

Goodwin, L. (1972) 'How suburban families view the work orientations of the welfare poor: problems in social stratification and social policy', *Social Problems*, 19, Winter, pp. 337–48.

Gough, I. (1979) *The Political Economy of the Welfare State*, London: Macmillan.

Government Statistical Service (1994) *Family Resources Survey: Great Britain, 1993/94*, London: DSS.

Government Statistical Service (1996) *Family Resources Survey: Great Britain 1994–1995*, London: DSS.

Graham, H. (1996) 'The health experiences of mothers and young children on income support', *Benefits*, 17, pp. 10–13.

Green, D. (1993) *Reinventing Civil Society: the rediscovery of welfare without politics*, London: Institute of Economic Affairs.

Greenwich, London Borough of (1987) *A Child in Mind: protection of children in a responsible society. The report of the Committee of Inquiry into the circumstances surrounding the death of Kimberley Carlile*, London: Borough of Greenwich.

Griffiths, R. (1988) *Community Care: an agenda for action: a report to the Secretary of State for Social Services*, London: HMSO.

Guardian (1993a) 'Welfare in sights of Portillo'; 'Portillo puts Whitehall big spenders on notice', 9 February, p. 1.

Guardian (1993b) 'Welfare review order by Lilley', 26 April, p. 4.

Guardian (1993c) 'Lilley puts knife into benefits', 5 June, p. 1.

Guardian (1993d) 'Lone mothers face council housing bar', 7 October, p. 7.

Guardian (1993e) 'Firms face full cost of sick pay', 15 November, p. 1.

Guardian (1994a) 'Benefit tourists face Lilley residence test', 5 February, p. 3.

Guardian (1994b) 'Housing groups hit back', 3 March, p. 3.

Guardian (1994c) 'Welfare safety net "is full of holes"', 23 April, p. 5.

Guardian (1994d) 'PM attacks "offensive" beggars', 28 May, p. 1.

Guardian (1994e) 'Please sir, I want to be a prostitute', 29 August, p. 2.

Guardian (1994f) 'Aitken wields spending axe over housing benefit', 6 September, p. 3.

Guardian (1994g) 'PM takes on yob culture', 10 September, p. 1.

Guardian (1994h) 'Funds crisis forces another council to cut care services', 16 November, p. 5.

Guardian (1995a) 'The taboo subject', 1 February, p. 9.

Guardian (1995b) 'Lilley targets £1.4bn benefit fraud', 11 July, p. 5.

Guardian (1995c) 'Children of the estates living in state of despair', 17 July, pp. 1–2.

Guardian (1995d) 'Justice amid enveloping air of chaos', 18 July, pp. 1–2.

Guardian (1995e) 'Welfare by Prozac as the safety net feels the strain', 19 July, pp. 1–2.

Guardian (1995f) 'A giant shadow over the mothers of Hope Street', 20 July, pp. 1–2.

Guardian (1995g) 'Council services "too expensive" for a fifth of disabled people', 23 August, p. 4.

Guardian (1996a) 'Poverty, what poverty? says Lilley', 17 April, pp. 1, 7.

Guardian (1996b) 'The end of the Welfare State', 8 May, pp. 1, 4.

Hadjipateras, A. and Witcher, S. (1991) *A Way out of Poverty and Disability: moving towards a comprehensive disability income scheme*, London: Disability Alliance.

Ham, C. and Hill, M. (1984) *The Policy Process in the Modern Capitalist State*, London: Wheatsheaf Books.

Handler, J. (1968) 'The coercive children's officer', *New Society*, 3 October, pp. 485–7.

Hardiker, P. and Barker, M. (1988) 'A window on child care, poverty and social work', in S. Becker and S. MacPherson (eds), *Public Issues Private Pain: poverty, social work and social policy*, London: Insight/Carematters Books, pp. 105–17.

Harding, S., Phillips, D. and Fogarty, M. (1986) *Contrasting Values in Western Europe*, London: Macmillan.

Harker, L. (1996) *A Secure Future: social security and the family in a changing world*, London: Child Poverty Action Group Ltd.

Hayball, J. (1993) 'Promoting take-up amongst home care clients', *Benefits*, 8, pp. 34–5.

Health Committee (1996) *Long-term Care: future provision and funding*, London: HMSO.

Henwood, M. (1992) *Through a Glass Darkly: community care and elderly people*, London: King's Fund Institute.

Her Majesty's Stationery Office (HMSO) (1957) *Royal Commission of Law Relating to Mental Illness*, London: HMSO.

HMSO (1969) *Report of the Committee of Inquiry into Allegations of Ill-Treatment of Patients and other Irregularities at the Ely Hospital, Cardiff*, Cmnd 3975, London: HMSO.

HMSO (1988) *The Report of the Inquiry into Child Abuse in Cleveland 1987*, Cmnd 412, London: HMSO.

HMSO (1995) *Social Welfare*, London: HMSO.

Heywood, J. S. and Allen, B. L. F. (1971) *Financial Help in Social Work*, Manchester: Manchester University Press.

Hill, M. (1985) 'The relationship between local authority social services and supplementary benefits since the 1980 supplementary benefit changes,' unpublished.

Hill, M. (1990) *Social Security Policy in Britain*, London: Edward Elgar.

Hills, J. (1993) *The Future of Welfare: a guide to the debate*, York: Joseph Rowntree Foundation.

Hollins, C. (1995) 'Charities and the welfare state', draft of a report, London: Family Welfare Association, mimeo.

Holman, B. (1973) 'Poverty: consensus and alternatives', *British Journal of Social Work*, 3, 4, pp. 431–46.

Holman, B. (1980) *Inequality in Child Care*, London: Child Poverty Action Group/Family Rights Group.

Holman, B. (1993) *A New Deal for Social Welfare*, Oxford: Lion Publishing.

Holman, B. (1996) 'Changing times', *Community Care*, 4–10 April, p. 25.

Huby, M. (1996) 'Reflections on the social fund', *Benefits*, 15, pp. 9–11.

Huby, M. and Dix, G. (1992) *Evaluating the Social Fund*, London: HMSO.

Hughes, B. (1993) 'Finance and management', *Community Care*, 25 February.

Hutton, W. (1995) *The State We're In*, London: Jonathan Cape.

Independent (1993) 'Portillo's review could mark end of welfare state', 1 June, p. 3.

Independent (1994a) 'Howard gives ground on the roots of crime', 27 April, p. 3.

Independent (1994b) 'Lilley wants "jobseekers, not job-shy"', 25 October, p. 1.

Independent (1994c) 'Limit to be set on £9bn cost of housing benefit', 10 November, p. 5.

Independent (1995a) 'CBI chief calls for training push', 11 February, p. 2.

Independent (1995b) 'Mentally ill face paying for after-care', 17 February, p. 8.

Independent (1995c) 'NHS guide "ends free cradle-to-grave care"', 24 February, p. 4.

Independent (1995d) 'Teenage mums: an idea out of control', 15 August, p. 11.

Independent (1996a) 'Clarke warns right on benefit savings', 7 February, p. 2.

Independent (1996b) 'Benefit offices to face £200m cutback', 26 March, p. 5.

Independent on Sunday (1993a) 'Pensioners told "sell assets"', 21 November, p. 2.

Independent on Sunday (1993b) 'How to end the welfare state', 5 December, p. 11.

Independent on Sunday (1995a) 'Old age pensioners hand over homes to beat care fees rule', 8 January, p. 9.

Independent on Sunday (1995b) 'Think-tank urges lone parents to give up their children', 5 March, p. 4.

International Year for the Eradication of Poverty UK Coalition (1996) *Poverty '96* (leaflet), London: IYEP UK Coalition.

Irvine, R. (1988) 'Child abuse and poverty', in S. Becker, and S. MacPherson (eds), *Public Issues Private Pain: poverty, social work and social policy*, London: Insight/Carematters Books, pp. 118–28.

Jani-Le Bris, H. (1993) *Family Care of Dependent Older People in the European Community*, Dublin: European Foundation for the Improvement of Living and Working Conditions.

Jenkins, S. (1994) *Winners and Losers: a portrait of UK income distribution during the 1980s*, Swansea: Swansea University.

Johnson, N. (1990) *Reconstructing the Welfare State: a decade of change*, Hemel Hempstead: Harvester Wheatsheaf.

Jones, B. (1989) 'Section one: at the crossroads', *Benefits Research*, 3, pp. 22–5.

Jones, K. (1972) *A History of the Mental Health Service*, London: Routledge and Kegan Paul.

Jones, K. (1991) *The Making of Social Policy in Britain, 1830–1990*, London: Athlone.

Jordan, B. (1974) *Poor Parents: social policy and the cycle of deprivation*, London: Routledge and Kegan Paul.

Jordan, B. (1984) *Invitation to Social Work*, London: Martin Robertson.

Jordan, B. (1990) *Social Work in an Unjust Society*, Hemel Hempstead: Harvester Wheatsheaf.

Jordan, B. (1996) *A Theory of Poverty and Social Exclusion*, Oxford: Polity Press.

Jowell, T. (1985) 'Foreword' in AMA *Caring for Unemployed People*, London: Bedford Square Press/ National Council for Voluntary Organisations.

Jowell, T. and Airey, C. (eds) (1984) *British Social Attitudes: the 1984 report:* Aldershot: Gower.

Jowell, R., Witherspoon, S. and Brook, L. (eds) (1987) *British Social Attitudes: the 1987 report*, Aldershot: Gower

Jowell, R., Witherspoon, S. and Brook, L. (eds) (1990) *British Social Attitudes: the 7th report*, Aldershot: Gower.

Kamerman, S. B. and Kahn, A. K. (1978) *Family Policy: government and families in fourteen countries*, New York: Columbia University Press.

Kemp, P. (1992) *Housing Benefit: an appraisal*, London: SSAC.

Kemp, P. *et al.* (1994) *The Effects of Benefit on Housing Decisions*, London: HMSO.

Kempson, E. (1996) *Life on a Low Income*, York: York Publishing Services.

Kempson, E., Bryson, A. and Rowlingson, K. (1994) *Hard Times? how poor families make ends meet*, Policy Studies Institute, London.

Kerbo, H. R. (1976) 'The stigma of welfare and a passive poor', *Sociology and Social Research*, 60, 2, pp. 173–87.

Kestenbaum, A. (1992) *Cash for Care*, Nottingham: Independent Living Fund.

Kestenbaum, A. (1996) *Independent Living: a review*, York: Joseph Rowntree Foundation.

Klein, R. (1989) *The Politics of the NHS*, London: Longman.

Knapp, M. *et al.* (1992) *Care in the Community: challenge and demonstration*, Aldershot: Ashgate.

Korman, N. and Glennerster, H. (1990) *Hospital Closure*, Milton Keynes: Open University Press.

KPMG Management Consulting (1992) *Improving Independent Sector Involvement in Community Care Planning*, London: KPMG.

Kumar, V. (1993) *Poverty and Inequality in the UK*, London: National Children's Bureau.

Labour Party (1996) *Welfare to Work*, London: Labour Party.

Laing, R. D. (1959) *The Divided Self*, Harmondsworth: Penguin.

Laing and Buisson (1991) *Care of Elderly People: market survey 1990/91*, 4th edn, London: Laing and Buisson.

Langan, M. (1993) 'The rise and fall of social work', in J. Clarke (ed.), *A Crisis in Care?*, London: Sage, pp. 47–66.

Lauer, R.H. (1971) 'The middle class looks at poverty', *Urban and Social Change Review*, 5, 1, pp. 8–10.

Le Grand, J. and Bartlett, W. (1993) *Quasi-Markets and Social Policy*, London: Macmillan.

Leicestershire County Council (1989) *Preventative Aid Payments, October 1987–September 1988*, Social Services Research Section Report, May.

Lilley, P. (1992) Speech to the 109th Conservative Party Conference, London: Conservative Central Office.

Lilley, P. (1993a) 'Benefits and costs: securing the future of social security', Mais Lecture to the London Business School, 23 June.

Lilley, P. (1993b) Social security statement to the House of Commons, 1 December.

Lilley, P. (1994) Social security statement to the House of Commons, 30 November.

Lilley, P. (1995a) Speech to the Social Market Foundation, London, 9 January.

Lilley, P. (1995b) *Winning the Welfare Debate*, London: Social Market Foundation.

Lilley, P. (1996) 'Equality, generosity and opportunity – welfare reform and Christian values', Speech, Southwark Cathedral, 13 June.

Lipsey, D. (1986) 'Poverty – the public does care', *New Society*, 4 October, pp. 12–14.

Lipsey, D. (1994) 'Do we really want more public spending?', in R. Jowell, J. Curtice, L. Brook and D. Ahrendt (eds), *British Social Attitudes: the 11th report*, Aldershot: Dartmouth.

Lister, R. (1986) *There is an Alternative: reforming social security*, London: Child Poverty Action Group.

Lister, R. (1989) 'Social security', in M. McCarthy (ed.), *The New Politics of Welfare: an agenda for the 1990s?* London: Macmillan, pp. 104–31.

Lister, R. (1990) *The Exclusive Society: citizenship and the poor*, London: Child Poverty Action Group Ltd.

Lister, R. (1994) 'Citizenship and difference', Paper presented at the fourth gender and welfare seminar, University of Bath, 12–13 December.

Lister, R. (1996a) 'Introduction: in search of the underclass', in R. Lister (ed.), *Charles Murray and the Underclass: the developing debate*, London: Institute of Economic Affairs, pp. 1–16.

Lister, R. (1996b) 'Permanent revolution: The politics of two decades of social security reform', Paper presented to the DSS Summer School, King's College Cambridge, July.

Lister, R. and Becker, S. (1994) 'Care and the community', in P. Allan, J. Benyon and B. McCormick (eds), *Focus on Britain: review of 1993*, Oxford: Perennial Publications, pp. 180–4.

Lister, R. and Beresford, P. (1991) *Working Together Against Poverty*, London: Open Services Project.

Lister, R. and Emmett, T. (1976) *Under the Safety Net*, London: Child Poverty Action Group.

Local Government Anti-Poverty Unit (LGAPU) (1995) *Survey of Charges for Social Care 1993–95*, London: Association of Metropolitan Authorities.

Lowe, R. (1993) *The Welfare State in Britain Since 1945*, London: Macmillan.

Macarov, D. (1981) 'Social work student attitudes towards poverty: a tri-national study', *Contemporary Social Work Education*, 4, 2, pp. 150–60.

Mack, J. and Lansley, S. (1985) *Poor Britain*, London: George Allen.

Macnicol, J. (1989) *Eugenics and the Campaign for Voluntary Sterilisation in Britain Between the Wars*, London: The Society for the History of Medicine.

Mail on Sunday (1990) 'The attack on innocence', 21 October, p. 9.

Marquand, D. and Seldon, A. (eds) (1996) *The Ideas that Shaped Post-War Britain*, London: Fontana Press.

Marsland, D. (1994) *The End of the Welfare State*, London: Adam Smith Institute.

Martin, J. P. (1984) *Hospitals in Trouble*, Oxford: Blackwell.

Martin, J. and White, A. (1988) *The Financial Circumstances of Disabled Adults Living in Private Households*, London: OPCS/HMSO.

Matza, D. (1969) *Becoming Deviant*, New Jersey: Prentice Hall.

McCormick, J. and Oppenheim, C. (1996) 'Options for change', *New Statesman*, 26 January, pp. 18–21.

McGrail, S. M. (1983) 'We shouldn't really be teaching this sort of thing', *Community Care*, 15 December, pp. 26–7.

McLaughlin, E. (1991) *Social Security and Community Care: the case of the invalid care allowance*, London: HMSO.

Mental Health Act Commission (1992) *Fourth Biennial Report of the Mental Health Act Commission 1989–1991*, London: HMSO.

Mess, H. A. (1948) *Voluntary Social Services Since 1918*, London: Kegan Paul.

Middleton, S., Ashworth, K. and Walker, R. (1994) *Family Fortunes: pressures on parents and children in the 1990s*, London: Child Poverty Action Group Ltd.

Milburn, A. (1996) 'Labour's policy for social services', speech to the ADSS, 6 February.

Millar, J. (1991) 'Bearing the cost', in S. Becker (ed.), *Windows of Opportunity: public policy and the poor*, London: Child Poverty Action Group Ltd, pp. 23–37.

Miller, A. H. (1978) 'Will public attitudes defeat welfare reform?', *Public Welfare*, 36, pp. 48–54.

Milne, K. (1995) 'Able to protest', *New Statesman and Society*, 10 February, pp. 25–30.

Mishra, R. (1984) *The Welfare State in Crisis: social thought and social change*, Brighton: Wheatsheaf Books.

Moore, J. (1989) 'The end of the line for poverty', speech to Greater London Area CPC, 11 May.

Morgan, P. (1995) *Farewell to the Family: public policy and family breakdown in Britain and the USA*, London: Institute of Economic Affairs.

Morley, R. (1990) 'Charities: the social fund and income support', *Benefits Research*, 5, pp. 10–13.

Morris, J. (1991) *Pride Against Prejudice: a personal politics of disability*, London: Women's Press.

Morris, J. (1993) *Independent Lives*, Basingstoke: Macmillan.

Morris, P. (1969) *Put Away*, London: Routledge and Kegan Paul.

Murray, C. (ed.) (1990) *The Emerging British Underclass*, London: Institute of Economic Affairs.

Murray, C. (1994) *Underclass: the crisis deepens*, London: Institute of Economic Affairs.

Murray, N. (1983) 'The politics of uselessness', *Community Care*, 3 November, pp. 18–20.

NACRO (1995) *Crime and Social Policy*, London: National Association for the Care and Resettlement of the Offender.

Nadash, P. and Zarb, G. (1994) *Cashing in on Independence: comparing the costs and benefits of cash and services for meeting disabled peoples' support needs*, London: British Council of Organisations for Disabled People.

Nash, A. (1983) 'Long shadow of unemployment', *Community Care*, 30 June.

National Children's Home (NCH) (1986) *Families Affected by Unemployment*, London: NCH.

National Children's Home (1994) *Victorian Values for Children in 1994 Britain*, London: NCH.

National Consumer Council (NCC) (1995) *Charging Consumers for Social Services*, London: NCC.

National Welfare Rights Officers Group (now National Association of Welfare Rights Advisers) (1991) 'Care in the Community: the role of welfare rights officers – a summary of planning, practice and ethical issues', London: NWROG, mimeo.

Neill, J. and Williams, J. (1992) *Leaving Hospital: elderly people and their discharge to community care*, London: NISW/ HMSO.

Nixon, J. (1988) 'Section one expenditures; insider views', in S. Becker and S. MacPherson (eds) *Public Issues Private Pain: poverty, social work and social policy*, London: Insight/Carematters Books, pp. 57–70.

Nocon, A. (1994) *Collaboration in Community Care in the 1990s*, Sunderland: Business Education Publishers.

Nottinghamshire County Council (1994) *Social Need in Nottinghamshire: the county disadvantaged area study, part 1*, Nottingham: Nottinghamshire County Council.

No Turning Back Group of Conservative MPs (1993) *Who Benefits? reinventing social security*, London: Conservative Political Centre.

Novak, T. (1988) *Poverty and the State*, Milton Keynes: Open University Press.
O'Brien, J. and Tyne, A. (1981) *The Principle of Normalisation: a foundation for effective services*, London: Values Into Action.
Observer (1990) 'Hard man's rage turns to despair', 16 September.
Observer (1993) 'Lilley sharpens the benefits axe', 25 April.
O'Connor, J. (1973) *The Fiscal Crisis of the State*, New York: St Martin's Press.
Oldfield, N. and Yu, A. C. S. (1993) *The Cost of a Child*, London: Child Poverty Action Group Ltd.
Oldman, C. (1991) *Paying for Care: personal sources of funding care*, York: Joseph Rowntree Foundation.
Oliver, M. (1990) *The Politics of Disablement*, London: Macmillan.
Oliver, M. and Barnes, C. (1993) 'Discrimination, disability and welfare: from needs to rights', in J. Swain, V. Finkelstein, S. French and M. Oliver (eds), *Disabling Barriers, Enabling Environments*, London: Sage, pp. 267–77.,
OPCS (1992) General Household Survey: carers in 1990, *OPCS Monitor*, London: OPCS.
Oppenheim, C. (1993a), *Poverty: the facts*, London: Child Poverty Action Group Ltd.
Oppenheim, C. (1993b), *Crisis – What Crisis?*, London: Child Poverty Action Group Ltd.
Oppenheim, C. and Harker, L. (1996) *Poverty: the facts*, 3rd edn, London: Child Poverty Action Group Ltd.
Orten, J. D. (1979) 'Experimentally influenced changes in students' attitudes towards the poor', University of Alabama, DSW, unpublished.
Page, D., Bochel, H. and Arnold, P. (1995) 'Community care, housing and benefits: integration through separation?', *Benefits*, 14, pp. 11–15.
Parker, H. (1989) *Instead of the Dole*, London: Routledge.
Parsloe, P. (1996) 'Another change', *Community Care*, 4–10 April, p. 24.
Payne, M. (1979) *Power, Authority and Responsibility in Social Services: social work in area teams*, London: Macmillan.
Payne, M. (1991) *Modern Social Work Theory: a critical introduction*, London: Macmillan.
Pearson, S., Alcock, P. and Craig, G. (1996) 'Welfare rights and local authority anti-poverty strategies', *Benefits*, 16, pp. 3–7.
Phillimore, T., Beattie, A. and Townsend, P. (1994) 'Widening inequality of health in Northern England', *British Medical Journal*, 308, pp. 1125–8.
Piachaud, D. (1974) 'Attitudes to pensions', *Journal of Social Policy*, 3, 2, pp. 137–46.
Piachaud, D. (1979) *The Cost of A Child*, London: Child Poverty Action Group.
Piachaud, D. (1987) 'Problems in the definition and measurement of poverty', *Journal of Social Policy*, 16, 2, pp. 147–64.
Piachaud, D. (1996) 'Means-testing and the Conservatives', *Benefits*, 15, pp. 5–8.
Pinker, R.A. (1982) 'An alternative view', in P. Barclay (ed.), *Social Workers: their roles and tasks*, London: Bedford Square Press.
Pirie, M. (1993) *The Radical Agenda: the privatisation of choice*, London: Adam Smith Institute.
Pitkeathley, J. (1989) *It's My Duty Isn't It?*, London: Souvenir Press.
Policy Studies Institute (1992) *Monitoring Change in Social Services Departments*, London: Policy Studies Institute.
Popay, J. and Dhooge, Y. (1985) *Unemployment and Health: what role for health and social services?*, London: Polytechnic of the South Bank.

Portillo, M. (1994) 'A Revolution in the public sector', speech at Hertford College, Oxford Deregulation Seminar, 7 January.

Prescott, J. (1994) 'Taking from the poor', *New Statesman and Society*, 14 October, p. 26.

Princess Royal Trust (1992) *Caring in Partnership*, London: Princess Royal Trust for Carers.

Pryke, R. (1995) *Taking the Measure of Poverty*, London: Institute of Economic Affairs.

Rainbow, H. (1985) 'No Money? Who Cares?', report on the work carried out jointly between Finsbury CAB and Finsbury social services area team in the London Borough of Islington, mimeo.

Rainbow, H. (1993) 'Income maximisation in community care assessment and in continuing care', *Benefits*, 7, pp. 11–14.

Redpath, A.D. (1979) 'Public attitudes to the unemployed', M.Phil., Edinburgh University, unpublished.

Room, G. (1995) 'Poverty in Europe: competing paradigms of analysis', *Policy and Politics*, 23, 2, pp. 103–13.

Root, A. (1995) 'A not so healthy nation', *Poverty*, 91, pp. 6–8.

Rose, M. (1971) *The English Poor Law, 1745–1834*, London: Macmillan.

Rosenthal, R. and Jacobson, L. (1968) *Pygmalion in the Classroom*, New York: Holt Rinehart and Winston.

Rowntree, S. (1901) *Poverty: a study of town life*, London: Macmillan.

Royal College of Psychiatrists (RCP) (1992) *Mental Health of the Nation: the contribution of psychiatry*, London: RCP.

Sainsbury, R. (1996) 'Rooting out fraud – innocent until proven fraudulent', *Poverty*, Spring, pp. 17–20.

Salonen, T. (1993) *Margins of Welfare: a study of modern functions of social assistance*, Lund: Hallestad Press.

Savage, S. and Robins, L. (1990) *Public Policy Under Thatcher*, London: Macmillan.

Scarman, L. G. (1982) *The Scarman Report*, Harmondsworth: Penguin.

Schaff, C. (1993) 'From dependency to self advocacy: redefining disability', *The American Journal of Occupational Therapy*, 47, 10, pp. 943–8.

Scheerenberger, R. C. (1983) *A History of Mental Retardation*, Baltimore: Brookes.

Schorr, A. (1992) *The Personal Social Services: an outsider view*, York: Joseph Rowntree Foundation.

Schlackman Research Organisation (1978) *Report on Research on Public Attitudes towards the Supplementary Benefit Scheme*, Report submitted to Central Office of Information, London: Schlackman Research Organisation.

Schur, E. M. (1971) *Labelling Deviant Behaviour: its sociological implications*, New York: Harper and Row.

Scott, J. (1994) *Poverty and Wealth: citizenship, deprivation and privilege*, London: Longman.

Scott, V. (1994) *Lessons from America: a study of the Americans with Disabilities Act*, London: RADAR.

Scott-Parker, S. and Holmstrom, R. (1995) 'The outsiders', *New Statesman and Society*, 10 February, pp. 27–30.

Searle, R. (1976) *Eugenics and Politics in Britain, 1900–1914*, Noordhoff: Leydon.

Seebohm, F. (1968) *Report of the Committee on Local Authorities and Allied Personal Social Services*, Cmnd 3707, London: HMSO.

Sen, A. (1983) 'Poor, relatively speaking', *Oxford Economic Papers*, 35, 1.

Silberman, G. (1977) 'A study of the relationship between education, dogmatism and concern for the poor in a public welfare agency', PhD., New York University, unpublished.

Silburn, L. (1993) 'A social model in a medical world: the development of the integrated living team as part of the strategy for younger physically disabled people', in J. Swain, V. Finklestein, S. French and M. Oliver (eds), *Disabling Barriers, Enabling Environments*, Milton Keynes: Open University Press.

Silburn, R. (1992) 'The changing landscape of poverty', in N. Manning and R. Page (eds), *Social Policy Review 4*, Canterbury: Social Policy Association, pp. 134–53.

Silburn, R. (1993) 'Introduction to Research Round-up', *Benefits*, 6, p. 16.

Silburn, R. (1994) Book Review, *Journal of Social Policy*, 23, 1, p. 122.

Silburn, R. (1995) 'Beveridge', in V. George, and R. Page (eds), *Modern Thinkers on Welfare*, Hemel Hempstead: Prentice Hall/Harvester Wheatsheaf, pp. 84–102.

Silburn, R., MacPherson, S. and Becker, S. (1984) 'Social workers and supplementary benefits', *Social Work Today*, 12 November, pp. 19–25.

Sinclair, I., Parker, R., Leat, D. and Williams, J. (1990) *The Kaleidoscope of Care: a review of research on welfare provision for elderly people*, London: HMSO.

Sinfield, A. (1969) *Which Way Forward for Social Work?*, London: Fabian Society.

Sinha, Y., Jain, U.C. and Pandey, J. (1980) 'Attribution of causality to poverty', *Journal of Social and Economic Studies*, 8, pp. 349–59.

Smale, G., Tuson, G., Ahmad, B., Darvill, G., Domoney, L. and Sainsbury, E. (1994) *Negotiating Care in the Community*, London: HMSO.

Smith, C. (1995) 'A letter to all CLPs and affiliated organisations', 18 December.

Smith, R. (1982) 'Living in the material world', *Social Work Today*, 17 December.

Social Security Advisory Committee (SSAC) (1987) *The Draft Social Fund Manual: report by the Social Security Advisory Committee*, London: HMSO.

Social Security Advisory Committee (1990) *Seventh Report*, London: HMSO.

Social Security Advisory Committee (1993) *Ninth Report*, London: HMSO.

Social Security Advisory Committee (1994) *State Benefits and Private Provision*, paper 2, Leeds: Benefits Agency Publishing Services Ltd.

Social Security Advisory Committee (1995a) *Housing Benefit – The Review of Social Security*, paper 3, Leeds: Benefits Agency Publishing Services Ltd.

Social Security Advisory Committee (1995b) *Tenth Report*, London: HMSO.

Social Security Committee (1995) *Low Income Statistics: low income families 1979–1992*, London: HMSO.

Social Security Committee (1996) *Third Report on Housing Benefit Fraud*, London: HMSO.

Social Security Research Consortium (SSRC) (1991) *Cash Limited, Limited Cash: the impact of the social fund on social services and voluntary agencies, and their users*, London: AMA.

Social Services Committee (1985) *Community Care: second report*, vol. 1, London: HMSO.

Social Services Committee (1990) *Community Care: carers, fifth report*, London: HMSO.

Social Services Inspectorate (SSI) (1992) *Capitalising on the Act*, London: SSI.
Social Services Inspectorate (1994) *Advice Note for Use by Social Services Inspectorate. Discretionary Charges for Adult Services*, London: SSI.
Social Work Today (1992) 'Yeo slams attitude', 6 August, p. 5.
Southwark, London Borough of, (1985) *Response to the Government's Green Paper*, Social Services Committee, September.
Spicker, P. (1993) *Poverty and Social Security*, London: Routledge.
Squires, P. (1990) *Anti-social Policy: welfare, ideology and the disciplinary state*, Hemel Hempstead: Harvester Wheatsheaf.
Stainton, T. (1992) 'A terrible danger to the race', *Community Living*, 5, 2.
Stevenson, O. (1995) 'Reviewing post-war welfare', in I. Allen (ed.), *Targeting Those Most in Need: winners and losers*, London: Policy Studies Institute.
Stewart, G. and Stewart. J. (1986) *Boundary Changes: social work and social security*, London: CPAG/BASW.
Stewart, G. and Stewart. J. (1988) 'Shifting the safety net: social services financial powers and social security policy', in S. Becker and S. MacPherson (eds), *Public Issues Private Pain: poverty, social work and social policy*, London: Insight/Carematters Books, pp. 71–83.
Stewart, G. and Stewart, J. (1991) *Relieving Poverty: use of the social fund by social work clients and other agencies*, London: Association of Metropolitan Authorities.
Stitt, S. and Grant, D. (1993) *Poverty: Rowntree revisited*, Aldershot: Avebury.
Strathclyde Regional Council (1985) *Unemployment – implications for regional services*, report commissioned by the Regional Deprivation Group, Chief Executive's Department, June.
Sullivan, M. (1996) *The Development of the British Welfare State*, London: Prentice Hall/ Harvester Wheatsheaf.
Sunday Telegraph (1995) 'Are the poor really worse off?', 12 February, pp. 20–21.
Sunday Times (1990) 'Children speared on the horns of a demonic dilemma', 30 September, p. 5.
Sunday Times (1994a) 'Oliver Twist charity lands in the soup', 6 February, p. 5.
Sunday Times (1994b) 'Homeowners lose mortgage safety net', 17 July, p. 11.
Sunday Times (1995) 'Surrey council seeks free care for the elderly', 15 January, p. 3.
Sunday Times (1996) 'Major pledges to let elderly keep homes', 31 March, p. 17.
Svenson, M. (1988) *Boundary Wars: local authority responses to the social fund*, Nottingham University: Benefits Research Unit.
Svenson, M. and MacPherson, S. (1988) 'Real losses and unreal figures' in S. Becker. and S. MacPherson (eds), *Public Issues Private Pain: poverty, social work and social policy*, London: Insight/Carematters Books, pp. 41–53.
Swain, J., Finklestein, V., French, S. and Oliver, M. (1993) *Disabling Barriers, Enabling Environments*, Milton Keynes: Open University Press.
Szasz, T. (1972) *The Myth of Mental Illness*, London: Granada Publishing Ltd.
Taylor-Gooby, P. (1985a) *Public Opinion, Ideology and State Welfare*, London: Routledge and Kegan Paul.
Taylor-Gooby, P. (1985b) 'Attitudes to Welfare', *Journal of Social Policy*, 14, 1, pp. 73–81.
Taylor-Gooby, P. (1995) 'Comfortable, marginal and excluded: who should pay higher taxes for a better welfare state?' in R. Jowell, J. Curtice, A. Park, L.

Brook, D. Ahrendt with K. Thompson, *British Social Attitudes: the 12th report*, Aldershot: Dartmouth, pp. 1–18.

Thane, P. (1982) *The Foundations of the Welfare State*, London: Longman.

Thompson, P. (1995) 'Residential care, benefits and charges' in NISW/LGAPU, *Charging for Social Care*, London: NISW/LGAPU, pp. 37–40.

Thompson, P., Lavery, J. and Curtice, J. (1990) *Short Changed by Disability*, London: Disablement Income Group.

Times (1993) 'Middle class faces threat to benefits', 21 May, pp. 1–2.

Times (1994a) 'Champions of privatisation seek to overthrow the welfare state', 28 February, p. 8.

Times (1994b) 'Pensioners win in home help claim', 6 December, p. 1.

Times (1995a) 'Disabled pensioners win community care battle', 17 June, p. 4.

Times (1995b) 'Poor man at the gate', 23 August, p. 16.

Times (1995c) 'Health Secretary stands firm on community care', 23 September, p. 4.

Times (1995d) 'Lilley hoping to save £600 million with fraud crackdown', 30 November, p. 10.

Timmins, N. (1995) *The Five Giant Evils: a biography of the welfare state*, London: Harper Collins.

Timmins, N. (1996) 'Fewer poor – a tall Tory tale?', *Independent on Sunday*, 30 June, p. 9.

Torkelson, R., Lynch, R. and Thomas, K. (1994) 'People with disabilities as victims: Changing an ill-advised paradigm', *Journal of Rehabilitation*, March, pp. 8–15.

Towell, D. (ed.) (1988) *An Ordinary Life in Practice*, London: King Edward Hospital Fund for London.

Townsend, D. (1996) 'A breed apart', *Community Care*, 4–10 April, pp. 26–7.

Townsend, P. (1962) *The Last Refuge: a survey of residential institutions and homes for the aged in England and Wales*, London: Routledge and Kegan Paul.

Townsend, P. (1970) 'The objectives of the new local social services', in P. Townsend *et al.* (eds), *The Fifth Social Services: nine Fabian essays*, London: Fabian Society.

Townsend, P. (1979) *Poverty in the UK*, Harmondsworth: Penguin.

Townsend, P. (1993a) *The International Analysis of Poverty*, Hemel Hempstead: Harvester Wheatsheaf.

Townsend, P. (1993b) 'The need for a new international poverty line' in Friederich Ebert Foundation, *Old and New Poverty in the Welfare States: a challenge to reform our social security systems?*, London: Friedrich Ebert Foundation.

Townsend, P., Davidson, N. and Whitehead, M. (1992) *Inequalities in Health: the Black Report and the health divide*, Harmondsworth: Penguin.

Townsend, P. and Donkor, K. (1996) *Global Restructuring and Social Policy: the need to establish an international welfare state*, Bristol: Policy Press.

Tree, D. (1996) 'What's so special about rural areas?' *County News*, Association of County Councils, March, p. 27.

Trenery, D. (1993) 'Coordination, implementation and community care', MA thesis, Loughborough University, unpublished.

Tropman, J. E. (1977) 'Reality or projection', *Public Welfare*, Winter, pp. 17–23.

Tropman, J. E. (1981) 'Copping out or chipping in', *The Humanist*, 41, 2, pp. 43–6.

Tunstill, J. (1995) 'Children in need: is targeting the answer?', in I. Allen (ed.),

Targeting Those Most in Need: winners and losers, London: Policy Studies Institute.

Twigg, J. (ed.) (1992) *Carers: research and practice*, London: HMSO.

Twigg, J. Atkin, K and Perring, C. (1990) *Carers and Services: a review of research*, London: HMSO.

Ungerson, C. (ed.) (1990) *Gender and Caring: work and welfare in Britain and Scandinavia*, Brighton: Harvester Wheatsheaf.

Utting, D., Bright, J. and Henricson, C. (1993) *Crime and the Family: improving child rearing and preventing delinquency*, London: Family Policy Studies Centre.

Utting, W. (Chairman) (1991) *Children in the Public Care: a review of residential care*, London: HMSO/DoH.

Valencia, B.M. and Jackson, M.P. (1979) *Financial Aid Through Social Work*, London: Routledge and Kegan Paul.

Vaux, G. and Alcock, P. (1995) 'Take-up work with home care clients', *Benefits*, 13, pp. 30–2.

Vaux, G. and Devine, D. (1988) 'Race and poverty', in S. Becker and S. MacPherson (eds), *Public Issues Private Pain: poverty, social work and social policy*, London: Insight/Carematters Books, pp. 208–19.

Veit-Wilson, J. (1986) 'Paradigms of poverty: a rehabilitation of B.S. Rowntree', *Journal of Social Policy*, 15, 1, pp. 69–99.

Veit-Wilson, J. (1994) *Dignity not Poverty: a minimum income standard for the UK*, London: IPPR.

Vernon, S. (1993) *Social Work and the Law*, London: Butterworths.

Vincent, D. (1991) *Poor Citizens: the state and the poor in twentieth century Britain*, London: Longman.

Wagstaff, G.F. (1983) 'Attitudes to poverty: the Protestant work ethic and political affiliation; a preliminary investigation', *Social Behaviour and Personality*, 11, 1, pp. 45–7.

Walker, A. and Walker, C. (eds) (1987) *The Growing Divide: a social audit 1979–87*, London: Child Poverty Action Group.

Walker, C. (1993) *Managing Poverty: the limits of social assistance*, London: Routledge.

Walker, R. (1987) 'Consensual approaches to the definition of poverty: towards an alternative methodology', *Journal of Social Policy*, 16, 2, pp. 213–26.

Walker, R., Dix, G. and Huby, M. (1992) *Working the Social Fund*, London: HMSO.

Ward, S. (1996) 'The 1995 Pensions Act', *Benefits*, 15, pp. 12–14.

Warner, N. (1994) *Community Care: just a fairy tale?*, London: Carers National Association.

Warner, N. (1995) *Better Tomorrows: report of a national study of carers and the community care changes*, London: Carers National Association.

Webb, A. (1980) 'The personal social services', in N. Bosanquet and P. Townsend (eds), *Labour and Equality: A Fabian study of Labour in power, 1974–79*, London: Heinemann.

Webb, A. (1991) 'Personal Social Services', in P. Catterall (ed.), *Contemporary Britain: an annual review 1991*, Oxford: Blackwell.

Webb, A. and Wistow, G. (1987) *Social Work, Social Care and Social Planning: the personal social services since Seebohm*, London: Longman.

Webb, S. (1995) *Poverty Dynamics in Great Britain: preliminary analysis from the British Household Panel Survey*, London: Institute for Fiscal Studies.

Weir, S. (1981) 'What do people think about social workers?', *New Society*, 7 May, pp. 216–18.

Weitz, D. (1994) 'Everybody must get stoned', *Changes: An International Journal of Psychology and Psychotherapy*, 12, 1, pp. 50–9.

Whitehead, M. (1987) *The Health Divide: inequalities in health in the 1980s*, London: Health Education Council.

Whiteley, P. (1981) 'Who are the labour activists?', *Political Quarterly*, 52, pp. 160–70.

Wilkinson, R. (1994) *Unequal Shares: the effects of widening income differences on the welfare of the young*, London: Barnardos.

Willetts, D. (1993) *The Age of Entitlement*, London: Social Market Foundation.

Williams, F. and Pillinger, J. (1996) 'New thinking on social policy research into inequality, social exclusion and poverty', in J. Millar and J. Bradshaw (eds), *Social Welfare Systems: towards a research agenda*, Bath: Centre for the Analysis of Social Policy, pp. 1–32.

Williamson, J. B. (1974) 'Beliefs about the motivation of the poor and attitudes toward poverty policy', *Social Problems*, XXI June, pp. 634–48.

Wills, T. (1978) 'Perceptions of clients by professional helpers', *Psychological Bulletin*, 85, pp. 968–95.

Wistow, G. (1995) 'Charges at the interface between health and social care', in National Institute of Social Work/Local Government Anti-Poverty Unit, *Charging for Social Care*, London: NISW/LGAPU, pp. 13–24.

Wistow, G., Knapp, M., Hardy, B. and Allen, C, (1994) *Social Care in a Mixed Economy*, Milton Keynes: Open University Press.

Wistow, G., Leedham, I. and Hardy, B. (1993) *Community Care Plans: a preliminary analysis of English community care plans*, London: Department of Health.

Wolfensberger, W. (1972) *The Principle of Normalisation in Human Services*, Toronto: National Institute on Mental Retardation.

Woodroofe, K. (1962) *From Charity to Social Work in England and the United States*, London: Routledge and Kegan Paul.

Young, H. (1989) *One of Us*, London: Macmillan.

INDEX

Abel-Smith, B. 24, 32
absolute poverty 6, 12, 21–2, 24
Adam Smith Institute 3, 70, 74, 77
Adams, R. 116, 117
Addison, P. 46
additional requirements 65, 98, 150
Adoption Bill (1996) 17
Airey, C. 9
Aitken, Jonathan 14, 76
Alaszewski, A. 52
Alcock, P. 2, 21, 23, 25–6, 63, 108, 148,
    155, 158
Aldgate, J. 104
Aldridge, J. 133
Allen, B.L.F. 100
Allsop, J. 121
Alston, J. 7
Americans with Disabilities Act 158
Andrews, K. 63
anti-institution critique 52–3, 121–2
anti-poverty movement 6, 22, 33, 37, 88,
    108–11, 114, 117, 119, 143, 163
anti-psychiatry movement 53–4
Arnold, P. 155
Arshey, H. 134
Ashley, P. 94
Ashworth, K. 26, 27, 31, 81
assessment process 136–9, 151, 155
Association of County Councils 98–9, 136
Association of Directors of Social
    Services (ADSS) 131, 136
Association of Metropolitan Authorities
    95, 98–9, 140, 143–4, 149, 150
asylum seekers 79
asylums 43–4
Atkin, K. 92, 133
attendance allowance 58, 146, 154
Audit Commission 124, 129, 132, 138–9

Bailey, R. 50, 117
Baldock, J. 92, 95
Baldwin, N. 109, 110, 112, 132
Baldwin, S. 145
Balloch, S. 108
Bamford, T. 51

Bank-Mikklesen, N. 54
Barclay, P. 3, 6, 25, 34
Barclay Report (1982) 51–2, 94–5, 106–7
Barker, M. 110
Barnes, C. 55, 159
Barnes, H. 158
Barr, N. 58
Bartlett, W. 13, 123
Bartley, M. 36
Bean, P. 53
Beattie, A. 36
Bebbington, A. 110
Becker, Saul 3, 6, 40, 46, 60, 65–7, 86,
    93–8, 100–6, 108–11, 113–18, 125,
    129, 131, 133, 148–9
Beckford, Jasmine 109
Bell, M. 74
benefit-to-work strategies 3, 4–5, 18–19,
    20, 39, 62, 83
benefits
    continuity/change 38–56
    contributory 4, 40, 58, 70, 135
    delivery of 17, 20, 85, 123, 175–7
    dependency 4–5, 9, 10, 15, 16, 82,
        161–3, 165
    fraud/abuse 19, 65, 68–9, 71, 74, 77–9,
        82
    integration policy 153–6
    localisation of 83–4
    means-tested see means-tested benefits
    non-contributory 58–9, 62
    privatising 17, 20, 72, 84–6, 177
    system simplification 81
    universal 59
    see also individual benefits
Benefits (journal) 102
Benefits Agency 77–9, 84–5, 149, 153–4
Benefits Research (newsletter) 102
Benefits Research Unit 96, 101–3, 105
Bennett, F. 3, 60, 80, 86
Benson, S. 96
Benyon, J. 35
Benzeval, M. 36
Beresford, P. 5, 18, 25, 34, 37, 111, 119,
    163–4

Berthoud, R. 96
Bevan, Aneurin 52
Beveridge Report (1942) 3, 41, 46–52, 56, 58, 83, 97
Black, Sir Douglas 36
Blair, Tony 18, 20, 73
Blane, D. 36
Blau, P. 114
Blom-Cooper, L. 109
Blunn, C. 95
Boards of Guardians 46, 130
Bochel, H. 155
Bolger, S. 51
Bond, H. 150
Booth, Charles 22
Borrie, Sir Gordon 17–18
Bottomley, Virginia 34, 129–30, 136, 150
Bowis, John 17, 139
Bradshaw, J. 15, 26, 29, 31, 64, 81, 123
Brake, M. 50, 117
Bransbury, L. 140, 145
Breakwell, G.M. 161
Brewer, C. 51
Bright, J. 35
Brisdenen, S. 54
British Association of Social Workers 98–9
British Social Attitudes Survey 11
Brook, L. 8, 11
Brown, Gordon 18
Brown, H. 54
Brown, M. 23, 32, 94
Brown, P. 51
Broxtowe incident 110, 111
Bryson, A. 83
budget standard approach 26–7, 29, 31, 81
Bull, D. 6, 114
Bulmer, M. 23, 119
Burns, D. 119
Burt, Alistair 76
Butcher, T. 48
Butterworth, E. 45
Bynoe, I. 158

Care in Action (1981) 123
care manager 91, 138–9
carers (family role) 132–5, 145, 154
Carers (Recognition and Services) Act (1995) 91, 134, 136
Carers National Association 132, 133
Caring for People (1989) 126–7, 128
Carlile, Kimberly 109–10
case advocacy 114
case managers 19
casework approach 50, 51, 116–18
cash and care
    direct payments *see* direct payments

historical perspective 38–56
integration policy 153–6
social reaction model 157–66
cash limits
    community care 135–9, 152–3, 156
    social fund 67, 97–8, 106, 135–6, 138
Central Council for Education and Training in Social Work 90, 95
Challenge 132
Change Programme 1, 17, 20, 85, 123, 175–6, 177
charges 139–48
Charging for Residential Accommodation Guide (CRAG) 141
charities 40–3, 48, 88, 92, 105
Charity Organisation Society 88, 105
Chartered Institute of Public Finance and Accountancy 130
Chemins, J. 111
Chetwynd, M. 145–6
Chief Inspector of Social Services 89–90, 120, 124
child benefit 9, 10, 17, 59, 74–5, 85
Child Care Act (1980) 99
    Section 1 98–101, 103, 152
    Section 12 98–101, 103
Child Poverty Action Group 3, 6, 14, 61, 73, 94, 179–80
Child Support Agency 69, 108
children
    abuse/neglect 93–4, 109–10
    direct payments 98–101, 103–5, 149–54, 156
    families with problems 89, 111–13, 119, 162
    lone parent families 15–17, 49, 65, 78, 82, 111
    residential care 89–91, 110–11, 118
    services for 88–94, 99, 103–4, 107–13, 117–18
Children Act (1948) 47, 49, 53
Children Act (1989) 51, 89, 91, 99, 103, 107, 108, 117, 119, 136
    Section 17 103–4, 105, 150, 152
Children and Young Persons Act (1963) 99
Chronically Sick and Disabled Persons Act (1970) 89, 137–8
Church House 25
Citizens Income Trust 3
citizenship 18–19, 23, 54, 56, 60, 119, 159, 163, 165, 166
civil rights 121–3, 146–7, 158–9, 163
Clapham, D. 155
Clarke, J. 44, 49, 113
Clarke, Kenneth 73–5, 126
Clasen, J. 57, 60
class advocacy 114

Cleveland Report (1988) 110
client-based premiums 62, 65, 98
Clode, D. 94
Coates, K. 24, 32
Coffield, F. 94
Cole-Hamilton, I. 36
collective responsibility 60, 146, 148
collectivism 41, 49
Colwell, Maria 94
Commission on the Future of the
    Voluntary Sector 48
Commission on Social Justice 3, 5, 17–19,
    36, 73
community care 49, 73, 89, 91, 106, 121
    case for 52–3
    cash limits 135–9
    charges 140–8
    direct payments 152–3
    funding 130–2
    Griffiths Report 51–2, 67, 125–30,
      133–4, 140, 183–4
    integration 153–6
    politics/policy formulation 122–5
    privately borne costs 132–5
    welfare rights 148–52
Community Care (magazine) 102, 129,
    136, 138, 143, 145
Community Care (Direct Payments) Bill
    (1995) 150–1, 188
Community Development Programme 50
Confederation of Scottish Local
    Authorities 98–9
Conservative Party 12–17, 68
    see also Major government; Thatcher
      government
Conservative Way Forward 74, 77
Considine, M. 114
continuing care 92, 123–4, 130, 146–7
contributory benefits 40, 58, 70
Cooke, F. 9
Cooper, A. 34
Cooper, J. 91, 181–2
Corden, A. 95
Corrigan, P. 50–1
Coser, L.A. 161
Coulshed, V. 117
Coulter, F. 58
Cousins, C. 118
Craig, G. 6, 34, 108
crime, poverty and 15, 16, 35–6
Croft, S. 25, 37, 119, 164
Crossman, Anthony 52
Curno, P. 117
Curtice, J. 55

Dahrendorf Commission 3–4, 19, 73
Davey Smith, G. 36

Davidson, N. 36
Davis, A. 41, 116
day care 90, 91, 142
Deacon, A. 9, 13, 25, 47, 56, 64
Deakin, N. 3, 13, 26
Dean, H. 16
Dean, K. 7
Dearden, C. 133
demand-led services 132, 135, 137
Dennis, N. 15–16
dependency 13, 120, 121
    on benefits 4–5, 9–10, 15, 16, 82,
      161–3, 165
    culture 14, 15, 16
deprivation 45, 94, 112, 144–5
    'standard' 24, 29, 32
Derber, C. 118
deserving poor 8–10, 12, 14, 43, 61–3,
    116, 165
determined advocacy 99, 106–7
Devine, D. 55
Dhooge, Y. 95
Dickens, R. 16
difference 1, 38, 115, 121, 123, 158–9,
    162–3
    poverty and 42–5
    redefining 53–6
Digby, A. 43
Dillon, M. 111
direct payments 154, 187–8
    income maintenance 152–3, 156
    welfare rights 149–52
disability 13, 89
    benefits 58–9, 62, 108, 146, 154–5
    community care 121–3, 130, 137–8,
      140, 142–3, 145–7, 149–55
    direct payments 58–9, 99, 146, 149–54
    family carers 132–5
    social model 54–5, 121, 158–9, 163
Disability Alliance 3
disability living allowance 58–9, 146, 154
Disabled Persons (Services, Consultation
    and Representation) Act (1986)
    136
disadvantaged groups 55–6, 158
discretionary social fund 66–7, 96, 97, 135
Dix, G. 65, 108
domiciliary care 123, 124, 131
    charges 141, 142–8
Donkor, K. 5
Donnison, D. 64, 73
Dorrell, Stephen 53, 139
Doyal, L. 24, 38

earnings-related supplements 64
earnings top-up benefit 83–4
Education Act (1914) 45

elderly people
  community care 140–3, 146–7, 149,
    151
  continuing care 92, 123–4, 130, 146–7
  pensions 17, 19, 58, 65, 70, 72–4, 80
  residential care 52–3, 73, 89–90, 123,
    130, 140–3, 147
eligibility criteria 136, 138, 151
Ellis, K. 138
Emmett, T. 100
Employment Service 77–8
empowerment 55, 117, 118–20
enabling social work 118–20
Enthoven, Alain 125, 129
Epstein, I. 114
Erdos, G. 15–16
Esping-Anderson, G. 57
eugenics movement 44, 45
Evans, M. 82
Evans, Roger 79
exceptional needs payments 64, 66–7, 106
exclusion 1, 5, 6, 25, 28, 56
  social reaction model 157–66

families 42
  carers in 132–5, 145, 154
  income 22, 28–31
  lone parents 15–17, 49, 65, 78, 82, 111
  with problems 89, 111–13, 119, 162
family credit 15, 58, 65, 75, 83
Family Expenditure Survey 28, 31
family income supplement 65
family planning 45
Feagin, J.R. 7
Feather, N.T. 7
feminisation of poverty 96
Fiegehen, G. 24
Field, Frank 4–5, 11, 16, 18–20, 68, 168
field social work 90
Fimister, G. 95, 148, 152, 153
Fitch, M. 154
Fogarty, M. 12
Fowler, Norman 127
Fowler Review 3, 10, 64–8, 95, 96, 97
fraud/abuse 5, 152
  benefits 19, 65, 68, 71, 74, 77–9, 82
Freeman, I. 111, 140
Friedrich Ebert Foundation 25, 157–8
Fry, V. 16
Fuller, R. 94, 113
funding policies 130–2, 135–9
Furnham, A. 11, 12

George, V. 12, 39, 44, 48
Gibbons, J. 104, 111, 117
Gibbs, I. 123
Gladstone, D. 50
Glazer, N. 12–13, 15

Glendinning, C. 30, 54, 61, 69, 92, 132,
    133–4, 135, 159
Glennerster, H. 43, 52
Goffman, E. 52, 161
Goldberg, E.M. 94
Golding, P. 2, 7–11, 23, 25–6, 43, 160
Gooding, C. 158
Goodman, A. 30
Goodwin, L. 7
Gough, I. 24, 38, 49
Graham, H. 29
Grant, D. 23
Green, D. 3, 5, 13, 18, 25, 34
Griffiths Report (1986) 51–2, 67, 125–30,
    133–4, 140, 183–4
Gunter, B. 12

Hadjipateras, A. 3
Hadley, R. 51
Ham, C. 125
Hambleton, R. 119
Handler, J. 153
Hardiker, P. 110
Harding, S. 12
Hardy, B. 128
Harker, L. 5, 6, 16, 23, 25, 29–30, 61, 73,
    179–80
Hayball, J. 148
health 35–6, 95, 142–3, 147
  see also disability; mental health
Health Committee 142, 147
Health Education Council 95
Health of the Nation strategy 36
Health Services and Public Health Act
    (1968) 149
Health and Social Services and Social
    Security Adjudication Act 142–3
Henricson, C. 35
Henwood, M. 129, 130
Heywood, J.S. 100
Hill, M. 56, 64, 100, 125
Hills, J. 34, 49, 73
Hoggett, P. 119
Hollins, C. 105
Holman, B. 45, 93, 110, 116, 118
Holman, R. 45
Holmstrom, R. 158
home helps 90, 142
Households Below Average Income
    statistics 28, 30–1
housing benefit 15, 65, 72, 74–8 *passim*,
    83, 154–5
Howard, Michael 16, 35
Huby, M. 65, 67, 108
Hughes, B. 118
Hunter, H. 82
Hutton, Will 3–4

ideology 35–7
    of casework 116–18
    political 11–20
    of welfare 7–8, 160, 161
Idiots Act (1886) 43
ill-health, poverty and 35, 36
illegitimacy 15, 16, 44
incapacity benefit 58, 70, 74
inclusion, partnership and 163–5
income maintenance 9, 46, 97–100
    direct payments 152–3, 156
income standard, minimum 27, 165–6
income support 8, 15, 27, 29–30, 58–60,
        62, 65, 77–9, 96, 98, 100, 107, 115,
        123, 140–2, 146
independent living, movement for
        53–6
Independent Living Fund 131, 149–50
independent sector 40–5, 129
individualisation of poverty 1, 7, 32, 46,
        112, 114, 115, 157, 163
individualism 41, 49, 56, 67, 146, 148
industrial injuries benefit 59
informal sector 40–5, 92, 132–5, 145,
        154
Institute of Economic Affairs 3, 15, 16
Institute for Fiscal Studies 28, 74
Institute for Public Policy Research 3
insurance
    health 44–5
    national *see* national insurance
    private 19, 72, 76, 79–80, 85
integration of cash and care 153–6
internal quasi-markets 123, 125, 127
International Year of Poverty
        Eradication 2, 6, 22
invalid care allowance 59, 62, 134, 135,
        154
invalidity benefits 70, 72, 74
Irvine, R. 109

Jackson, M.P. 100
Jacobs, J. 63
Jacobson, L. 165
Jain, U.C. 7
Jani-Le Bris, H. 42
Jenkin, Patrick 36
Jenkins, S. 30
jobseekers allowance 19, 70–1, 74, 77, 84
Johnson, N. 13, 25, 56, 64
Jones, B. 100, 108
Jones, K. 43, 45
Jordan, B. 25, 55, 116, 159
Joseph, Sir Keith 45, 93–4
Jowell, R. 8, 11
Jowell, T. 117
Judge, K. 36

Kahn, A.K. 42
Kamerman, S.B. 42
Kay, H. 155
Kemp, P. 60, 76
Kempson, E. 6, 16, 35, 64
Kerbo, H.R. 161
Kestenbaum, A. 150
King's Fund Institute 129–30
Klein, R. 52
Knapp, M. 123
Korman, N. 43, 52
Kumar, V. 29

Labour Party
    New 4, 17–20, 84, 87, 120, 146, 169,
        185–6
    Social Justice Commission 3, 5,
        17–19, 36, 73
Laing, R.D. 53
Lait, J. 51
Langan, M. 47, 49, 51
Lansley, P. 24
Lansley, S. 8, 9, 10, 26, 27
Lauer, R.H. 7
Lavery, J. 55
learning difficulties 43–5, 52–4, 91, 151
Leedham, I. 128
Le Grand, J. 13, 123
Leonard, P. 50–1
Lewis, J. 23
Lilley, Peter 3–4, 6, 19, 25, 27–8, 30, 34,
        57, 74–80, 82–4, 170–1
    Change Programme 17, 20, 85, 123,
        175–6, 177
    'Little List' 78, 173–4
    Portillo/Lilley review 68–73
Lipsey, D. 8, 10
Lister, R. 5, 16, 23, 25, 60, 64, 69, 100,
        125, 157–8
loans 66, 97, 98
local authority social services *see* social
        services
Local Authority Social Services Act 50
Local Government Act (1929) 46
Local Government Anti Poverty Unit
        143–5
Local Government Information Unit 140,
        143–4
Lockhart, F. 111
lone parent families 15–17, 49, 65, 78, 82,
        111
low income families 22, 28–30, 31
Low Pay Unit 3
Lowe, R. 47, 49, 50
Lunatics Act (1845) 43
Lunt, N. 145
Lynch, R. 54
Lynes, T. 64

Macarov, D. 113, 114
McCormick, J. 18
McGrail, S.M. 94
Mack, J. 8, 9, 10, 26, 27
McLaughlin, E. 134
Macnicol, J. 44, 45
MacPherson, S. 40, 93–8, 100, 109, 111,
    113, 117, 148–9
Madge, N. 32, 94
Major government 12–14, 17, 25, 35–6,
    57, 71–2, 73, 111, 123, 142
managerialism 118
Marquand, D. 49
Marsh, A. 83
Marsland, D. 35–6
Martin, J. 55
Martin, J.P. 52
Matza, D. 161
meals on wheels 90, 142
means-tested benefits 4, 29, 40, 46–8,
    57–60, 62, 65, 82, 139, 141, 147
media (role) 31–4, 71–3
medical-pathology model 7, 36, 56, 121,
    158, 162, 166
Mental Deficiency Bills 44, 45
mental health 43–5, 52–4
    community care 121–2, 138, 149–51
Mental Health Act (1983) 143
Mental Health Act Commission 138
Mess, H.A. 48
Middleton, S. 7–10, 26, 27, 31, 43, 81
Milburn, A. 120, 146, 185–6
Miles, J. 110
Millar, J. 15, 25, 26, 30
Miller, A.H. 7
Milne, K. 158
minimum income standard 27, 165–6
Mishra, R. 49
mixed economy of welfare 10, 12, 17, 41,
    42–5, 86, 88, 122–3, 125, 127–9,
    132
Monks, John 71
Monro, M. 155
Moore, John 23, 27–8
Morgan, P. 17
Morley, R. 105
Morris, J. 55, 121
Morris, P. 52
mortgages 76, 77, 79–80
Murray, Charles 14–15, 17
Murray, N. 94

NACRO 35
Nadash, P. 149
Nash, A. 94
national assistance 46–7, 49, 59, 140,
    149

National Association of Welfare Rights
    Advisers (NAWRA) 148
National Children's Homes 33, 109
National Council for Civil Liberties 52
National Health Insurance Act (1911) 44
National Health Service 46–8, 124–5, 130,
    146–7
National Institute for Social Work 94
national insurance 44, 46–7, 61, 70, 75
    benefits 4, 40, 58, 62, 70, 84, 135
National Welfare Rights Officers Group
    (NWROG) 148
needs 38–41, 62–3, 132–9
Neill, J. 129
New Labour 4, 17–20, 84, 87, 120, 146,
    169, 185–6
New Right 12, 49, 122, 125
NHS and Community Care Act (1990) 51,
    89, 91, 127–8, 136, 138, 154
Nixon, J. 100
No Turning Back Group 72
Nocon, A. 129
non-contributory benefits 58–9, 62
normalisation 54, 122
Novak, T. 33, 43, 63
Nye, R. 34

O'Brien, J. 54
O'Connor, J. 49
Oldfield, N. 26, 29, 31, 81
Oldman, C. 146, 147
Oliver, M. 54, 55, 159
Oppenheim, C. 5, 6, 15, 16, 18, 23, 25,
    29, 30, 73
Orten, J.D. 113, 114

Page, D. 155
Page, R. 39, 44, 48
Pandey, J. 7
Parker, H. 3
Parker, J. 111
Parsloe, P. 93
participation 18, 55, 56
partnership 65, 142, 163–5
Pashardes, P. 16
Payne, M. 49–50, 117
Payne, S. 23
Pearson, S. 108
pensions 17, 19, 58
    private schemes 65, 70, 72, 80
    SERPS 65, 74–5, 80, 86
Perring, C. 92, 133
personal social services 40, 88–120
Phillimore, T. 36
Phillips, D. 12
Piachaud, D. 9, 23, 26, 36, 58–9, 81–2
Pillinger, J. 1, 25, 157

Pinker, R.A. 51
Pirie, M. 70
Pitkeathley, J. 55
Policy Studies Institute 94, 129
politicians 5–7
politics
    of poverty 1–7, 11–20, 21–37
    of the social fund 96–9
poor
    deserving *see* deserving poor
    families 89, 111–13
    managing (social service role) 88–120
    social construction of 1–20
    social workers' attitudes 113–16
    undeserving *see* undeserving poor
    'victims' 5, 7, 9, 12–13, 25, 33, 55, 115
    'villains' 5, 9, 12, 33, 82, 165
Poor Law 33, 42–3, 46, 49–50, 52, 83, 113
Poor Law Act (1930) 46
Poor Relief Act (1601) 42–3
Popay, J. 95
Portillo, Michael 13, 14, 74, 172
    Portillo/Lilley review 68–73
poverty
    absolute 6, 12, 21–2, 24, 26–8
    agenda (refocusing) 157–9
    awareness of 42–5, 93–6, 114, 164
    definitions 21–8
    difference and 42–5
    effects 35–7
    individualisation of 1, 7, 32, 46, 112, 114–15, 157, 163
    measurement 28–34
    perspective (denial of) 109–11
    politics of 1–7, 11–20, 21–37
    relief (social security function) 60
    relative 21, 22, 23–8
    research/policies (1990s) 107–9
    social attitudes 7–20
    social construction of 1–20
    social reaction model 157–66
    social workers' attitudes 113–16
    see also anti-poverty movement
power/powerlessness 25, 115
premiums (client-based) 62, 65, 98
Prescott, J. 22
Princess Royal Trust 133
prioritisation strategy 136, 137–9
Private Finance Initiative 85
private insurance 19, 72, 76, 79–80, 85
private pensions 65, 70, 72, 80
private sector 40–5, 123–4, 129
privatising benefits 17, 20, 72, 84–6, 177
'problem families' 89, 111–13, 119, 162
Pryke, R. 30, 34
Public Assistance Committees 46

Public Health Acts 44
public spending
    Change Programme 1, 17, 20, 85, 123, 175–6, 177
    Fowler Review 3, 10, 64–8, 95, 96, 97
    Portillo/Lilley review 68–73
purchaser–provider split 20, 85–6, 123, 125, 127, 136

quasi-markets 123, 125, 127

Rainbow, H. 100, 148
Redpath, A.D. 8
Redwood, John 17
regulation (of the poor) 57–87
relative poverty 21, 22, 23–8
residential care 73, 89–90, 111
    anti-institutional critique 52–6
    charges 140–2
    continuing care 92, 123–4, 130, 146–7
Revenue Suppport Grant 143
Robins, L. 64
Robinson, P. 94
Room, G. 157
Root, A. 36
Rose, M. 43
Rosenthal, R. 165
Rowntree Inquiry (1995) 5, 17–18, 22, 34, 36, 73
Rowntree Report (1901) 22–3, 27
Royal Association for Disability and Rehabilitation 137
Royal College of Psychiatrists 138
Royal Commission on the Care and Control of the Feeble Minded 44
Royal Commission of Law Relating to Mental Illness and Deficiency 52

Sainsbury, R. 78, 79
Salonen, T. 114
Sarsby, J. 94
Savage, S. 64
Scarman Report (1982) 35
Schaff, C. 54
Scheerenberger, R.C. 45
Schlackman Research Organisation 8
Schorr, A. 109
Schur, E.M. 53
Scott, J. 43
Scott, V. 158
Scott-Parker, S. 158
Searle, R. 44
Section 1 payments 98–101, 103, 152
Section 12 payments 98–101, 103
Section 17 payments 103–4, 105, 150, 152
Seebohm Report (1968) 49–52, 56, 93, 96
Seldon, A. 49

self-interest 4, 5, 10, 13, 34, 132
Sen, A. 26
severe disablement allowance 59, 154
sickness benefits 70, 72, 74
Silberman, G. 114
Silburn, L. 54
Silburn, R. 16, 24, 27, 32, 40, 46–7, 65–7,
    94–5, 98, 100–6, 108, 148, 159
Sinclair, I. 124, 145
Sinfield, A. 93
single payment grants 64–5, 66, 96, 97
Sinha, Y. 7
Smale, G. 107, 119
Small, M. 95
Smith, A. 24
Smith, Chris 18–19
Smith, H. 54
Smith, R. 95
social attitudes 7–12
social construction of poverty 1–20
social exclusion 1, 5, 6, 25, 28, 56,
    157–66
social fund 65–6, 100, 106–8, 139, 154
    cash-limited 67, 97–8, 106, 135–6, 138
    monitoring impact of 101–4, 105
    politics of 96–9
social housing 154–5
social insurance 19, 40, 46, 50, 56–8
social justice 3, 5, 17–19, 36, 73
Social Market Foundation 3, 83
social model of disability 54–5, 121,
    158–9, 163
social reaction model 157–66
Social Sciences Research Council 94
social security 106
    benefits *see* benefits
    costs/structure 57–60
    functions 60–3
    historical perspective 38–56
    political views 12–20
    reform (New Labour) 4, 17, 19, 84,
        169
    reforms (1980s) 63–8
    reforms (1990s) 13–14, 68–80
    regulatory role 9, 57–87
    social reaction model 160–1
    transfer 130–2
Social Security Acts 64
Social Security Advisory Committee 65,
    73, 75–9, 86, 108, 178
Social Security Research Consortium
    101–3, 105
social services 181–2
    community care and 121–56
    departments 40, 89–90, 92, 120, 125,
        127–32, 134–41, 145–56
    historical perspective 38–56

payments
    Section 1 98–101, 103, 152
    Section 12 98–101, 103
    Section 17 103–4, 105, 150, 152
    managing the poor 88–120
    social reaction model 160–1
    state provision 40–52
Social Services Committee (House of
    Commons) 124, 133
Social Services Inspectorate 136, 143
social work 49–51, 53, 90–2
    enabling/empowering 118–20
    impact of social fund 101–6
    in 1990s 107–9
    methods 116–18
Social Work Today 129
social workers 50, 90–3, 97–8
    attitudes to poverty/poor 113–16
    Barclay Report 51–2, 94–5, 106–7
    in 1990s 107–9
Special Transitional Grant 130–1
Spencer, N. 109, 110, 112
Spicker, P. 23, 32
Spotlight on Benefit Cheats campaign 79
Squires, P. 33, 43, 63
Stainton, T. 45
stakeholders 4, 122, 128–9
Standard Spending Assessment 131, 138,
    154
state
    local authority services 50, 88–120
    social service provision 40–52
state earnings-related pension (SERPS) 65,
    74–5, 80, 86
statutory sick pay 72, 74
sterilisation policy 45
Stevenson, Olive 3, 47, 53, 94, 113
Stewart, G. 95, 97, 100, 102
Stewart, J. 95, 97, 100, 102
Stitt, S. 23
Strathclyde Regional Council 95–6, 111
structural reform 72
subsistence lifestyle 21, 23, 24, 29
Sullivan, M. 47, 49, 64
supplementary benefits 9, 59, 62, 64–6,
    94, 96, 100, 115, 123
Supplementary Benefits Commission 53
supply-led services 132, 135
Svenson, M. 98, 100
Swain, J. 54
Szasz, T. 54

Taylor-Gooby, P. 10–11, 16
Thane, P. 43
Thatcher government 12, 25, 34–5, 48, 57,
    64, 73, 95, 122, 123, 126
Thomas, K. 54

Thompson, P. 55, 144
Thorpe, S. 111
Timmins, N. 3, 31, 47–8, 64, 93
Thomas, K. 54
Torkelson, R. 54
Towell, D. 54
Townsend, P. 5, 23–5, 29, 32, 36, 50–1,
    52, 93, 161
Tree, D. 108
Trenery, D. 128
Tropman, J.E. 8
TUC 71
Tunstill, J. 103–4, 111
Twigg, J. 92, 132, 133–4
Tyne, A. 54

UN Economic and Social Council 2
UN Summit on Social Development 6
underclass 9, 14–17, 33, 82
undeserving poor 2, 8–11, 33, 38, 42–4,
    52, 116, 161–3
    political views of 12–20
    regulation of 61–3, 82
unemployment 75, 94, 95, 96
    benefit 9, 14, 19, 70–2, 74, 78, 84
    jobseekers allowance 19, 70–1, 74, 77,
        84
Ungerson, C. 42
Unified Budget (1993) 72, 73–6
universal benefits 59
Utting, D. 35, 90

Valencia, B.M. 100
Vaux, G. 55, 148, 155
Veit-Wilson, J. 23–4, 27, 31, 165–6
Vernon, S. 89
Vincent, D. 47
voluntary sector 13, 42, 48, 92, 129, 149
vulnerability/vulnerable people 61–3, 71,
    91, 101–2, 121–2

Wagstaff, G.F. 11
Walker, A. 6
Walker, C. 6, 33
Walker, R. 26, 27, 31, 65, 81
Warburton, R.W. 94

Ward, S. 80
Warner, N. 133, 134
Webb, A. 49, 110, 125
Webb, B. 52
Webb, S. 30, 31, 52
Wedgewood, Josiah 45, 52
Weir, S. 94
Weitz, D. 54
welfare
    attitudes to 9–11
    historical perspective 38–56
    ideologies 7–8, 160, 161
    meeting needs for 38–41
    mixed economy of 10, 12, 17, 41–5,
        86, 88, 122–3, 125, 127–9, 132
    political views of 12–20
    rights (community care) 148–52
    rights services 90, 93, 95–6, 99, 109
White, A. 55
White, K.J. 51
Whitehead, M. 36
Whiteley, P. 11
Wicks, Malcolm 30
Wilding, P. 6, 12
Wilkinson, P. 111
Wilkinson, R. 34
Willetts, David 73
Williams, F. 1, 25, 157
Williams, J. 129
Williams, S. 96
Williamson, J.B. 11
Wills, T. 165
Wistow, G. 123, 124, 125, 128, 146–7
Witcher, S. 3
Wolfensberger, W. 54
Woodroofe, K. 43, 48, 50, 116
work ethic 11, 82
workfare schemes 14
workhouse 43, 44, 52, 53

Yeo, Tim 129, 131
Young, Sir George 16
Young, H. 64
Yu, A.C.S. 26, 29, 31, 81

Zarb, G. 149